BE WISE NOW

BE WISE
NOW

A GUIDE TO

CONSCIOUS

LIVING

GAEL McCOOL

FOR ENLIGHTENED EMOTIONAL LIVING

DISCLAIMER
This book is presented solely for personal growth and self-development purposes. The author is not offering it as a substitute for therapeutic, medical, or other professional advice. Every personal development approach is different, and the advice and strategies contained herein may not be suitable for your situation. Every effort has been made to give appropriate credit to the people cited in this book. If there have been any errors or misattributions, it has been accidental, and the author will make appropriate adjustments on notification.

BE WISE NOW

A Guide to Conscious Living

ISBN   978-1-5445-0210-6 *Paperback*

978-1-5445-0209-0 *Ebook*

For Nico and Jesse,
who helped me to see the light.

CONTENTS

"We don't receive wisdom; we must discover it for ourselves after a journey that no one can take for us or spare us."

—MARCEL PROUST

ACKNOWLEDGMENTS

My first debt of gratitude goes to my clients, who nudged, cajoled, and encouraged me to write this book. The writings here are based on everything they taught me about deep listening. For the rare gift of their trust, I am sincerely grateful.

Next, I wish to acknowledge my most important teachers: my children, Nico and Jesse. More than anyone else, they taught me the meaning of unconditional love and accountability. When you raise children to be truth tellers, watch out! They will hold your feet to the fire. For keeping mine warm all these years, I thank you both from the depths of my heart.

So many people offered their unconditional mental, emotional, spiritual, and material support along the way. Thanks go to Teri McArter, for being my muse and sounding board; Sandie O'Brian, for her generous material and spiritual support; Diane Johnson, for holding the space and for her endless encouragement; Karin Konstantynowicz, for resourceful assistance; and Fran Diamond for her loving editorial ear. Thanks also to the women who helped me define this material through courses and retreats, especially Jacqueline Peters, Leah Rowntree, Bonnie Wilson, Teri Tatchell, and Jennifer Johnson. To my writing group buddies, Sandi Bojm and Mary MacDonald, I can only say thanks for keeping my feet on this path. Thanks also to Caroline Durstan for providing a healing space in which to write.

There have been many positive influences on my work, but recently the contributions of three women stand out: Cindy Wigglesworth of Deep Change and author of the *SQ21: The 21 Skills of Spiritual Intelligence*; Laura Belsten, the founder of the Institute for Social and Emotional Intelligence; and Bonnie Bright, the founder of the Depth Psychology Alliance.

I also want to acknowledge my late friends and mentors, Dr. Ted Merrill, Bill Merrill, and Navajo Elder Leon Secatero, whose influences continued to affect me through this entire project. Thanks also to Drs. Ed and Julia Levy for believing in me and challenging my ideas.

I was privileged to have the invaluable editorial assistance of Mary Beth Conlee, who helped me breathe life and organization into this book, and who immeasurably improved the quality and clarity of my expression in it. Her patience and persistence were a godsend. I also want to acknowledge Tamara Cooper, who designed my graphic for the multidimensional self.

A special expression of heartfelt gratitude goes to my husband, Doug Allan, for the loving and supportive way he listened deeply and advised gently, which made all the difference in the world. I could not have completed this without him.

To my readers, I thank you in advance for taking the time to become curious about your own deep wisdom and its conscious application in the world.

INTRODUCTION

Every life is a sacred work of art—an assemblage of real and surreal, fact and fiction, order and chaos—a divine mix of mess and magic. What holds it all together is your capacity to create stories, extract meaning from your experience, and assemble the pieces into an evolving narrative about who you are and your place in the world.

Your everyday story unfolds naturally as you cruise along on autopilot, but when life presents you with an unexpected plot twist, a fantastic opportunity emerges: the chance to consciously engage in the **deeper story of your life**.

It doesn't matter whether that twist presents as health problems, relationship trouble, parenting difficulties, career complications, or any other bump in the road of life; challenge and change provide incredible opportunities for self-discovery, learning, and growth. During such turmoil, you have unprecedented opportunities to re-evaluate your needs, priorities, and direction.

When sudden changes occur, or your path no longer appears to be taking you where you thought you were going, it's easy to become disoriented. Things you once thought were rock solid can be called into question, and your sense of identity and security can be disrupted as conflicting inner directions emerge.

Such moments of confusion bring perfectly normal, successful, high-functioning people to my door: clients who unexpectedly find themselves unmoored by some difficult life circumstance. In such situations, people instinctively reach out to gain perspective. My job is to teach them how to reach inward.

At life's critical turning points, you can't rely on someone else for your answers. Regardless of how brilliant or well-intentioned an advisor, therapist, or coach may be, there is no other person in the world who inhabits your unique set of perceptions and experiences. Nobody else can say what's right for you; all they can do is support you in discovering your own truth.

This doesn't mean you shouldn't seek feedback and guidance; we all need support along the way. It simply means that, in the end, you alone must decide what is in keeping with your deepest integrity.

Deep down, a part of you always knows the answer you seek—but that doesn't necessarily mean it is easy to uncover. Getting to your deepest truth can be complicated because just like the outer world, your inner world is filled with conflicting ideas, feelings, contradictions, and paradoxes. To find genuinely meaningful answers, you need to learn how to dive beneath the surface and move through the usual defenses so you can listen deeply and discriminately to inner prompts. Those very prompts can take you to the deeper story of your life.

Imagine how different your life would be if, during your most challenging moments, you could:

- Connect with a deeper sense of **purpose**
- Inhabit your body's **wisdom**
- Rewire your **survival** mechanisms
- Wholeheartedly embrace your **emotion**al nature
- Apply the subtle workings of your **intuition**
- Employ the creative genius of your **imagination**
- Utilize the discerning power of your **intellect**
- Ground yourself in a **social** support system
- Work with the catalytic energies behind your **wound**ing, your **ego**, your **judgment**, and your **shadow** to inspire higher consciousness

- Activate the subconscious value in your **dreams**
- Rewrite the **narratives** with which you make sense of yourself and the world around you

In accepting and working deeply with every part of yourself, you would move from fragmentation to wholeness, and toward the possibility of living a fully conscious and accountable life. And that, my friend, is a rare and beautiful thing.

This book is an invitation to start that journey toward a deeper life, and it all begins with your story.

TURNING INWARD

You've heard it a million times: "The answer lies within." But where exactly are those essential answers when you most need them? Is it best to use your head, listen to your heart, or follow your gut instincts? How can you tell if the answers that emerge are products of logic, a bit of wishful thinking, or a deeper kind of intelligence at work?

What if one part of you wants one thing while another wants something else? Which one should you listen to? These questions represent an old way of thinking that polarizes and pits one part of self against another—head versus heart, mind versus body, ego versus spirit, self versus other, and so on. That approach leads to fragmentation. It limits the richness and complexity of your inner being and the deeper holistic perspective you can bring to the resolution of any problem.

Maturity and inner authority come from the ability to successfully engage the dynamic tension of opposites within you and come to a new sense of wholeness as a result.

YOU HAVE NO SPARE PARTS

Western culture teaches us to extinguish what we don't understand or see as imperfect, flawed, negative, or difficult. We attempt to eliminate what we believe is "wrong" with us without exploring the truths contained within these parts of ourselves. We talk about getting over "old stories," ridding ourselves of negative emotions, eliminating our ego, and eradicating obstacles with sheer will. Somehow, this unconscious process of elimination is supposed to help us become authentic.

When people discuss the process of becoming authentic, they often use the metaphor of a sculptor, chipping away at the stone to release the ideal figure within. This implies that finding one's true self is achieved by removing what is in the way. But in my experience, often what we typically consider "in the way" *is the way* to understanding ourselves at a deeper level.

We have no spare parts that need to be removed. Working with even the most troublesome aspects of yourself and your behavior is often what leads you to consciousness of the deepest authenticity possible.

HOW I CAME TO MY OWN DEEPER STORY

I came to my sense of calling honestly, out of my own struggle to understand myself and others. As a child, I was taught to respect external authority and to trust that others had the answers I needed, but I often experienced difficulty reconciling others' advice with my own sense of inner knowing. I was told, however, that if you can't explain how or why you know something, then knowing doesn't "count."

The home in which I was raised was predominantly left-brained, competitive, and testosterone-driven (I was the only girl among five boys in my family). We were taught that logic, reason, and intellect were everything. Intuition and insight were deemed suspect at best, and feelings were definitely not to be trusted. This was a problem for me, since feelings were my main navigational tool.

I didn't understand the need to negate and deny feelings. They were patently undeniable, and yet everyone seemed to pretend they either didn't exist or didn't matter. I was taught that emotional expression indicated weakness, stoicism was strength, and being sensitive was a liability.

My brothers, who were also sensitive, worked hard to conceal any signs of vulnerability, while my parents hid from their feelings behind their intellect. This was very challenging for me because not only was I tuned into my own feelings, I was also acutely aware of emotions in others, even when they denied feeling anything at all.

My emotional radar worked overtime as I tried to decipher who was feeling what and why. While other kids were outside playing, I spent my time around adults, trying to make sense of their conversations and interactions. I quickly discovered that it wasn't just my family who said one thing while feeling another; most people seemed to exhibit this same kind of self-denying behavior. It was incredibly confusing.

At first, I was uncertain whether this withholding of feeling was deliberate, or whether people were simply unaware of the internal conflict they were broadcasting. I tried to understand what was going on beneath the surface. I questioned people's incongruities, but this did not go over well. I was told it was impolite and intrusive to ask personal questions. I eventually learned it was better not to point out the mismatch between words and feelings, but I desperately wanted to understand why people engaged in such pretense.

I wrestled with why no one else seemed to be disturbed by this. I thought there might be something wrong with me and my way of seeing things. I felt different and isolated, and even though I learned to keep my questions to myself, my curiosity never went away.

I continued to wonder about how people formed meaning out of their experiences, how they arrived at their conclusions, and why different people's versions of the same events often varied so dramatically. In learning to keep quiet all those years, I also learned how to listen.

The more I listened, the more adept I became at recognizing when things were left unsaid. I noticed contradictions, gaps in memory, and the places where stories trailed off into mumbles or caught in a person's throat. I became especially sensitive to the degree of animation with which people expressed themselves and tried to understand what opened or closed their conversational flow. I noticed patterns in people's stories—underlying themes, motifs, and repetitive elements that seemed to elude the storytellers themselves.

I promised myself that I would never do what I saw others doing: ignoring and overriding inner promptings, pretending not to know what I felt. But without being conscious of it, as I got older, I, too, became adept at overriding feelings and inner knowing. In my early twenties, I was given a devastating reminder of the dire consequences that kind of denial can have.

"POST-TRAUMATIC STORY DISORDER"

For me, those consequences came from denying an inner warning. When something in my gut told me to run, I didn't, and I paid a terrible price for that inner betrayal. I overrode a danger signal in an effort to prove that I was a "good person." A man was asking for help, and a good person shouldn't turn away from those in need. At least that was the story I told myself, and that story, combined with my refusal to honor my own knowing, set me up for a brutal assault.

The attack itself felt unendurable, but as if surviving it wasn't bad enough, it also left behind a traumatic imprint. I wrestled with Post-traumatic Stress Disorder (PTSD) and found myself sinking into a period of suicidal depression. It was during that dark time that I came to understand the profound impact of what I now call *Post-traumatic Story Disorder*—a distorted way in which we learn to interpret, manufacture meaning from, and re-create our deepest wounds.

The notion of Post-traumatic Story Disorder arose unexpectedly from one of my dark nights of the soul. On that particularly black night, I was struggling with despair and suicidal feelings. I felt broken and filled with fear, pain, and rage. Suicide was not only enticing, it seemed like the best and only solution. But I also knew it was impossible: I had two young children who needed me, and I couldn't abandon them that way.

Feeling totally trapped in my dark state, I paced the family room of our home, back and forth like a caged animal. As I passed the bookcase for the umpteenth time, I randomly reached out and grabbed a book, taking the first one that came to hand. I latched onto a thin hardcover volume I had purchased at a second-hand book sale years before but had not opened since. It was a companion prayer book for the *Tibetan Book of the Dead*. Its contents were to be read as a guide to a person to help them make the transition from dying to rebirth. It seemed oddly fitting to my circumstance, so I took it with me to read in bed.

LIFE, DEATH, AND LIBERATION

I knew nothing about Buddhist beliefs, so I opened the book with a mixture of curiosity and skepticism, but I soon found myself drawn into the strange undertow of the book's revelations. According to its teachings, at any moment, one could liberate themselves from the entire karmic cycle of life, death, and rebirth by simply facing and "becoming one" with the bright light within them. This was a totally foreign notion to me, but the book indicated that this was all that was required to achieve enlightenment, or Buddhahood. I had never had those aspirations, but I liked the implication of an end to suffering.

The book went on to say that, to accomplish this, one must accept fear, confusion, and suffering without becoming attached to it. I had no idea what that meant.

The book then described the stages in the "dying" process. In the first phase, the main trial or challenge was accepting your departure from the life you had known. During this stage, you would likely feel lost, confused, alone, and powerless. I could certainly relate to those feelings.

The book said that you would feel regret and experience difficulty in letting go of the life you had to leave behind. I knew this feeling, too. I felt like my previously innocent life had ended with the assault, and now I didn't know how to live or die.

The book went on to say that the remedy for transforming that confusion and discomfort would come from turning toward a numinous light. If you could look directly into its brilliance and become one with it, you would become enlightened. I did not believe in light of any kind at that point, but I continued reading. It cautioned that if you were unable to face that light, you would miss your chance for liberation and would have to move on to the next phase.

Feeling nothing but blackness inside me, I missed that opportunity for liberation, so I read on to the next stage. The book said this one would be infinitely more challenging. In this phase, you would be confronted by your greatest fears—in fact, every fear imaginable, a relentless series of horrors. This was referred to as entering the plane of "frightening karmic illusions."

During this terrifying passage, you would encounter not only your own dark deeds, but also monsters—half animal, half human creatures who would attack and rip you apart. This got my full attention; I had intimate knowledge of such monsters. I also felt a stab of shame, fearing I was somehow responsible for unconsciously allowing such a monster into my life.

According to the book, you were supposed to face such horrors and your part in them without becoming overwhelmed. The goal was to remain detached and free from getting caught up in those images. But then the book, which was already confusing, started to make absolutely no sense at all. It insisted that you needed to see those monsters for what they *really* were: illusions, manifestations of compulsive thought forms, and the reflection of your own dark consciousness!

I found this notion outrageous. How was I supposed to do that? Especially if the darkness wasn't just some illusion or thought form of my own conjuring? I didn't make up that monster. What if the monsters and the tearing apart were real, and the pain and suffering they cause also, real?

I felt duped and was suddenly furious at myself for getting sucked into that ridiculous book. Overwhelmed with anger, I jumped out of bed and threw it as hard as I could across the room. It skidded across my desk, hit the wall, and fell to the floor. My stomach went into a spasm, and my chest tightened.

It felt like a typical case of blaming the victim. It reminded me of all the times when, as a child, I was told that my feelings weren't real or that I shouldn't be feeling what I was feeling. My anger felt pretty real in that moment, and I argued, too, for the realness of my pain. After fuming for a while, the anger gradually flamed out. I was left alone again in my pain, so I cried myself into a stupor.

Eventually, I was able to breathe again. I felt emptied out. But into that emptiness crept the stirrings of anger again.

Feeling defensive and annoyed, I decided to prove that book wrong. I wasn't going to let it have the last word on what was real for me!

I got up to retrieve it, but when I crossed the room to pick it up, I noticed it had knocked something off my desk: the tiny, cockeyed clay mouse that lived there, a gift from my four-year-old daughter. I picked it up carefully, examined it, and noticed with gratitude that the fall hadn't damaged it. Something about that mouse gave me resolve. I placed it on my bedside table and crawled back into bed with the book.

I took a deep breath and paused, steeling myself before opening the book. I felt determined—oddly stronger and calmer than I had been since the attack. Maybe this was a new beginning. Maybe it was a good thing to actually stand up for myself and fight for my feelings.

But with that thought, something strange occurred. It was as though everything switched into slow motion, and I was somehow outside of my body, watching myself. I could see myself reaching for my familiar fear and pain, and to do this, I was going to have to conjure up and rerun a memory of the attack. Suddenly, a different kind of alarm went off inside me. I felt shocked and confused. Why on earth would I want to do that? It seemed like a totally crazy thing to do. Why would I choose to re-engage the very feelings that made me want to take my own life? Why was I arguing for the right to hang onto this?

And then it struck me...I was doing exactly what the book had been talking about. It had warned that an undisciplined mind would automatically be compelled toward dark thoughts and feelings, would experience the addictive pull toward suffering, would fixate itself on pain and frightening illusions. I was feeling that pull, and not only was it compelling, it was feeling just a little *too* familiar.

I was suspended in time as I witnessed myself desperately trying to decipher what was really happening. I grasped for the truth but didn't know where to find it...so I began surveying the facts.

This is what I noticed: I was alone, at home, perfectly safe and secure in my own bed, and yet, even with the certain knowledge of my safety, I was seeking to re-traumatize myself by conjuring up a memory that would make me re-live the horror of the worst moment of my life!

That realization was both terrible and profound. It meant that, in that particular instant, I alone was responsible for my own fear and suffering. *It didn't mean I hadn't been grievously violated or that I had to deny my pain, but it did mean I needed to stop re-running it and re-inflicting it upon myself.* By incessantly replaying that memory, I had been keeping myself trapped (as the book described it) on that plane of frightening karmic illusions, suspended in that dark territory between life and death. I was caught in my own Post-traumatic Story.

I was stunned. I took a breath, picked up the book, and continued reading. It said that when we are ensnared in this kind of illusion, we perpetuate an endless cycle of suffering, and until we liberate ourselves, we are doomed to repeat the same lessons over and over again. That definitely got my attention. I knew for certain I never wanted to re-experience that lesson.

I also knew I couldn't pretend the assault hadn't happened. Somehow, I had to acknowledge that painful experience without making it the focus of my existence. In that moment, I realized I had never really wanted to end my life; I had just wanted to end the pain I was feeling. I needed to learn how to accept the pain and somehow have a good life anyway.

The book also identified a third and final stage of transition: the preparation for rebirth. To avoid the pitfalls of re-creating the same lessons in a new life, it suggested that one must move through the darkness while actively choosing the light. Again with the light!

I tried to evoke an image of a bright light but couldn't. I

didn't know where to turn or how to find such a thing... but then I saw the mouse. I remembered the love in my daughter's face when she gave it to me, and I knew then I'd found my source of light. I focused on the love I had for my children, and as I did, my darkness lifted. I knew I had a powerful reason for living, and I wanted to be around to teach my kids how to find and face their own light.

Of course, I didn't achieve enlightenment or Buddhahood through this experience, and that moment of realization was only the beginning of a lifelong journey of learning and healing. I did study Buddhism, and even though I never became a Buddhist, I am incredibly grateful for my timely encounter with it and all I have learned as a result.

The story of my life is not about being assaulted; that was just one painful event. When I examined that trauma, however, I discovered that it was actually reinforcing a previously-established story that had already been running in the background of my psyche: a story about feeling alone and powerless in an unfeeling world. I had been unconsciously attached to that idea even before the assault. I knew I had a lot of work to do to decipher what other unconscious stories were running in the background and keeping me from turning toward the light of my deeper self.

I knew that hanging onto my insight wouldn't sustain me; I needed a way to stay connected to the source of that wisdom. I committed to my own version of a spiritual practice and began meditating daily, but that wasn't enough. So, I went back to university, thinking I might find answers there. I studied psychology, neurophysiology, and ultimately, clinical behavioral medicine but found trying to translate clinical concepts into the considerations of everyday life very frustrating. Science and critical thinking were invaluable allies, but I craved more than theories and proofs. I wanted to become conscious of what was going on in the background, and I wanted hands-on exploration and experiential learning.

I discovered there is no substitute for direct experience and feedback. In the classroom of everyday life, my learning came serendipitously, by following inner promptings and challenging underlying stories. I had to learn how to move beyond the instant answers my mind offered, so I could inhabit many different dimensions of myself and follow their life-giving directions.

It wasn't easy at first, but the more skillful I became at bypassing mental interference, the more I realized those inner promptings were not random. My contemplative practice became less an act of will and more a yielding to my calling. By following a deeper wisdom within, I became a lightning rod for new learning, and an unexpected world opened before me.

I discovered that teachers come in all forms, and sometimes our highest education arrives through hardship. I have had the privilege of learning from academics, scientists, indigenous elders, and traditional medicine people from around the world. I have also learned from my children, grandchildren, friends, clients, colleagues, strangers, and animals. Ultimately, no matter what the experience, I discovered that, in remaining open, life itself is the greatest teacher of all.

WHAT LISTENING TO CLIENTS TAUGHT ME

Initially, I wrestled with how to best share what I was learning with others. I didn't want to be an authority on anyone's experience except my own, but I did want to encourage others to learn how to consciously honor their own experience. I became a professional listener, and nearly thirty-six years later, I am still amazed at how much you can learn just by listening.

I listen to clients to discover how they have put their worlds together, to understand the influences that have shaped them, to discover their beliefs and biases, and to learn how they have worked with the feedback life has given them.

I notice the point of view they assume when recounting their tales and whose version of their lives they seem to be reporting. I observe what they protect, reinforce, or make sacred in their telling. I note their degree of self-awareness, how conscious and accountable they are, and to what extent they have made a connection between their inner world and their outer circumstance.

I also listen for the part of them that is rebelling beneath the surface of their presented identity, the deeper sense of self that is fighting to break through their pretense and set them free.

I listen with all of my senses so that I can teach clients how to listen to themselves in this same way—openly, with curiosity and wonder, free from resistance or judgment. I tell my clients that I won't be teaching them anything they don't already know, but I will provide them with a framework through which they can tap into their own deep wisdom. In learning how to listen to every part of themselves, they discover their own answers. In consciously reclaiming themselves, they become integrated and whole again. And so can you.

WHAT YOUR EXPERIENCES CAN TEACH YOU

When clients first arrive, they are often afraid of what will emerge from exploring their inner world. They have learned from experience that self-disclosure can be a risky business. Mostly, they are afraid that they'll discover some way in which they are wrong or inadequate. They are used to judging themselves harshly and are often full of rules and "shoulds" about what and how they are supposed to feel. They would rather erase their discomfort than seek answers from it.

It isn't until they begin to genuinely explore their automatic reactions to things that they discover how important their inner promptings are and how those promptings reveal what truly matters. Ultimately, clients discover that inner conflict can be a valuable ally, announcing change in the making—a new story emerging from within.

YOUR DEEPER STORY REVEALS PURPOSE

Through listening to people's stories, I have come to see that we each have a purpose, and that every life is an integral part of something much larger than the individual. Each person is uniquely endowed with the potential to activate something important in the world.

Just as there are no irrelevant parts of one's being, there are also no unnecessary experiences. Every experience plays an integral role in shaping who you are and what you are meant to bring to the world. Each personal pain reflects a growing pain in the evolving consciousness of the world, and every blessing is a call to give more from the deep reservoir of your individual being. Like a hologram, each aspect of the self reflects not only personal wholeness at the individual level but also an evolving wholeness in the world.

Wholeness can seem like an abstract concept but is an undeniable feeling. When all parts of yourself are balanced and integrated, you experience a harmonious flow in your life, a buzzing in every cell that insists you do something of value with the unique bit of life force you possess.

THE IMPORTANCE OF YOUR STORIES

Stories are how we make sense of our experience, and to a certain extent, we all suffer from some measure of Post-traumatic Story Disorder—not because we all have huge traumas we need to uncover and heal, but because we are all part of a social conditioning process that can unconsciously and inadvertently wound us and thwart the expression of our deepest self. Meaning derived from our early life experience contributes to the unconscious content of our automatic pilot. Until we bring that content to light, we are not really functioning from a place of conscious choice.

There is always a deeper story at work beneath the visible

surface of people's lives. That crucial story is both sensory and symbolic. It is encoded in our feelings, and to access and integrate its meaning, we must delve beneath our unconscious conditioning to meet it where it lives: in our emotions, sensory information, intuition, imagination, and in our dreams. There is a story at work beneath each challenge and change in our lives.

Nothing is ever quite what it seems to be at first glance. This is what makes stories such rich territory for exploration—they offer vehicles for wading through the complexities, paradoxes, and contradictions in life. They make the mercurial nature of existence graspable. The trick is to not grasp too tightly at any point along the way.

APPROACHING YOUR STORY WITH LOVE

Think back to a time when you first fell in love with someone. Remember how excited you were to learn everything about them? How you took special care to build rapport and establish trust, gazing at them lovingly and hanging on their every word? Wanting to know their entire life story, you listened carefully and responded empathetically, comforting them in the places they were hurt and standing up for them in ways they couldn't yet stand up for themselves. You worked hard to discover and respond to their needs, accepting them wholeheartedly, acknowledging their strengths, forgiving their weaknesses, and shoring them up as they developed and grew in those areas. You delighted in their gifts and quirks, supported their dreams, and encouraged them to realize their potential. This is how you turned *love* into a verb.

Imagine the relationship you could create with *yourself* if you used the same approach you take with a new love in your life.

The journey toward self-awareness is usually catalyzed when things go sideways in our lives. In our desperation to get to the bottom of the "problem," we can be hard on ourselves and come at things too harshly, proceeding as though we need to smash through an impenetrable layer of defense. And while it's true we all have some armoring, it's also important to understand why those barriers were erected in the first place.

All the hammering and prying in the world is not nearly as effective as honoring the longing from within to be known and accepted for who we really are. Only in an atmosphere of love and safety can defenses be dropped.

As you explore yourself with loving kindness, you uncover the unconscious narrative working in the background and begin to consciously connect with the deeper story of your life.

USING THIS BOOK TO FIND YOUR DEEPER STORY

I remember the agitation I felt as a teenager when I first heard Descarte's famous declaration, "I think, therefore I am." The notion that I was nothing more than my thoughts was deeply disturbing. I started taking note of many other aspects of my being. In noticing and acknowledging different dimensions of myself, I found it much easier to reflect on the nature of my experience.

To help you undertake your own exploration, I developed the Multi-dimensional Model of the Self contained in this book. The distinctions provided here are figurative rather than literal. The definitions I use are my own, although the concepts for them are synthesized from many sources. You have no such perfectly distinct and discreet parts, but you can think of each of these as a translucent layer of inner being contributing to a more complete picture of who you are. These parts act as a set of interrelated filters through which you experience the world. Each one has its own structure, intelligence, and unique form of expression.

To develop a more integrated and stable sense of self, we need to look at all these aspects and rebalance them within our system as a whole.

The following image shows fifteen interrelated aspects of self.

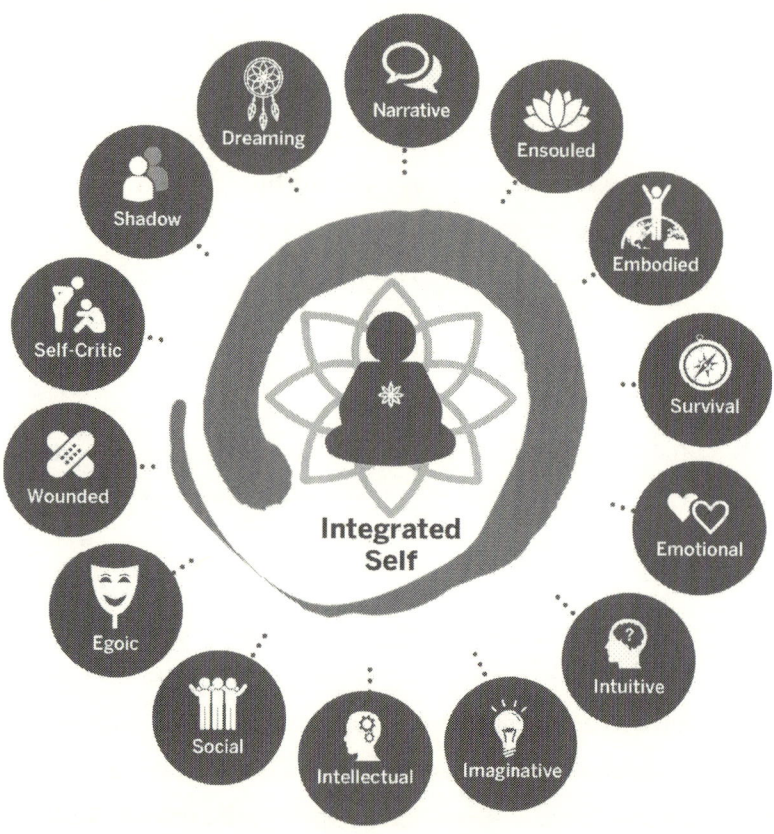

You will undoubtedly have greater fluency in and familiarity with some of these aspects more than others, but I encourage you to stay open and give yourself permission to explore each one as a potential source of insight.

You are more than the sum of your parts. Your deeper story emerges from integrating the wisdom contained within the stories you have encoded at every level of being.

By asking questions and connecting the dots between each part of yourself, a more cohesive and integrated set of responses can emerge. Those answers help to redefine your focus, shifting it away from the question, "What is the matter with me?" to the more essential one: "What *matters* to me?"

EXPLORING THE ASPECTS OF YOUR SELF

In this book, you will have a chance to explore how the various aspects of self are organized and how your deeper story pulsates through each part of you.

Each chapter in this book:

- Outlines one particular aspect of self
- Defines its role and function
- Provides examples of how that aspect shows up in your life
- Offers you an opportunity to reflect on and interact with that part

Here's the overview of each part that we will explore in depth in the ensuing chapters.

You were brought into existence as an **Ensouled** spark of life, called into being for a purpose. This is the initiating spark of consciousness with which you began your human journey. You rode into life on the first wave of air, when your breath and the breath of the world entwined. That initiating consciousness underlies and informs each new layer of self as you grow.

Then, as an **Embodied** being, you were swept up in a sudden synthesis of stimuli: newly developing senses emerged in relationship to your surroundings, rooting you in the time and place of your birth, family, and culture.

Nobody had to tell you when to eat or sleep; your innate **Survival** needs and impulses were perfectly intact. Your nervous system was a work in progress, and you began developing a range of responses to life's challenges. That early survival encoding makes you react automatically to potential threats.

As a feeling creature, your early **Emotional** needs were received and responded to by those responsible for your survival. How those needs were addressed ultimately became another layer of conditioning. Those early emotions also helped you to form the bonds and attachments that mark the unconscious beginnings of your social self.

Both sensitive and sensing, you had innate **Intuitive** and perceptual acuity. You were alert and attuned to subtle shifts of energy in your environment and to the feelings of those around you.

Feelings, sensations, and perceptions merged and coalesced within your mind's eye. Through **Imaginative** play, you experimented, learning about life and empathy through pretending and role-playing, and the creative impulse to reshape your world began to emerge.

Up to this point, you were the center of your own little universe and remained blissfully ignorant of the fact that the world was full of invisible lines called rules. But as **Social** consciousness began to emerge, you started to realize that your well-being depended on the good graces of others. You needed to decide who you were and where you fit.

As your cognitive mind developed, authority and rules began to exert a bigger influence in your life. You learned how to step away from your feelings to engage in the **Intellectual** and abstract thinking necessary for the larger world of school and social institutions. Because you could now anticipate consequences, you learned to make choices in relationship to the power around you. You also made your own rules in order to control your destiny.

Subject to both the vagaries of power and peer pressure, you learned about expectations and experienced the treachery of labels that sometimes left you **Wounded**. No matter how hard you tried, it would not be enough to protect you from having your innocence shattered—from being hurt and experiencing life's inevitable losses. Your wounding caused you to dim the light of your expectations about life.

As hormones came on stream, you rode out the highs and lows of emotional and sexual tension during your adolescent and teen years. You engaged in epic battles with your **Self-Critic**: doubting yourself, seeing yourself through the eyes of others, and wrestling with the standards that were set for you by others. You wanted to take back the power to define yourself.

You railed internally and externally against the definition others imposed on you and struggled to find a sense of **Ego** identity that would work for you. Passionate about life and wanting to make your own mark, you vowed not to fall into the mediocrity and entrapment of the adults around you.

By this point, you had become very strategic, having learned what parts of you were permitted expression and which parts were deemed unacceptable. There was plenty of feedback from the world around you, against which you developed a system of defense, a bulletproof way of being. Your **Shadow** became fully engaged to keep your real self safely under wraps while you navigated the minefields of life.

Emotional adaptation and adjustment carried you into young adulthood, where you wrestled with the challenges of independence and responsibility: how to manage and balance desire, expectation, effort, pain, and results. There were important decisions to be made about your future, even before the part of your brain that could process long-term consequences was fully developed.

As you moved into adulthood, you formed significant social bonds and connections with others and entered intimate long-term relationships—perhaps you chose to raise a family. You contributed as a member of groups, social movements, and organizations, investing time and energy into community and civic responsibilities to earn your place in the world.

During mid-life, you began to wonder what had happened to the life you thought you were going to have. A desire for a deeper life was awakened. You started to acquire new capacities for self-reflection and contemplation. You experienced new perspectives on your life circumstances, and you wanted to explore the meaning of your life with self-awareness and awakening consciousness.

Dreaming began to awaken and stir the unconscious depths of your psyche, calling you to re-examine the myth you were living.

It was time to review your **Narrative**—the story you accumulated along the way. You discovered how hindsight had blurred the edges of stories and memories into a continuous narrative flow. You decided to consciously interact with this story to get at its deeper truths and see your life as a whole.

You worked hard to blend your **Integrated** wisdom with that of the world's. In doing so, you moved from fragmentation to wholeness and were able to freely offer the wisdom harvested from your life's journey to the world.

INTEGRATING THE ASPECTS OF YOUR SELF

When you reflect on your life in context, you can see how each piece of your puzzle fits together. Organized around your reason for being, you recognize a deeper story that has always been running in the background.

With new perspective, you can see how even your wounded and most difficult moments were calling you to become more conscious and to refocus on what really mattered.

Looking beyond yourself, you also recognize that your struggles were not yours alone. All wounds are shared by others and show up in many ways in the world. You can see how a lack of consciousness in the world can also lead to devastatingly unintended consequences. In seeing the interconnectedness of your own experiences, you see how the same cry for healing works in the world.

But here's the thing. You don't have to wait until your elder years to sort yourself out. You can **be wise now**, despite whatever difficulty is presenting itself, by consciously engaging and integrating the wisdom that is already alive within you.

GOING DEEPER: GETTING THE MOST OUT OF THIS BOOK

To get the most out of this book, you can begin by simply having a question or issue in mind you would like to explore. As you read each chapter and complete the exercises and reflections, you are gathering insights that can be brought together at the end to honor and move forward with what really matters.

You can work with *The Deeper Story* questions alone, in partnership, or within a group. It is always useful to share your stories with others, as they will see elements that you may overlook. In workshop settings, this is the part clients enjoy the most: listening to each person's stories and helping one another find hidden value within them.

As you ask the questions of each dimension at the end

of the chapters, you can begin to weave a new narrative about your life and put your themes to work for you.

Here are some ways to approach the questions:

- Release the need to do anything but be fully present.
- Drop out of your head and into your body (feel your bum in the seat, feet on the floor, etc.).
- Breathe and settle yourself.
- Get grounded and centered.
- Focus on each question and allow answers to come to you.
- Resist the urge to judge or evaluate; simply write your answer and move to the next question.

Things you may notice when tuning in (either for yourself or when listening to others):

- Sensations arising in your body. Simply let those sensations, feelings, or emotions arise. Do not interpret or evaluate them; just allow your feelings to wax and wane as you continue to be present.
- Shifts or animation of energy. Notice where energy expands or contracts in your body, gets lighter or heavier, intensifies or lessens, becomes more fluid or congested, etc.
- Images that arise spontaneously. Acknowledge them and let them pass—you can make a note of them, but

there is no need to grasp or interpret anything. Later you can learn how to inhabit and embody the images to bring their hidden content to light.

- Fragments of memory may also surface. Again, don't get attached; just make a note.
- Sounds: auditory impressions from your environment, fragments of music or songs, or random words or phrases in your mind may trigger associations.
- Scents or tastes may arise.
- Patterns, themes, motifs, or repetitive elements may show up.
- Notice places where focus and attention fades.

There will be a feeling of completion when you have stayed present with a story for a time. Afterward, make notes, drawings, or recordings from which you can later interact with the information.

CHAPTER 1

THE DEEPER STORY
OF YOUR SOUL

Many years ago, I went to see the Dalai Lama at a crowded stadium. He slowly moved through the crowd of people that lined the passageway leading to the stage, offering a personal greeting to each one. Eventually, he climbed the steps to take his seat. Settling into his position, he took time to adjust his robes, rocked back and forth, pursed his lips, adjusted his visor, and scratched his head. As time passed, a hush fell over the crowd. In that vast space, 20,000 people waited for his first holy utterance. You could've heard a pin drop. Finally, he spoke. "Stop trying to be Buddhists," he said. There was a great (and possibly relieved) laugh from the crowd.

Continuing, he asserted, "It is more important to be yourself, to practice loving-kindness, compassion, and mindfulness in your own way. The goal is not to be spiritual but to be a better human being."

I wholeheartedly agreed.

When it comes to the topic of spirituality, or being "ensouled," I feel the same way. Whatever your orientation may be toward the concept of *soul*, I invite you to let go of its religious connotation so you may consider it within the larger framework of becoming a better human being and living your life in a meaningful way.

We enter our exploration of your deeper story by considering the original spark of consciousness with which you began your life's journey. Your soul holds the key to your reason for being, and in working with its promptings, you discover what makes you feel most alive.

THE ROLE OF THE ENSOULED SELF IN YOUR DEEPER STORY

Function: Encoded with your reason for being, your soul stirs your innate potential and guides you toward fulfillment of both your individual and larger purpose.

When out of alignment, you feel void of purpose and direction, disconnected from yourself and others, disempowered or cynical. You engage in self-defeating or destructive patterns, feel you have nothing meaningful to contribute, and may feel that your existence makes no difference to the world.

When in alignment, you feel on track in your life, engaged and fulfilled; you have a sense of purpose, accept your place in the scheme of life, and work toward meaningful contribution.

Key Areas of Development: Spiritual Intelligence,[1] Interconnectedness, Personal and Transpersonal Consciousness, Non-dual[2] or Unitive Consciousness, and Values that Provide Meaning and Significance

Dominant Questions: Who am I? What calls me? What is my purpose?

Arc of Development: From unconscious individualism to interconnected consciousness

THE CALL OF THE ENSOULED SELF

You are born to be and become a certain way; the mark of your distinctive essence or character is present at birth. Any parent knows this about their children—from the very beginning, each child is distinctly different from the next. Even with common history and shared similarities, every being is unique. The ways in which you fit in and stand apart are at the core of healthy individuation and self-actualization. Discovering the value of your unique identity is foundational to living a fulfilled life and activating your greater purpose.

The human journey is about coming to terms with your reason for being. At the soul level, this means elevating your consciousness, refining your character, becoming deeply attuned to a sense of inner calling, and living with a sense of meaning and purpose.

> *"We do not 'come into' this world; we come out of it, as leaves from a tree. As the ocean 'waves,' the universe 'peoples.'"*
>
> —ALAN WATTS[3]

Through conception, you were brought to life as an individual spark of consciousness, a short-term custodian of a particular bit of life force inextricably connected within a greater whole. It is impossible to separate yourself from the living field of intelligence you inhabit. This is the paradox of being *ensouled*: you are both individual and indivisible at the same time.

Soul is your point of connection to the eternal awakened presence within you. It provides the interface between the individual and the collective, the personal and transpersonal, the known and unknowable.

One of the great challenges of life is learning how to reconcile your individuality with your essential interconnectedness, remaining true to your individual nature while maintaining a sense of responsibility to the whole. To do this, you must become aware of your impact and acknowledge that your life, and the choices you make, matter. As part of a dynamic energy exchange, you are not only affected by the world around you, but also exert your influence on the world. Your existence leaves an imprint on the living field of consciousness from which you emerged.

In the Western worldview, oftentimes the idea of living one's purpose is tied to some notion of work and success, but soul purpose has nothing to do with accomplishment. It is about absolute acceptance, alignment, and refinement of what is already within you.

THE JOB OF YOUR SOUL

Your soul coordinates your individual journey within that context. It operates at a subconscious level, propelling you toward fulfillment of your innate potential. A compelling internal force at the core of being, your soul makes you conscious that you are more than the ephemera of day-to-day existence or the material trappings of your life. It constantly reminds you of your true nature and encourages its expression.

Your soul is not attached to issues or worldly drama. Its aim is to evolve your level of consciousness and bring the unconscious material that holds you back from expressing your true potential to the surface. When some kind of loss, difficulty, or challenge occurs, the very things you avoid, resist, or abhor are all opportunities for your soul to advance your level of consciousness.

Your soul not only illuminates you from within, awakening consciousness of your particular gifts and activating your highest potential, but it is the evolutionary healing force underlying both personal and planetary transformation.

At the personal level, your soul focuses you on what matters. It can show up as the burning question that lives inside you, the mystery you were born to solve, the thing that keeps you up at night, or a deep sense of purpose that guides you. Your soul's agenda pulsates beneath each thing you love and feel drawn to, and it activates your life force accordingly. It can awaken you to the opportunity present in any given situation. It also constricts the application of your energy and enthusiasm when you are out of integrity with yourself and have lost sight of what's important. Your soul helps keep you accountable.

Soul expression is simply about being wholly and uniquely yourself, releasing the full measure of your *creative life force* into the world. At the interconnected level, your purpose is to feed back the wisdom gleaned from your lived experience into the evolving consciousness of the whole.

Life circumstances can either thwart or facilitate this inner drive toward expression of one's true self. There are many things that turn us away from authentic expression, and whenever we deny, repress, or suppress our true nature, we become fragmented. These denied parts of oneself become the soul's dark counterpart—the shadow.

Your soul metabolizes your life experience, and like an alchemist, it can transform your darkest moments into gold if you let it. You must learn to recognize its call within you and yield to those inner nudges. The more you become present to the nudging of your soul and allow it to guide you, the less interested you become in controlling your experience. You become open to life's mysteries, attuned to your own creative flow and the personal hum of life in your cells.

BEING WHOLLY ORIGINAL

Despite social pressure to conform, we value originality, authenticity, and clear expression of individual purpose. When someone trades their uniqueness for a more generic, acceptable, or profitable form of self-expression, we say they have "sold their soul." We equate being soulful with having a deep, profound, and passionate nature and see people who have lost their inner center of gravity as "lost souls." Openness, honesty, and authenticity are often described as "baring one's soul."

If you think about the people you admire most, you will notice they exhibit a kind of authenticity and nobility of character. People who are in alignment with their soul's purpose demonstrate heightened awareness, operate beyond mere self-interest, see how things are interrelated, and make choices accordingly. They often devote a lifetime to working toward betterment in some area of existence. They hold a rare integrity and do not get derailed by drama or blaming others but seek to improve conditions for all.

Knowing your own deep nature—what you came in with and what you have to offer the world—is not a new concept. The ancient Greeks used the term *arête*, meaning the innate gift of one's true potential. Psychotherapist James Hillman[4] speaks of the soul as an acorn: just as the acorn holds the full potential of the oak tree within it, an inner map is already present within each person's soul at birth, containing instructions for their full actualization.

During one of my earliest discussions with Navajo Elder Leon Secatero, he explained the meaning of *Nilch'i*. According to Leon, this breath of spirit, or sacred wind, first swirled its way into your being at conception, carrying with it what he called your "original instructions," your reason for being. As its currents swirled around and through your developing body, it formed the distinctive whorls, loops, and arches of your fingerprints, indelibly imprinting your individuality. The soul-breath not only connects you to everything, it is also responsible for making you (and the mark you leave on the world) wholly individual.

As author James Kale McNeley expounds, "In the Navajo way, *Nilch'i* has no direct English equivalent. It refers to the air or holy atmosphere that pervades all life, connecting and communicating among the elements, animating through thought, word, and movement."[5]

The Greeks used another term, *entelechy,* to describe how one's original instructions are brought to life. According to writer Jean Houston,[6] entelechy is an inner coding that acts as dynamic inner propulsion toward the realization of one's true potential.

First Nations people speak about a person's *medicine* in this same way: an inner guiding gift that attracts the individual to their *sacred path*. In his book *Being and Vibration,*[7] Pueblo Medicine Man Joseph Rael describes how within each person there is an inborn heart vibration that keeps them attuned to the song of their soul purpose. Each of these terms describes a connection that goes beyond a temporal sense of self.

INTEGRATING YOUR ENSOULED SELF
BREATHING LIFE INTO YOUR DEEPER STORY

Many cultures and religions refer to the notion of a soul as an immaterial living essence, a life force or energy that is dispersed back to the universe at death. That life force is animated through breath, from your first inhalation at birth to your last at death. The Hindus refer to this as *prana*, the "divine breath" of the cosmos, on which all things depend for health and life.

Interestingly, the verb *to be* comes from the Sanskrit word *bhu*, "to grow, or make grow," while the English forms *am* and *is* have evolved from the same root as the Sanskrit *asmi*, to breathe.[8] Breath and life force are entwined.

When you flow with the breath of life, you can dissolve artificial boundaries and separations created by the mind. This is why meditation practices begin with focusing on the breath—to calm and center you—to go beyond distracted habits of thought and awaken to a deeper sense of presence within you. When you connect through breath to this deeper presence, you are alert to the potential for growth and expansion within each experience.

Just as connecting to your soul through breath helps you dissolve boundaries around you, it also dissolves them within you. Breathing through every part of your multi-dimensional self helps to activate your potential for wholeness.

Emerson speaks to this important awareness: "Soul is not a function but the illumined presence that animates all functioning—when it breathes through intellect it is genius, when it breathes through will it is virtue, when it breathes through affection, it is love." [9]

Reconnecting with the life force within you stirs to consciousness parts of you that have gone numb or been shut down along the way. No matter which dimension of self is experiencing challenges, through regulating your breath, your soul can refocus you on what is essential.

Through conscious breathing you can begin to notice when you are in or out of alignment with your deeper purpose or true intentions. You will discover that your energy and breath become irregular and contracted when you are stressed, conflicted, and incongruent. Feeling a lack of flow, being stuck, unable to gain traction, and feeling disconnected or isolated are all indicators of having lost contact with your soul's inner guidance.

When you are triggered into a reactive state, you hold

your breath. This becomes an important cue for recognizing your state of flow. Reconnecting with your breath also connects you with what is essential in your experience. When you are in a fully expanded and expressive state, you breathe freely and easily.

OTHER PRACTICES TO INVITE THE SOUL

Experiences of soul are often expressed as a sense of oneness—a unitive experience in which you go beyond the confines of your everyday concerns and tune into the larger sense of the universe at work. In this state, we recognize that everything contains elements of everything else and nothing is wholly separate or independent; everything is connected.

The soul helps us gravitate both toward the center and the edges of things where distinctions blur—where things meet, cross over, and transform into one another. From the soul's point of view, we not only inhabit the world, we are an integral part of it. Being in nature, practicing presence, meditating, praying, or engaging in contemplative states can induce this nameless sense of interconnectivity.

As a child, my first experience of soul came through time spent in nature. I escaped the chaos of home to find peace in the nearby fields, woods, and wetlands. My senses were attuned and alert, but my mind would go quiet as

I settled into my favorite spot between the saplings. I would lose track of myself as I merged with my surroundings—light flickering through leaves, air alive with the sound of insects, the pungent scent of soil and swamp. I sensed an awakened presence within and all around me, a continuum of consciousness both me and not me at the same time. This is my definition of soul—an awakened presence that allows one to harmonize with and find their "place in the family of things."[10]

HOW PATTERNS REVEAL THE SOUL

"What is not brought to consciousness comes to us as fate."

—CARL JUNG

When people say that everything happens for a reason, they are acknowledging an underlying intelligence in the way events unfold in peoples' lives. This becomes clear when you examine the repetitive patterns we all exhibit. There is an internal gravitational force that inexorably pulls people toward specific types of experience and expression. Seemingly unrelated and random events take on entirely new meaning when seen in the light of your soul's purpose. This was true for a client named Greg.

Greg's Story

Greg loved outdoor sports of all kinds: hiking, mountain biking and climbing, whitewater rafting, camping, etc. He worked for a summer at Outward Bound just after high school and wanted to lead nature expeditions professionally...until he discovered there were few jobs available and the pay would never support him. Instead, he took a decent-paying job at an IT company as a means to support his outdoor adventures.

By his mid-thirties, he was bored and dissatisfied at this job. The long hours sitting staring at a screen were, by his own definition, "soul crushing." He felt listless and disheartened, so he decided to take some time off and went for a hike on the West Coast Trail.

Along the trail, he encountered and befriended a couple. They hiked together through the day and spent evenings around the fire telling their life stories. It seemed that for every topic or issue raised, Greg had an analogy from one of his misadventures in the outdoors.

As the days went on, Greg's spirit was recharged, and he began to feel more like his former self. At the end of the hike, the couple asked him if he had ever considered counseling as a career. At the time, he laughed at the idea. He enjoyed helping people but couldn't imagine sitting in a room all day long listening to peoples' tales of woe. After returning to work for a few days, the notion started to tug at his consciousness. While on a coffee break at work, he picked up an outdoors magazine and discovered an ad for a Wilderness Therapy Program. He found his calling and never looked back. Greg now runs wilderness adventures for troubled youth to help them learn life skills from nature.

People sometimes refuse their sense of inner calling, but when they do, they invariably find themselves circling back around to it in some way. Like moths returning to an illuminated area, people repeatedly turn toward their inner light. They are unconsciously attracted to their soul purpose and to the kinds of circumstances that bring them face to face with it.

FIGHTING THE CALL OF YOUR SOUL

I have a friend who is a brilliant psychologist. She had a thriving practice for years, was renowned for her success, and had a lengthy list of people waiting to see her. She was grateful for the gift that helped so many people and also provided her with a great reputation and a good living. Her real passion, however, was writing, another way in which she was extraordinarily gifted. Although she loved it and felt fulfilled when writing, in comparison to working with clients, it seemed like an indulgence. For years, she was torn, lamenting her lack of time for serious writing. She became increasingly burnt out in her work with clients. It wasn't until she was forced to stop working through repeated serious illnesses that she finally accepted her calling. She came to realize that just because she was good at something, it didn't mean she was obliged to offer her energy in that particular form. Now, she hears from all kinds of people about how emotionally transformative and meaningful her writing has been for them. She eventually became a strong advocate for writers, and she enjoys teaching the healing potential of writing to others. What once seemed like indulgence is now her deepest source of satisfaction. Her health returned when she stopped fighting the call of her soul.

> *"You don't get to choose what you get famous for and you don't get to control which of your life's many struggles gets to stand for you. The best you can do is work at not caring too much about the outer symbols and continuing to do whatever it is that centers you and makes you remember your true self."*
>
> —ERICA JONG[11]

UNEXPECTED EXPRESSIONS OF SOUL

When I work with clients, we generally start by identifying patterns to determine where they are out of sync with themselves. Gradually, the nature of their repetitive challenges gives context to the work of their soul.

Toward the end of our time together, we work a bit more

directly by taking an inner journey that leads them right to the core of their being, to their soul. This is not something they are anticipating in the session, so their experience is spontaneous and unexpected.

In more than thirty-five years of working with people, I have come to discover that people's patterns are pretty much generic and derivative, but I have never heard any two people describe their experience of their soul in the same way. Soul qualities may be universal—wise, timeless, compassionate, and connected—but the individual experiences of it and how it shows up in one's life are completely unique to each individual.

THE REWARDS OF THE SOUL

People often point to Joseph Campbell's "follow your bliss" teaching as though it was the full prescription for getting in touch with one's purpose. Although your soul can awaken you to your purpose through joy, it can also awaken you through challenges. Challenges invite you to reflect on how you may be out of touch with your own deep nature. My psychologist friend's story is a good example of that.

There is another thing Joseph Campbell used to say that I think captures this other side of soul work: "If you are falling anyway, make your falling a voluntary act." In other words, work with whatever is presented and see where it takes you. Let your soul be your guide.

If you feel trapped in a dead-end career, relationship, or pattern of any kind, don't run away from it, run *toward* it. Let it teach you what you have been ignoring about your needs and your true nature. In the end, you may or may not choose to change the job, leave the relationship, or heal the pattern, but if you have worked with your soul's directional guidance, you will have a higher purpose in doing so. All circumstances are learning opportunities to get in touch with your deeper needs, values, and principles.

When you feel incongruent and out of sorts in your life, take a breath and let the wisdom of your Ensouled Self help you transcend the dramas, trials, and constrictions of everyday life and turn you toward what is essential, evolving, and eternal. Let your choices be driven by higher aspirations to fulfill your potential.

People often seek a purpose in the world without recognizing that their purpose is entirely evident within them, and all it takes is noticing what makes you come alive.

You are a work in progress, and when you work toward balance and what matters, you can honor and offer your original strengths to the world.

DEEPER PERSONAL REFLECTION

Take a moment to settle yourself comfortably. Be sure you are in a space where you can be undisturbed for a period of time. This is soul time, time to simply reflect on the nature of your existence.

Breathe in and open yourself to possibility. Feel that breath animating you, activating the life force at the center of your being. Let your breath intermingle with the breath of the world. Feel your breath animating the larger field of energy that you inhabit and share with all life.

Your breath contains the same life force that moves the tides and carries seeds on the wind across plains, fields, and forests. Sun-warmed breath touches the earth, connecting with minerals borne from fresh mountain streams that deliver nutrients to life forms germinating within the soil. Thousands of organisms working together produce nourishment for all the world's inhabitants: plants, insects, animals, and humans. All drawing from that same essential source, and each adding its own unique ripple in the sea of life.

Creating and procreating, making new life out of the same raw elements, each breath drawn, then releasing its particular magic into the world. Everything affecting everything else, each contribution interconnected but specific in its expression.

Feel that life force moving in you. Notice where it flows freely, where it gets stuck, where you withhold it. What would happen if it simply flowed fully and freely? What would change? What would be different? What would come alive in you? What would grow and take on a life of its own? That animated life force—of you and beyond you—what beautiful thing does it bring into the world through you?

Life begets life, and each thing influences other things. What are you influencing and what are you influenced by? What inspires you? When do you feel most vibrant, alive, and expressive? How do you give life to what matters?

What were you born to initiate, change, resolve, activate, or bring to the collective consciousness? It doesn't have to be grandiose. It only has to come from that wellspring of love and life within you.

Love and life force are strengthened by each other. Love moves mountains and makes people come alive. Not love in the small "l" romantic sense but *Love* in its most powerful sense. When you love something, you tend it, protect it, nurture it, and make it grow. By investing your interest, care, and attention, you breathe life into what matters to you.

It may be that your soul's calling is the very thing that

makes you feel or see yourself as "different" from others. Embrace and explore what makes you unique. Not everyone shares the same calling or can see the value in another's preoccupation. Only you know when you have been captivated by a calling because you feel it every time you are engaged in something you truly love.

Everyone does not operate at the same level of consciousness; we are all here to teach each other how to evolve. What are the things that you love and the challenges you face trying to evolve in you?

DEEPER QUESTIONS FOR YOUR SOUL

This is a time to notice, listen, feel, and record the responses from your Ensouled Self. When wrestling with a specific issue and needing soul guidance, you can reflect on these questions.

- What does my soul want me to know about this?
- Is the way I am handling this issue consistent with expression of my true nature?
- How might this issue be related to my highest aspirations or sense of purpose?
- What step could I take to bring myself into alignment with my soul's guidance?
- What deeper story is my soul trying to awaken in me?

LIVING THE DEEPER STORY OF YOUR SOUL

Your soul catalyzes the potential for integration, not just within yourself but also integrating what you have to offer to the world. Your purpose is not something outside of you that you must aspire to; it is a life force within that you must yield to.

When you are out of sync with yourself or going against the grain of your own nature, your soul will nudge you back onto your path. Your soul won't let you off the hook or allow you to coast through life on cruise control; it provides constant reminders of the unexpressed potential that lies within you. It doesn't lament when things fall apart; it celebrates the opportunity to steer you back toward a deeper and more fulfilling expression of your potential.

All living things are ensouled, endowed with unique life force, so the more you honor that force within you, the more deeply interconnected you will be with the living world around you.

I AM

A spark of consciousness carried me into this world and clothed itself in my being, its immaterial essence and animating presence binding me to the web of life. Interwoven within the fabric and fate of all that is, my soul's imminent guiding force insists that I live up to the sacred potential of my life. **I am ensouled; therefore, I am.**

CHAPTER 2

THE DEEPER STORY OF YOUR EMBODIED SELF

Your body is beautifully and sensitively calibrated to alert you to any imbalance occurring within you, and you can trust it to yield valuable information about the source and nature of that imbalance. Whether the origin of the disturbance is mental, emotional, or spiritual, your body can bring unconscious material to the surface, where it can be processed and integrated to free up your vital energy.

Getting quiet in your body—noticing and acknowledging sensation as it arises without mental interference—is what embodiment is all about. In an age of instant gratification and instant answers, it is critically important to learn how to slow down enough to listen to the wisdom of your body.

THE ROLE OF YOUR EMBODIMENT IN YOUR DEEPER STORY

Function: Your body's job is to perceive, experience, and engage life through your senses and to physically manifest your potential in the world.

When out of alignment: You become disconnected from your senses, from others, and from the earth. You ignore, override, or deny bodily signals. You lose contact with your essential needs and become trapped in the mind and its insatiable appetites.

When in alignment: You are grounded and attuned to the pulse of life within and all around you. You are present, discerning, and responsive to both internal signals and external feedback. You exercise appropriate self-care.

Key Areas of Development: Sensate intelligence,[12] somatic awareness, health-promoting behavior, boundary setting, awareness of both internal and external ecology, awakened wildness.

Dominant Questions: Where do I begin and end? How do I fit into the ecology of the world?

Arc of Development: From head-driven to fully embodied.

THE CALL OF THE EMBODIED SELF

From the moment of conception, you pulsated with life force embodied in the rhythmic expansion and contraction of heart and lung, muscles, and synapses. While in the womb, you learned to stretch and bend, and at birth, your vocal chords announced your arrival in no uncertain terms. Your earliest needs were expressed through sound and movement, crying to be fed and rooting for a breast. Your senses were awakened through smell, taste, and touch, while your eyes and ears tried to decipher the world around you. You reached out to find the boundaries of your being, hands flailing and then grasping a toe.

As you developed, your repertoire of expression grew. You gurgled and cooed, laughed, and yelped in protest. Eventually you learned to coordinate your movements—to walk, climb, tumble, and dance. Your body was limber, sensual, and alive with feeling. You experienced and expressed your needs without inhibition, crying for food when hungry and reaching out for consolation and comfort when required. You had your own timetable, dictated by bodily processes alone.

Entrainment of those processes began at day one, as your caregivers gently nudged you toward a reality that had nothing to do with your feelings—an adult world governed by concepts, clocks, and convenience.

Later on, school required you to sit still, to abandon the urge to move or make noise. It dislocated your attention, moving it away from your body toward the development of your mind. Through this conditioning, your body/mind connection was ruptured, creating an artificial separation. Eventually, you learned to use your mind to manage, subdue, and control bodily urges. As you grew, you became adept at overriding bodily signals, learning to squelch your body's cries for sleep, movement, nourishment, and nurturance. You learned to sit still, hold your tongue, speak when spoken to, pay attention, and to do as you were told.

Having a measure of control over bodily urges is necessary, but when you fail to respect natural bodily rhythms and processes, you dislocate from the ground of being and lose touch with a powerful and passionate dimension of self. When physicality is repressed, so too are playfulness, imagination, independence, creativity, curiosity, and your connection to the living Earth.

As a child, you were in touch with the natural world. You engaged it with every sense, smelling the rain-washed earth, watching the clouds overhead, skipping, sliding, and somersaulting your way through a day. Children love everything, from mud puddles to stars. Trees, bugs, and animals are experienced as living wonders, as are rocks, shells, and the man in the moon.

"We love our bodies by staying in them and feeling them fully. The body thrives on love...acceptance of all its functions and parts."

—STEPHEN KAPLAN-WILLIAMS

Adults are often too preoccupied to notice and respond to the natural world surrounding them. Our connection to the Earth is made even more tenuous when manmade ingenuity lengthens our days with artificial light, alters the seasons with indoor climate control, and de-natures our food.

When we talk about nature as though it is something separate or outside of us, we deny our physical rootedness—our interconnection and interdependence with the Earth. With that disconnection, we lose contact with a source of sustenance beyond mere creature comfort. When we dominate nature and exert too much control, we create an imbalance that puts us in danger of becoming the kind of parasite that kills the host.

In her song "Big Yellow Taxi," Joni Mitchell sang, "We paved paradise and put up a parking lot." In the same way we alter and cover what is sacred and natural in the Earth, we now do the same with our bodies, valuing body image over health, caring more about how we appear than how we inhabit the body we are given. We mold our bodies to mimic abstract ideas of perfection, adding and subtracting with a surgeon's knife. Control, striving for perfection, taming our wildness, and worshipping our own cleverness can cause us to ignore or deny critical warning signs from our body and our world.

"The physical world of our bodies gets remodeled by our psychic and conceptual worlds."

—STEPHEN COLE

WHEN YOUR BODY SPEAKS

The human body is incredibly complex. Even with everything modern medicine and technology has illuminated, there are still many mysteries that run deeper than our reach. There is much to learn about how to listen to your body and how to take responsibility for deciphering its messages.

When it comes to health and inner harmony, there is no one answer or formula that fits all. Science and medicine can only approximate and account for statistical averages rather than individual differences, and because you are unique, it is critically important that you become an expert on your own physical well-being.

Ted's Story

My friend Ted provided a good example of this. Ted had

been a small-town family doctor in John Day, Oregon. He was known for his deep caring and attentiveness. He retired late in life as congestive heart failure started to get the better of him. He focused on his writing, wood carving, and feeding the endless stream of wildlife that wandered into his yard. One evening while I was visiting, he began to feel faint and asked me to take him to the hospital.

I took him to the town's gleaming new facility where everyone seemed to know and adore Ted—he had delivered and doctored more than half the staff who worked there. He was whisked into a treatment room and as the on-call doctor arrived, I got up to leave, but Ted asked me to stay while he was being examined.

A caring young cardiologist spoke with Ted about his symptoms, ordered some blood work, and had a nurse set him up with an IV Lasix drip to reduce his edema. Ted was hooked up to various monitors, and some type of a scan was done. The doctor departed to await the test results. When he returned, he spoke briefly with Ted about his symptoms and told him he was setting up an appointment at the larger hospital in Bend, Oregon, so Ted could receive a cardioversion procedure to regulate his heartbeat.

When the doctor left the room, Ted asked me what I

thought about his treatment. I told him I was impressed with how caring everyone was and how quick and efficient the whole process seemed, but that I also noticed there had been no real physical examination. I was surprised that Ted had hardly been touched at all, except for when he was being hooked up to machines. He agreed.

I asked him what the doctor would have noticed if he had done a physical examination, and Ted said he probably would have noticed an odd pulse that he was feeling somewhere between his heart and his liver. There was something in his voice when he said this, so I asked him if he thought the doctor had missed something important. He said he wasn't sure.

I asked him if he was confident that the cardioversion procedure was the right thing for him, and I sensed the hesitation and reservation contained in his reply. Although he could see that it made sense medically, something in his body didn't seem to agree. I asked Ted if he knew any old-time cardiologists who could give him a hands-on examination and listen to his concerns.

We sat out the night until his IV treatment was done, alternately chatting, dozing, and communing with the numerous people on shift who dropped by to check on Ted and wish him well. When we got home, he tracked down one of the older cardiologists and booked an appointment right away. He was driven up to Bend to see that doctor, and immediately afterward, an echocardiogram was done. The cardioversion procedure was cancelled, and Ted was taken in for an emergency heart valve replacement.

Listening to his body saved Ted's life, and after surgery, he said he felt like a new person. We took a bit of the extra time allotted to him to sort through some things that had been "troubling his heart" in other areas of his life.

Ted needed the doctors, the medicine, and the technology, but he also needed to include the wisdom from his own body for his healing.

People with chronic or life-threatening illness discover the need to listen to their body in entirely new ways. Limited resources demand a reassessment of the distribution of one's energy. Illness is the kind of gift that forces you to make a fearless inventory of the places you have been leaking energy and to learn how to set healthy boundaries. A period of illness often rebalances a person's life and restores well-being in unexpected ways. Healing is not just about eliminating illness; it is a process through which you are restored to wholeness. By listening and responding to bodily needs, you build resiliency.

LEARNING THE LANGUAGE OF YOUR BODY

In your daily haste, you may not even notice when your mind is pushing you past the needs and requests of your body. The plans and demands of life dictated by your mind don't necessarily include consultation with your physical being.

Healthy embodiment means inhabiting, feeling, and responding to your body's signals. To do this, you must shift your attention and orientation away from being head-driven and attend to the responsive language of your body. This begins with getting grounded, getting present, setting healthy boundaries, and developing discipline. Knowing when and where to set your own lines in the sand is not something someone else can teach you—but your body can, if you are willing to listen.

Some people are naturally fluent in the language of their body and find it easy to tune into specific sensations that speak to them, but the majority of people I work with need a little practice at giving themselves permission to feel and express their bodily sensations without mental interference.

Part of this challenge is that your body doesn't use the language of logic to communicate, and it doesn't yield pat, packaged, or necessarily pretty answers. Your body has a vast repertoire of attention-getting devices, some subtle and some downright undeniable. But to yield the benefit of bodily wisdom, you must learn how to stay in your feelings rather than jumping to the need to figure things out and come up with an explanation.

North American culture (and schooling) conditions us to believe that if you are asked a question, you must immediately have an answer at the ready—but the answers your body gives may not be immediately obvious.

Staying with your feelings is like developing a photograph. First, you must capture an image and then work with it in the dark. You need to apply the right chemistry and focus on it with the right equipment. Most difficult of all is the process of waiting patiently as the image slowly emerges in the developing tray. You can't rush the process without damaging the integrity of the image.

The information your body yields is not immediately logical or explicable, but it "makes sense" at an entirely different level. In the same way a symptom is not the actual problem but merely an indicator of an underlying issue, your body responses cannot necessarily be taken at face value alone. Attention and exploration are required to get to the deeper story.

You can become clued in to bodily requests through sensations of pleasure, tension, or pain, or even more subtle feelings of expansion or contraction. You can notice when your body feels unsettled, agitated, or antsy. You can engage awareness through the use of sensory association—noticing when something "doesn't sit right" with you, or when "something smells fishy," and so on. You can also notice when excitement is stirred: when you feel drawn, attracted, or particularly curious about something.

Stress, pain, and illness can all be extremely useful sources of information. Your body may be speaking to you in physical terms, but it may be indicating an imbalance that is occurring in some other dimension of your being. Using these physical signals wisely and engaging the healing power of embodiment moves you toward your unfolding wholeness.

> *"Often the hands will solve a mystery that the intellect has struggled with in vain."*
>
> —CARL JUNG

Adaptability can be a great asset, but it can also be a liability when you use it to adapt to unhealthy ways of being. You can get used to anything. You can adapt to operating at a high level of stress and think it is normal—just the way things are.

People have differing tolerances for pain, tension, and

dysregulation. You may tend to be hyper-reactive, easily overwhelmed, and to feel things intensely. Conversely, you may be overly buffered, withdrawn, shut down, or "comfortably numb." Your body can express or constrain your sense of aliveness, freeing or freezing your vital energy.

THE GIFTS OF TRAUMA

Your body is part of a larger field of energy that moves through you as stimulation and information. When trauma occurs through violations of physical, emotional, or energetic boundaries, healthy self-regulation is disrupted, and your nervous system is reorganized. Energy and information stored as cellular memory affects your well-being at both the conscious and unconscious level. Unresolved trauma will interfere with healthy bodily functioning until it is released.

> "...Someday the body will present its bill, for it is as incorruptible as a child who, still whole in spirit, will accept no compromises or excuses, and it will not stop tormenting us until we stop evading the truth."
> —ALICE MILLER, *THE DRAMA OF THE GIFTED CHILD*

Little things can disconnect you from embodiment, and those same things can reawaken and restore your sensual nature when you choose to listen to your body's story.

Tom's Story

Many years ago, I worked with a lovely young man called Tom. Tom felt crippled by inhibition. He lived in fear of being judged and humiliated by others. He felt physically shy and awkward. He told me a story from his childhood that haunted him. When he was about five years old, he and his family were leaving their home on a Sunday to go to church. They stepped outside into the fresh morning air that had been cleansed by a storm the night before.

The world was sparkling and alive. Swept up in the pure sensual joy of it, Tom dashed across the yard and shoved his whole head into a fragrant flowering bush. He drank in its intoxicating aliveness. His entire family was taken aback by this uninhibited expression of delight. They responded to his passionate embrace of beauty with derision and laughter. They teased him about it and never let him live it down.

Tom felt humiliated. That moment of magical communion with nature was stolen from him and replaced with a feeling of shame. This was the beginning of Tom's departure from his sensual nature.

The mocking from his family took on a life of its own within Tom's mind. It developed into a belief that it was unsafe to feel or express his feelings. He worked hard to stifle any spontaneous expression. To avoid potential vulnerability and humiliation, he fought against his body's cries for aliveness. He became stilted and inhibited in his bodily expression and tried to avoid attention. He became withdrawn and inwardly focused—except when he drank. In a state of disinhibition, Tom said he became something of a wild man. He used alcohol to dissolve the wall he had erected against his feelings.

I worked with Tom to help him reclaim his childlike sense of embodiment. He had to dissolve that frozen moment of trauma and re-engage with his feelings. He worked hard to reconnect with his inner child, and when he did, he discovered a lovable little guy he likened to the character "Tigger" in *Winnie the Pooh*—a character so full of life and joy that he literally bounced off the forest walls. His inner child's natural mode of expression was diametrically opposed to the stiff and self-conscious physical being that Tom had trained himself to become.

Reconnecting with the embodied and expressive enthusiasm of his inner child, Tom was able to free his energy to find his passion again. He worked to heal and integrate that moment of childhood humiliation as part of the deeper physical story of his destiny, and when he did, he was able to express himself more authentically.

With his natural intensity and lively humor, he found he no longer needed to rely upon alcohol as a social lubricant. His energy was freed to focus on what was truly important to him. He combined his aesthetic sensibilities with his love of nature in practical and meaningful ways in his work as a developer of green housing projects.

> *"When the body is finally listened to, it becomes eloquent. It's like changing a fiddle into a Stradivarius."*
>
> —MARION WOODMAN

INTEGRATING YOUR EMBODIED DIMENSION

There are many ways to reconnect with your body and its story, but to begin, you must learn to inhabit your flesh and bones, to ground and connect with the living presence that is your body. You must enter your body as a sacred space, gently and with respect, with tenderness and consideration, with warmth and loving attention. You need to breathe love and mercy into every nook and cranny of your physical being so it can release its tension and sorrows, yield its information, and tell its story on its own terms.

Learn where you start and end. A good place to begin an embodiment practice is to reconnect with the physical boundaries of your body—to fully inhabit the physical space in which you begin and end. This is important especially if you are used to being in your head all the time, or if you have had an experience that made you want to vacate your body due to physical or emotional pain.

Take a moment to check in with yourself and notice how connected you are with your core strength, and how familiar you are with the boundaries of your physical space.

Many years ago, as part of an embodiment exercise, a teacher started moving toward me, telling me he was going to harm me. I didn't do anything to stop him until he was within inches of me. He asked me why I would let anyone who was threatening me come so close without responding. He kept repeating the exercise until I finally used the power in my body to take my own space. As he moved toward me, I stood up, felt a surge of strength, focused my energy, engaged eye contact, stretched out my arm, put up my hand, and told him to STOP. He did, and I felt strong and rooted to my spot. It was a valuable lesson that I never forgot.

I hadn't realized my tendency to shrink inward in the face of conflict rather than stand up for myself from a place of strength and confidence. This body lesson applied to other areas of my life as well. I worked on grounding myself, centering in my core, and experimented with martial arts and energy work to learn how to claim my physical space.

In his brilliant books about healing trauma (*Waking the Tiger* and *Healing Trauma*), Peter Levine talks about ways to release energy that has been trapped and frozen in your body through traumatic events. He suggests a practice in which you physically mark your territory and claim your space by defining its edges. You can do this by making a circle with tape, string, or wool. Or if standing on paper, you can draw or cut out a circle that is the size of the area you take up when standing with your arms outstretched. Placing yourself in the middle of that circle and recognizing it as the energetic extension of your body in space helps to define where you begin and end.

I have done a similar practice in a class with a Celtic teacher, who had us stand with arms fully extended from our sides. She encouraged us to expand our personal energy and fill the entire space outward to the end of our fingertips. We were then told to lower our arms into their natural position while maintaining that same energetic boundary as though they were extended. Maintaining that circumference, we then walked through a crowded marketplace. It was amazing to see people move out of the way to accommodate the full extent of the space we claimed. It was also gratifying to feel the full flow of life force through our bodies as we did this. It is both grounding and strengthening to claim the piece of Earth on which you stand.

GROUNDING

Once you have felt every part of your body and focused your energy within the boundaried space, you can then feel your feet making contact with the Earth. Imagine and allow roots like those from a tree to extend down from the bottoms of your feet into the welcoming ground beneath you. As you breathe and feel that energy moving up from the ground through the bottoms of your feet, through your legs, buttocks, and groin area, up through the trunk of your body, breathe it all the way up to the top of your head. Feel yourself connecting and drawing the living energy of the Earth into your body and filling you out to the boundary of your skin.

Scan your body, checking your bones, muscles, tendons, and joints, feeling the structural elements that give your body strength. Feel your organs and sensory system and feel the hum of energy through your living cells.

Imagine someone you love—a child, a grandparent, your partner or pet—and feel your love for them spreading like warmth across your chest. Breathe into that feeling of love and circulate it throughout your entire system.

ASK YOUR BODY QUESTIONS

Start a conversation. Feel your own center of gravity and breathe all the way down into it. Stay in contact with it as you walk and talk. You can enter a dialogue with your body about any question you have. All you have to do is ask the question, let go of the need to figure out an answer, and attend to your bodily response. Just breathe and allow information to come to you, and when it surfaces, just stay with it, whether it is an image or sensation. Allow yourself to merge with the sensation or the image you receive. Move into it and inhabit it.

Allow your body to use movement and gesture to express whatever presents itself. Stay with the process until you feel the embodied answer emerging. Embodying your feelings, your thoughts, emotions, intuitions, and dreams yields an entirely new dimension of integrated awareness.

You can also do this with any part of you that feels numbness or pain, or areas where illness has visited. Invite your body to share information through sensation, vision, or movement. Let that part of you speak about its purpose and about what might be required for healing. Express gratitude to your body for its amazing support, for all the things it makes possible, from brushing your teeth to making love.

Notice your judgment. Wherever you feel physically hurt, disabled, or in some way different than others is another potential source of body knowledge. How you embody self-judgment, judgment of others, and how you embrace differences and diversity are all important aspects of your body's deeper story.

Notice your behaviors. Your body provides many clues to the source of behavioral imbalances in your life. Examine your excesses and deprivations—overworking, overeating, lack of sleep, sedentary lifestyle, medicinal and recreational drug use, etc. Engage with the bodily needs and sensations that underlie these behaviors. Forgive yourself for past abuses or ways in which you have mistreated your body and learn how to exercise self-care.

Notice your language. It is also important to notice the words and phrases you commonly use when referring to your body. Notice how you speak about yourself.

Practice loving-kindness. Release any judgments you have about your appearance or how your body functions. Practice loving-kindness toward your body, loving it as it is, while taking steps to improve the way you feel. As Mary Oliver says in her poem "Wild Geese," "You only have to let the soft animal of your body love what it loves."[13]

Get out into nature. Give yourself a break from technology and get outside. There are many scientifically proven benefits to spending time in nature. It reduces stress and inflammation, strengthens your immune system, lowers blood pressure, and improves mood and mental clarity. Let your body rediscover its own natural rhythm.

Embodiment practices. Embodiment practices such as yoga, bodywork, martial arts, and physical exercise strengthen your sensate intelligence, physical awareness, and well-being.

‖‖‖

DEEPER PERSONAL REFLECTION

Take a moment to settle into a place where you will be free from disturbance or distraction for a few moments. Breathe into your body and allow yourself to become fully conscious of your body. Feel your whole body, from the top of your head to the bottoms of your feet. Notice the feeling of your bottom making contact with the seat beneath you, the position of your limbs, the rhythm of your breath, and anything that your body is currently feeling—warmth or coolness, comfort or discomfort—just be aware without evaluation.

As you discovered in your ensouled meditation, with breath comes your sense of life, and on those currents, you draw the world into yourself. Sometimes, that world announces itself with a particular scent. So notice the scents that surround you now. Breathe in the world you are inhabiting.

Scent can be particularly evocative. Engage your scent

memory to recall the warm fragrance of bread right out of the oven; the familiar, welcoming smell of your grandmother's house; the scent of newly-mowed grass; or freshly cleansed air after a spring rain. Or, maybe there's a special person in your life whose scent evokes a strong response—pheromones are a big part of our attraction and connection to others.

Your sense of vision is another gift of embodiment, taking in the sights of the world around you. Look at your current surroundings and notice light and shadow, color and contrast, and the objects that surround you.

When you see a beautiful scene in nature, your body responds with feelings of awe. Picture a place in nature that awakens that feeling in you or imagine gazing at the face of someone who is dear to your heart. Feel the sense of pleasure that fills your whole body.

Your sense of sound can awaken you to the world around you: the rhythmic sound of wind through the trees, rain on rooftops, water lapping on a rocky shore, or the sound of your lover's heartbeat as you lay your head on their chest. You can be transported by an exquisite piece of music or have your heart stirred by the sound of a loved one's voice. Feel sound waves travelling through your body.

There are so many gustatory delights to be experienced.

You can taste the world's abundance in an earth-kissed carrot freshly pulled from the ground, or in a burst of tangy sweetness when biting into a newly picked apple. Your sense of taste can also bring with it a sense of connection with others; this is why so many of our celebrations revolve around the sharing of meals.

And then there is the incredible sensual joy of touch: touch that sends shivers down your spine, loving touch that comforts and reminds you that you are not alone, one that offers strength and support through a squeeze of shoulder or an encompassing hug. Or you can feel your body's sheer delight in feeling diverse textures of sand, grass, stone, wood, the soft peach fuzz of a baby's head, or the warm fur of your favorite animal companion.

Check in with your body's wisdom on a regular basis, and you will discover that it is always telling you what you need. Trust its messages and guidance and be grateful for its ongoing feedback. Learn how to inhabit your body with grace and treat it with kindness.

Feel the boundaries of your body and its connectedness to everything else at the same time. Feel the sensitivity of your skin as it makes contact with the world around you. Feel the strength of the muscles that help you to walk and bend and stretch. Feel your heartbeat and the pulse of life through your veins. Feel the flow of oxygen entering, circulating, and exiting back into the world. By simply surrendering to the embodied current of life, you are connected, not only within yourself but to everything around you.

DEEPER QUESTIONS FOR YOUR BODY

This is a time to notice, listen, feel, and record the responses from your Embodied Self. When you're wrestling with a specific issue and need your body's guidance, you can reflect upon these questions.

1. What does my body want me to know about this?
2. What physical sensations are present?
3. What are my senses telling me?
4. What steps could I take to become grounded and embodied—to become present to the authentic strength within me?

LIVING THE DEEPER STORY OF YOUR BODY

When consciously engaged, your sensual nature provides a unique form of awareness. Use your sense of sight to acknowledge both the beauty and the tragedy in the world. Notice what things attract you and call your energy forward to engage. Utilize your hearing consciously to tune into the sounds of life and of others around you, listening for opportunities to respond. Awaken your sense of touch, and consciously and responsibly give and receive comfort and pleasure with it. Learn to respect boundaries—your own and those of others. Allow your sense of smell to inform you when something needs attention, either because it is not right, or to stop and appreciate the gifts of nature around you. Eat consciously, nourish your body, and enjoy and give thanks for the life-giving sustenance provided by the Earth. Stay connected and feel all your sensations, allowing them to inform you about what is important.

Consciously listening to and caring for your body is what connects you with its deeper story. And if you stay present to the embodied pulse of life itself, it will connect you with the heartbeat of the world.

I AM

My body is a sentient miracle composed of earthly elements and stardust—the bridge between spirit and matter. I bump up against the world in my skin suit, but boundaries blur in this sensory symphony called life. I exchange a continuous flow of energy and information with forests and streams, riding waves of light and sound, my heartbeat harmonizing with the rhythms of the earth. Gravity anchors me, but my backbone defies the pull, and muscles engage to carry me upright through the landscapes of my life. Rooted in physicality and part of the living ecology of Earth, **I am embodied; therefore, I am.**

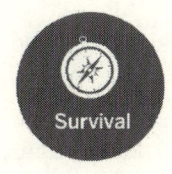

Survival

CHAPTER 3

THE DEEPER STORY OF YOUR SURVIVAL SELF

For the most part, we go about our daily lives as if existence is no big deal. We forget that we are living miracles with countless internal processes conspiring to keep us alive. It's only when a threat appears that we suddenly remember we are *alive* and want to stay that way. We become conscious that existence is not only a time-limited offer but one that comes without guarantees.

Survival instincts awaken us to both the precariousness and preciousness of life. When worked with effectively, they force us to face issues of vulnerability, acquire strengths, learn, adapt, and evolve. But sometimes what seems like a threat is really a wake-up call of another order.

THE ROLE OF YOUR SURVIVAL SELF IN YOUR DEEPER STORY

Function: Your Survival Self expresses your innate drive for self-preservation. It is designed to keep you alive long enough to fulfill your evolutionary potential. You develop survival strategies at every level of being.

When out of alignment: You become reactive, and perceptions of danger can become distorted. Driven by self-preservation and self-interest, you may become aggressive in addressing perceived threats. Erecting unnecessary barriers, you can become disconnected and lose empathy. You may become shortsighted and behave in ways that are detrimental to others, to the Earth, and ultimately, to your own long-term interests.

When in alignment: You proactively engage your senses, intuition, imagination, and intellect to anticipate and avert potential danger. You work toward improving potential survival for yourself, for others, and ultimately, for the world around you.

Key Areas of Development: Adaptive Intelligence,[14] Mindfulness,[15] Risk-Assessment

Dominant Questions: What part feels threatened or needs protection? How can I respond proactively?

Arc of Development: From Mindless Reaction to Mindful Responsiveness

THE CALL OF THE SURVIVAL DIMENSION

Our evolutionary heritage layered us with survival instincts that operate at the species, community, and individual level. Biological urges to procreate ensure continuity of human presence on the planet, while recognition of common ancestry leads us to protect our families, communities, territories, and ways of life. At the individual level, we are born with reflexes designed for self-preservation that are operative long before we are capable of understanding there is a "self" to protect.

Most people think of survival instincts in terms of our "fight or flight" mechanisms, but survival drives, reflexes, and strategies function at every level of being. Survival response can be unconscious and reactionary, or it can be consciously and skillfully engaged to elevate the human condition.

In the pyramid that represents Maslow's hierarchy of needs, physiological survival and safety are foundational, suggesting that our basic needs must be met before we can function at higher levels of consciousness. This is true, but survival challenges occur at all stages of the journey toward self-actualization.

At the purely physiological level, your CSO, or Chief Survival Officer, is your limbic system. This area of the brain regulates many critical functions related to survival, including your emotions, visceral responses, motivation, mood, sensations of pleasure and pain, associations, memory, and behavior. All sensory input is processed and distributed to higher cortical areas through your limbic system.

This brain system controls your autonomic nervous system (ANS), which functions mostly below your level of consciousness to regulate involuntary visceral responses: everything from blinking to digestion. You can consciously regulate a few of its functions, such as breathing and heart rate, but for the most part, your ANS goes about its business without your conscious participation.

It is divided into three parts: the sympathetic system, which is responsible for fight or flight reactions; the parasympathetic system, which is involved in rest and recuperation; and the enteric system, which regulates your gastrointestinal activity.

The sympathetic nervous system is your gas pedal, and the parasympathetic is your brake. Along with the neuronal meshwork of your gut, these systems kick into high gear to react to danger long before your conscious mind can evaluate the nature of the threat.

When it comes to potential threats, your brain is a short-cut junkie, valuing speed of response over accuracy of threat assessment. When a threat is perceived, the limbic areas of your brain take command of your entire system. Your amygdala (which is responsible for sensory associations) activates response in your hypothalamus, (which controls your ANS and your neuroendocrine system). Hormones and neurotransmitters arouse the tried and true evolutionary responses of fight, flight, or freeze.

Meanwhile, the "luxury" functions of your mind/body, such as complex thinking and immune response, are suppressed to conserve energy. Having a cold is irrelevant in the face of imminent death, and you don't need to calculate the velocity of the car careening toward you before leaping out of its path. Reaction is king in the land of survival—but not all perceived survival threats are created equal or should be treated equally.

You are hardwired to react to anything that looks like, sounds like, smells like, or in any way resembles any previously-identified threat. This emergency alert system shoots firsts and asks questions later; that's why a garden hose can accidentally activate your snake phobia, or a backfiring car can make you duck for cover.

This hair-trigger hyperarousal system was necessary for survival in the heyday of our Jurassic Park-like past. Fight, flight, and freeze reactions are perfectly designed for eat-or-be-eaten type situations, or circumstances involving acute stress. In the short term, these unconscious reflexes make us strong, resilient, and capable of handling significant survival challenges. We want these unconscious responses available for emergency situations, and certainly need them in the early stages of our lives before we develop the cognitive skills and maturity to make accurate risk assessments.

However, what was a threat to your three-year-old self may not require the same degree of reaction when you are thirty, so becoming conscious of these unconscious survival patterns is a necessary part of our maturing process. We need to update our system from time to time to ensure we aren't dependent on reflexes we've outgrown. The vestigial remains of outgrown reactions can be reactivated, especially during times of vulnerability.

When our systems are overtaxed with stress, we lose our powers of discernment. We tend to perceive and react to non-life-threatening events as though they were threatening our survival. Our overloaded system defaults to survival mode.

USING SURVIVAL MODE CONSCIOUSLY (OR NOT)

If there actually *is* an emergency to which you need to

respond with immediate action, you can utilize the elevated energy of your survival response, and once your action has been taken, your parasympathetic nervous system can calm things down and bring you back into a state of homeostasis.

If, on the other hand, you can't or don't take immediate action, you may become trapped in a survival state that can take a serious toll on your health. When we continually keep our foot on the gas pedal, things rapidly spin out of control. The physiological consequences of survival circuitry in overdrive are well documented.

- When you perceive a threat, your blood immediately goes from the frontal lobes to the back, "fight or flight" centers of the brain. Blood moves from your digestive centers to your large skeletal muscles. Glucose is released, requiring insulin from your pancreas. Over a prolonged period, this may contribute to diabetic conditions.
- Your adrenal glands release stress hormones to increase breathing, heart rate, and blood pressure, which can contribute to hypertension over time.
- Your blood manufactures cholesterol for energy. To prevent excessive bleeding, your blood-clotting mechanism becomes engaged. This can eventually leave deposits in your arteries, increasing the potential for arteriosclerosis or stroke.

- Cortisol released from your adrenal glands affects your thymus and suppresses your immune system, so when this response is prolonged, it can leave you susceptible to opportunistic viruses, bacteria, or activation of genetic predispositions to disease.
- Muscle tension along your shoulders, spine, and legs, designed to prepare you for fight or flight, can ultimately lead to chronic muscular pain if unrelieved.
- Your blood/brain barrier, which normally protects your brain from toxic incursion, becomes more permeable during heightened stress, so chemicals have increased opportunity to enter and affect your brain.
- Chronic stress creates acidity in your system, which can contribute to inflammatory conditions over time.
- When the threat is over, your blood moves to the organs of detoxification and elimination—your lungs, liver, and kidneys—which can be overwhelmed with toxic overload.

HOW SURVIVAL MODE KEEPS US REACTIVE

Survival is a stressful business. If overused, the very responses designed to keep us alive can ultimately jeopardize our survival.

Being in survival mode also affects your emotions, thinking, and behavior. Once triggered, you can't access the forebrain areas that govern your inhibitory responses and executive functioning. These are the areas necessary for objective thinking, planning, and creative problem solving—the very skills required for proactive rather than reactive response.

Once you are in a reactive mode, logic leaps out the window, and perceptual and cognitive distortions ensue. Emotional reactivity takes over; you think, speak, and behave in ways that would be foreign to you at times when you are in your "right mind" or in a balanced state of consciousness.

Your brain signaling becomes less efficient under extended duress, so you become more easily aroused and irritable, prone to negativity, resentment, and paranoia. Your judgment is impaired, and as discernment deteriorates, you are more likely to interpret benign situations as threats.

In the heat of the moment, people don't always recognize when they have been triggered into survival mode and how it can skew their perceptions. In fact, far from acknowledging their judgment as impaired or questionable, people in survival mode often cling to a desperate sense of certainty, believing their thinking is accurate and their emotional reactions justified. They may not be in their right mind, but they certainly believe they are right.

Andrea's Story

A good example of this occurred to a client of mine named Andrea. Andrea experienced an extreme reaction to a newly-appointed member of her department, a man named Brian. Whenever this coworker came near, Andrea felt a surge of dread and imminent panic. She had a strong defensive reaction to him but couldn't account for her intense aversion. She assumed her reactions meant there was something untrustworthy about Brian. She developed a strong antipathy toward him and actively engaged in subterfuge to get him removed from her department. Andrea's boss was alarmed by this uncharacteristic behavior and sent her for coaching.

Much to Andrea's surprise and embarrassment, it turned out that the source of the problem was not the new employee but her own unconscious reaction to the cologne he was wearing! Whenever she was near Brian, the scent of his cologne triggered a traumatic association from Andrea's past. She was reliving a Post-traumatic Story based on unprocessed memories of an abusive uncle, who just happened to use this same aftershave. Before she had been able to consciously recall that incident, Andrea was totally convinced that the source of her discomfort was Brian himself, and she felt fully justified in her reaction toward him.

This is just one extreme example of what most people

do all the time: filter current circumstances through past experience and learning. When a past imprint is unconsciously associated with our survival, our biophysical response to ordinary experiences can overwhelm our rationality and lead to extreme reactions.

When Survival is Threatened

At its most basic, our survival conditioning can be as simple as activating our startle reflex. When taken to its extreme, we can have a full-blown Post-traumatic Stress/Story response. Most of our survival reactions fall between these two ends of the spectrum.

Many years ago, I took a course at the Hermann Brain Dominance Institute in North Carolina to understand the role hemispheric dominance plays in people's perceptions and behavior. Many of the participants were Human Resources professionals, but there were also a number of military educators present. One of them was a colonel working at the Pentagon who was responsible for developing training programs for the US Armed Forces. We had several interesting discussions about the value of self-assessment tools. The colonel and I agreed about their limited value if they were only administered and evaluated under ideal circumstances. We both knew how radically self-perception and behavior change under duress and how quickly the ideal self disappears when triggered in a survival response.

In her book *A Natural History of Love*, Diane Ackerman provides a striking example. She tells the story of an anthropologist who witnessed the cultural breakdown and dark descent of a Ugandan hill tribe of hunter-gatherers after they were forbidden access to their traditional hunting grounds.[16] When starvation set in, so too did survival instincts that ultimately unraveled the previous peaceful and cooperative social fabric of the tribe. Scarcity led to hostility, competition, and cruelty, highlighting the dramatic turn human behavior can take when survival is threatened.

SURVIVAL MODE AND THE SHADOW SELF

When you perceive threats to your well-being, family, livelihood, or property, it can activate aspects of character that reside deep within both your survival and your shadow self. The dark and primal side of human nature is brought to the surface whenever one feels threatened. Even the most mild-mannered and agreeable person can exhibit extreme or even violent behavior when they perceive a threat to their security. Relationships disintegrate into battlegrounds when feelings of emotional safety are disrupted, and wars are waged when nations feel security is threatened.

Operating at the survival level can narrow focus to the point where we lose sight of the big picture. It replaces inclusivity and collective interest with self-interest. It diminishes tolerance for diversity and undermines our capacity for expressing empathy, compassion, and humanitarian ideals. It breaks the web of life, disconnecting us from one another and from nature. The consequences of unchecked survival response, with its inability to see beyond the immediate, may imperil life on the planet altogether.

Ultimately, survival is a matter of adaptation and adjustment, of balancing the need for safety and the need to learn and grow as conditions change. When looking at the multiple dimensions of yourself, it is also important to investigate what happens when that part is challenged or threatened in some way. Only when we consciously learn to work with and embrace both the brilliant *and* the shadow side of our survival self can we truly begin to live fully and introduce thriving into the baseline of the human condition.

INTEGRATING YOUR SURVIVAL DIMENSION

We are all subject to errors of perception—to being unconsciously triggered and, at times, unnecessarily reactive and defensive. It comes with the territory of having a "self" to protect. Usually we understand these moments in retrospect, after we have reacted, but we can also learn to anticipate and desensitize ourselves to triggers.

IDENTIFYING AND CHALLENGING YOUR SURVIVAL REACTIONS

Changing survival reactivity requires the willingness to become self-aware and conscious of your responses. When you feel flooded and overwhelmed, it's time to be curious about the roots of your response. There are specific cues that can help you determine whether you are reacting to something real or imagined—whether you are engaging an overlay from the past, or factually and accurately assessing the content of your current experience. You may not be discerning once you become caught in the reactive mode, but you can at least notice that you are reactive and vow to evaluate the situation more objectively once you have settled down. Later on, you can reconsider your response in honest self-reflection, without judgment or blame.

Here are some ways you can begin to reclaim conscious choice and empower yourself to respond with a greater level of awareness and accountability. Make note of the following cues and then compare how these reactions differ from times when you are in a balanced and healthy state of responsiveness.

- Become familiar with the bodily sensations that accompany your reactive and defensive state.
- Attend to areas of vulnerability and the emotional triggers that activate your defenses.
- Notice the type of thinking you employ in such circumstances. Evaluate the veracity of your inner dialogue in these moments.
- Identify what part of you is feeling threatened, and why.
- Ask yourself where you may have experienced these feelings in the past. Are you replaying an old pattern?
- Assess whether your behavior is in keeping with your usual value system. Notice if your reaction solved the problem or got you the result you were looking for.
- Have a greater level of objective scrutiny and conscious perspective. Is there another way you might interpret and respond to this situation?
- Review your past for clues about where you might be vulnerable to having a survival reaction triggered. Note times when you have felt under attack, when you have been traumatized, where you felt overwhelmed, threatened, or unable to cope, or where you felt extremely challenged in your sense of security and safety.

As you work through each layer of your multi-dimensional self, notice the themes and patterns that emerge. In each survival reaction, there are opportunities to consciously grow and evolve *new* patterns of response that more accurately reflect the deeper truth of your being.

DEEPER PERSONAL REFLECTION

Take a moment to settle yourself in a place where you will be free from distraction or disturbance for a few moments. Breathe in through your heart and send calming waves of loving energy and attention down into your tummy and solar plexus area.

The sensitive circuitry in this area of our body is often where you feel survival prompts—we call these gut reactions. Keep breathing and sending calming energy to and through your solar plexus. Feel that calmness deepening and allow it to move outward and to radiate through your entire body, sending waves of comforting peaceful energy through every part of you. Feel calmness flowing into your bones and peace and safety relaxing your muscles.

Notice if there are any areas that resist this comfort and consciously give them loving attention, letting go of tension and releasing defensive responses. Speak reassuringly to those places in yourself and feel them soften.

Thank your nervous system for the great job it does in ensuring your safety. Remind it that you are continually growing, learning, and gathering new skills. You are working to free your mind and heart from stress by becoming increasingly conscious, clear, and proactive.

You cannot control life—you can only control your response to it—so the goal is not to be safe all the time, but to build the strength and resilience necessary to consciously face and deal with challenges as they arise. Think of the many times you have already done this in your life, all you have come through. Your challenges have been building your center of gravity—the thing that rebalances you when the winds of change try to knock you over.

Breathing into your solar plexus and down into your lower body, connect with the earth beneath you and feel its grounding support. Give yourself permission to learn and grow and become increasingly adept at consciously building feelings of strength, calmness, and security. Know that you can access these feelings when you need them. Let life continue to stretch your comfort zone and be willing to take some risks as you focus on what truly matters.

Remind yourself of how fortunate you are to live in a part of the world where you can take the time to reflect on feelings of safety. Reflect on ways that you can bring greater feelings of safety to your world.

This is a time to notice, listen, feel, and record the responses from your Survival Self. When you're wrestling with a perceived threat and need your Survival Self's guidance, you can reflect on these questions.

- What does my Survival Self want me to know about this?
- What part of me is feeling threatened?
- What is at stake?
- Am I accurately assessing this situation, or am I caught in a Post-traumatic Story response?
- What steps can I take to calm my nervous system so I can gain better perspective in this situation?

LIVING THE DEEPER STORY OF YOUR SURVIVAL SELF

In the ideal of Maslow's hierarchy, all people would have an opportunity to have their basic life needs met, and thus would have opportunities for connection, growth, and the realization of their potential. A sense of safety is the most basic personal and universal prerequisite to any advancement in the human condition.

Understand what is required to meet *your* basic needs. Learn what promotes a sense of safety for you. When you are secure, you can be more present and help to establish a greater sense of safety for others.

Threats, both real and imagined, can wake us up and initiate necessary change at both the personal and global level. We may not be able to control all the events that unfold in our lives, but we can certainly control the way we respond to them. If we focus on honoring the warning, using discernment and proactive response, we will create greater levels of security for ourselves and the world.

Working constructively with the deeper story and instinctive wisdom of your survival system is the best prescription for dealing with mortality. When you do, you truly honor the gift of this one, precious life.

I AM

Every day, beyond my conscious awareness, my survival is negotiated at a purely organic level. Swirling strands of recombinant DNA bark out their orders. Cells are born, proliferate, and die, while electrochemical sparks ignite my brain, heart, and gut. Elements combine, cooperate, and conspire to sustain my vital energy. Muscles and reflexes remain at the ready, sensitive, and alert to environmental cues. I evolve in safety, bursting forth in animated glory like a butterfly shedding its chrysalis, but with the remotest of perceived threats I instinctively recoil and regress cocoon-ward. I am an organism with a biological imperative to survive. **I survive; therefore, I am.**

CHAPTER 4

THE DEEPER STORY OF YOUR EMOTIONAL SELF

"Emotions are the heart of our aliveness and the source of our individuality."

—SAM KEEN

Imagine if one day's routines simply blended into the next, with each moment taking on a dull sameness. With only cool calculation to influence your choices, you are not particularly invested in anything and have nothing compelling to strive toward. Consequently, you have no concerns about missed opportunities or wasted potential. There is no excitement, enthusiasm, or sense of wonder to motivate you; no passion, love, or joy to be experienced; and no anger to fuel activism or promote positive change. Without empathy, you experience no guilt or regret, and there is no sense of loss when people pass from your life. This is a world experienced without the benefit of emotions.

Emotions wake us up and make us feel alive. They illuminate what we care about and fuel our determination to make the most out of life. They can teach us about what is important and how to survive and thrive in an uncertain world. When we accept and embrace our emotions, they make life worth living—but if they are over-activated or under-developed, they can make our existence a living nightmare.

THE ROLE OF YOUR EMOTIONAL SELF

Function: Closely tied to both survival and thriving, emotions allow you to identify experiences of discomfort and well-being. Emotions provide essential feedback and motivation for identifying and addressing your needs and your unique expression. Emotions also support formation of bonds with others.

When out of alignment: You feel overwhelmed or powerless to respond in emotional situations. You may generate drama and act out, or shut down and withdraw, breaking the connection with both your inner world and with others.

When in alignment: You are able to feel your feelings,

identify their source, and express those feelings in healthy ways, balancing joys and sorrows to maintain stability. You are able to establish healthy bonds with others.

Key Areas of Development: Affective Intelligence,[17] Self-Awareness, Resilience, Thriving, Empathy and Compassion

Dominant Questions: What are my feelings? How can they help me thrive and evolve?

Arc of Development: From Numb to Fully Expressive

THE CALL OF THE EMOTIONAL DIMENSION
HOW YOUR BRAIN PROCESSES EMOTIONS

In chapter 3, we looked at the role of the limbic system and its critical role in our survival, but it also plays a significant role in the processing of our emotions. In fact, the word "limbic" is derived from the Latin word for "border." It is aptly named, due to its position between the brain stem and the cerebral cortex. This allows the limbic system to integrate information from both unconscious and conscious sources and help to bridge what neuroscientist Antonio Damasio calls the "gap" between the rational and non-rational aspects of ourselves.[18]

This is the place we process the raw instantaneous signals

of our emotions, such as a quickened pulse or the rush of adrenaline that accompanies states of joy, fear, anger, and so on. Our basic emotions are part of our survival system, but they also have a sophisticated and discerning role to play in our ability to thrive.

The lower parts of our limbic system handle basic unconscious physiological and instinctive responses, while the higher areas handle the conscious dimension of our emotional experience. The conscious part of our emotional response takes place in what is known as the limbic cortex: the inner core of the frontal, parietal, and temporal lobes. This is where we not only experience our feelings consciously but can gain some level of control over them. These areas are influenced and modified by learning and conditioning at the social and cultural level. The lower limbic structures, however, respond instinctively.

Emotions add another nuanced layer to our complex bio-psycho-social self-regulatory system. They provide an adaptive and integrative role within us but are also crucial in the development and regulation of our interpersonal relationships.

THE STORIES WE TELL ABOUT FEELINGS

Emotions influence our perceptions, cognition, and expectations, affect how we appraise and interpret our circumstances, and play a significant role in the storage and retrieval of memories.

Research tells us that basic emotions only last seconds to a few minutes at most. But while the emotion itself may quickly diminish, how we interpret that feeling and the story we run about it can keep us ensnared for much longer. Emotions tend to get a bad rap because we don't distinguish the emotion itself from our (preconditioned) interpretation of its meaning. Moods—as well as emotion's most maladaptive counterparts, emotional disorders—are often mistakenly described as emotions.

According to psychologist Paul Ekman, who is known for his research on emotions and their micro-expressions (made famous in the show *Lie to Me*), "Moods are highly saturated with one or another emotion and can be distinguished from basic emotions in what calls them forth, the length of time they are inhabited, the way they are interpreted, appraised and given meaning, and their physiological substrate."[19]

Ekman also discusses what he calls emotional plots: the stories we tell ourselves that evoke a variety of complex emotions, in which our previous experience has primed us with preset expectations about what is going to or "should" occur. This is how so many anticipated situations lead to self-fulfilling prophecies—we are already primed and running a preset emotional pattern before anything has actually happened.

In these situations, your body is reliving an emotion from your past that overtakes your present circumstance. In other words, your Post-traumatic Story has taken over. In its more extreme form, this is known as autonomic lability, in which your neuro-hormonal system tends to overreact to an over-interpretation of the situation. Not only is your brain and nervous system experiencing an intense chemical bath, known as *flooding*, but your system is also undergoing what Daniel Goleman calls an "amygdala hijacking." [20] This is how your emotional past propels you into survival mode. In these situations, we experience ourselves as caught in the grip of an emotion and perceive it as something "happening to" us, rather than as a response we are choosing.

Based on his research in cognitive appraisal theory, social psychologist Stanley Schacter concluded that emotions have two factors: physiological arousal and cognitive labeling. [21] First, we feel something in our body and *then* come up with reasons for having our feelings. His experiments demonstrated that when people don't know why they are feeling what they are feeling, they are more likely to search for an external reason to justify those feelings. In *Feeling Good*, David Burns describes this same process as a cognitive distortion known as emotional reasoning. [22]

So, our *emotions*, which arrive pre-consciously as visceral and glandular responses, are experienced as *feelings*. Those "feeling signals" transfer information into our working memory, where it is stored symbolically. Working memory is not simply a collection of individual feelings or thoughts, but the place where the two combine to form complex cognitive and emotional meaning. We form associations and attach language and meaning to interpret our experience after the fact. We feel first and then tell ourselves a story about what just occurred.

Norma and John's Story

Norma had a long history of feeling rejected. She had been neglected as a child and had a series of unsuccessful relationships. Shortly after marrying her adoring husband, John, Norma began to feel vulnerable. She felt afraid of losing John's affection. They had returned from a trip in which John had become ill, and Norma began interpreting his symptoms as a sign that John was turning away from her. She also began having nightmares about John cheating on her, which added fuel to her emotional belief that he was about to reject her. John tried to reassure her of his love to no avail. She described the following scenario as proof that John was losing interest: while at a drugstore to pick up a prescription, Norma started trying on new perfumes she thought John might like. After spraying a couple of samples on her wrist, she approached John and put her wrist under his nose. He gasped and pushed her arm away. Norma felt devastated and withdrew. She nursed this personal wound without ever saying anything to John. I encouraged her to ask him about it.

She returned with the following explanation: John had contracted hepatitis while they were away, and one of the symptoms he experienced was nausea that could be induced by his hypersensitive sense of smell. In fact, they were in the drugstore specifically to get a prescription to help him with his nausea. When she put her wrist under his nose, John was overwhelmed with nausea. He assumed Norma had understood his response. When she told him about her feelings, he apologized for his reaction and explained that he would never want to do anything to make Norma feel unwanted. Norma realized in that moment that her fear had made her so self-absorbed in her own rejection story that she had been completely oblivious to her husband's condition.

That is an example of how interpretation can overtake underlying desire. In reality, Norma just wanted to maintain the feeling of love between herself and John, but her fear of loss got in the way.

Bob's Story

Emotional states don't always behave predictably. An

acquaintance named Bob, who is prone to intractable bouts of depression, told me about waking one morning to a feeling of creeping depression setting in. He wanted to head it off at the pass before it really took hold. Often, taking a motorcycle ride up the coast would shift his emotional state, so he donned his gear and took off up the highway. Despite the sunshine, fresh air, and beautiful scenery along the way, Bob felt the heaviness enveloping him. He couldn't shake it. In despair, he stopped in a small town to get a cup of coffee to go. He sat on a bench outside the café and reconciled himself to the fact that he was not going to be able to disrupt the onset of this depression. At least that was the story he told himself, but when he settled on the bench, he happened to look down at the ground beside him and saw a lone Iceland poppy growing there. Somehow that bright orange bit of life simply snapped him out of it, and he felt a sudden rush of happiness. He was completely mystified. The "depression" had arrived without reason, and it receded even more quickly and mysteriously.

HOW CULTURE INFLUENCES OUR EMOTIONAL STORIES

In North American culture, emotions are often treated as though they are second-class citizens of the mind. Rationality is good; emotionality is bad. Emotional or passionate response to any situation often makes people feel uncomfortable. In fact, the term "emotional" is frequently used as a pejorative term. Many stereotypes reinforce this. The stereotypical male hero is often idealized as the "strong silent type," as is the female martyr type who subjugates her personal needs and feelings to care for others.

Emotions definitely disrupt our illusion of control, and people in Western culture are deeply attached to a sense of control. Not only are we supposed to be cool all the time, but we are also supposed to be happy. Our obsession with the pursuit of happiness has made being happy the gold standard against which all other feeling states are judged. Anything less than everything being "all good" is seen as evidence of personal failure. Consequently, we learn to ignore, resist, override, deny, and judge our feelings. As one client put it, we condition ourselves to become "overrideaholics."

We often shoot the emotional messenger before we have a chance to experience the message being conveyed. In order to redeem the value of any emotion, we must be able to feel it, but we rarely allow ourselves to simply inhabit a feeling without superimposing our conditioned beliefs about the emotion's acceptability. Many unspoken social and cultural rules dictate what, when, and how we are permitted to express our feelings. This leaves us wondering: How much fear is normal? Is it healthy to express anger? How vulnerable should we make ourselves to love? What is the "correct" amount of sadness to experience in the face of a loss?

A week after his wife of nearly sixty years passed away, my friend Bill went to a previously scheduled doctor's appointment to be assessed for a hip replacement. When the doctor asked him how he was doing, Bill teared up and told him that since his wife had died, he was often overwhelmed with grief. Without looking at him or saying a word, the surgeon took out his pad, wrote something on it, and slid the paper upside down toward him. It wasn't until after the appointment that Bill realized it was a prescription for antidepressants. He was offended by the doctor's response and disposed of the prescription, but it also reinforced a feeling that he should be able control his expression of grief.

We don't know the doctor's motivation, but it symbolizes a typical response to a display of emotion. We often just want the other person's emotional expression to stop. Even the most empathetic people sometimes employ their comforting skills not only out of concern for the other person, but as a means to relieve their own discomfort about the other person's feelings.

In many cultures, the expression of strong feelings is acceptable, and they find our North American emotional denial downright strange. I worked with a man of Greek origin who was completely mystified by his British wife's need to count to ten and calm herself down before responding. He felt insulted by his wife's tempering of her emotions and wanted her to feel safe enough with him to share her genuine feelings.

INTEGRATING YOUR EMOTIONAL DIMENSION

Beneath our conscious awareness, emotions continuously respond to the internal and external conditions of our lives. Without consciously realizing it, our emotions filter how we respond to the world. Imagine coming home from a frustrating meeting at work at which you felt thwarted at every turn. If, when you arrived home, you happened to encounter your child's bicycle blocking the front door, you are more likely to react with more frustration, or even anger, at having your way blocked once more. If the meeting had gone your way and you left work happy and satisfied, you might not even perceive the bike as an impediment and might simply move it aside to enter.

As children, we were often thwarted in our ability to express feelings rather than given direction about healthy ways to express them. You may need to update the information stored about emotions in your memory banks. It helps to have an emotional vocabulary to name and work with the states you feel. It is also useful to notice that we rarely feel just one emotion at a time. Our feelings are layered, nuanced, and fluid. One emotion quickly flows into the next. Even in grief, people often find moments of peace, gratitude, and even humor.

Not all forms of emotional expression are "healthy," but every emotional signal can serve a useful purpose in pointing us toward what matters. The job is to get to the raw signal and *experience it in the moment*, rather than reacting from old stories we have accumulated from the past.

INHABITING ANGER AND SADNESS

Anger is often a misunderstood emotion. Anger is an important and useful survival skill, because it releases a burst of adrenalin for immediate response. If that adrenalin is allowed to fulfill its potential, it can be incredibly clarifying. In its healthy expression, anger does not require us to raise our voice or make demands. When you allow yourself to experience it, anger can provide clarity about what does or doesn't work for you. The pure energy of anger can be used to stop a violation, set a boundary, or change a direction. It is a form of pure determination and can be incredibly useful when applied as a motivation for changing your circumstance. If you think of any substantial change you have made in your life, you will probably find that feelings of agitation and anger provided the impetus to move on.

Rather than discerning anger's true purpose, people often suppress anger for fear that it will become its maladaptive counterpart, rage.

The unhealthy expression of anger occurs when it becomes distorted by a story of fear of domination, victimization, or the need to assert power over another. In its maladaptive form, anger leads to the opposite of its intended purpose: it violates boundaries, can be violent, confuses things, and becomes reactive rather than proactive. Rather than being a focused expression toward a goal, it is often a fear-based reaction to a perceived loss of control.

Likewise, people are often afraid to express sadness or grief for fear of being perceived as a downer or someone who doesn't have it all together. Sadness is often imagined as a gateway emotion to depression. I would argue that you are far more likely to experience depression if you are never allowed to fully experience and integrate your sadness. Sadness can be a valuable signal, indicating the loss of someone or something that is precious to you. It helps you remember what is important. Loss and sadness are real experiences in life and need their due. What you don't express as sadness often finds other distorted forms of expression, but you can't outrun pain or sadness. Eventually, it will catch up with you.

TRYING TO FEEL (OR NOT)

Emotions are closely tied to our reward system: our fundamental drive to seek pleasure and avoid pain. Unfortunately, these drives are not quite as straightforward as they sound and can often overlap and backfire in unintended ways. Self-destructive behaviors can be cultivated in the process of trying to *feel something* (think of adrenaline junkies or people who engage in self-harm practices such as cutting). Conversely, self-destructive behavior can also develop in pursuit of *feeling nothing* (such as addictions designed to numb or drown out pain).

We may rail against our pain, but we can also cling to it, stoking its fires with repetitive stories. Think of people who get caught in continual patterns of victimhood, or those who career from one drama to the next in their life. But the patterns are not the emotions themselves—they are the way the adaptive signal of the emotion has been interpreted, distorted, and reinforced over time.

Stephen's Story: Depression Masking Activism

Throughout his life, my friend Stephen experienced crippling bouts of depression that laid him flat for months at a time. He told me he could feel when the depression was about to come on, and he always had medication on hand to buffer his dark descent into pain.

In the first few months of knowing him, I watched Stephen successfully change several habits: he gave up meat, coffee, and sugar. He also let go of alcohol, and I knew that some time previously, he had given up smoking. I was impressed by the disciplined ease with which he was able to change his behavior.

I asked him, since he was so good at giving things up, if he had ever considered giving up depression. He laughed and said he had never thought of that.

So, we looked at how he had been supporting his depression habit. I asked him to identify the steps of his depressive pattern. He easily recalled the sequence of the thoughts, feelings, and behaviors that triggered his downward spirals.

Because he cared about what was happening in the world, he spent hours watching the news and searching the internet to stay in touch with current affairs. He focused primarily on the topics of climate change, violence, and injustice. He considered himself to be a champion of the underdog, hated bullying in any form, and rebelled against authority.

As he watched the news, he focused on all that was wrong with the world and grew increasingly agitated, negative, and embittered. He ranted about injustice and tried to engage others in the fight against what he saw as the corruption of those in power. He felt hurt and frustrated when others didn't share his anger. If people suggested an alternative view, he became critical, poked holes in their arguments, or accused them of being naïve or uninformed.

He believed others were caught up in their own little worlds and didn't care nearly as much as he did. Instead of bringing people together to work on these issues, he inadvertently pushed them away with his intensity, anger, and superior attitude. He felt alone and isolated.

Overwhelmed by things beyond his control and powerless to make a difference, he eventually slipped into feelings of futility and despair. The underlying emotional theme of this pattern was a sense of powerlessness—a familiar feeling that had been with him all his life.

Stephen had been a sensitive kid whose father berated him, belittled his ideas, and tried to recruit him into fights. In the same way he had felt helpless as a child, he felt completely powerless against all authority. He felt victimized, placed responsibility for his feelings outside himself, and blamed everything and everyone else for his unhappiness.

It had never occurred to him that his own behavior contributed to his growing isolation. His focus on negativity, and his anger and sense of superiority, made others shy away from him. When he examined his behavior, he realized he had actually been using his father's tactics, a bullying intensity designed to get others to see things his way. He vowed to change the steps of his pattern and began to look at what he could do to break the cycle.

He gave up on waiting for the rest of the world to change and began by changing himself. He stopped watching the news and scanning the internet for things that fueled his sense of frustration. Instead of focusing on violence in the external world, he looked at how he could work with his own angry reactions more effectively.

To address some of his environmental concerns, he reduced his own ecological footprint by moving onto a cooperative farm, planting a garden, learning about permaculture, and experimenting with alternative energy sources.

He took a communications course and worked on his listening skills. He tried learning how to be expressive without being pushy. He now practices being more present and compassionate. He admits that he is still a work in progress with more healing to do, but it has been over ten years now since his last bout of depression.

Instead of watching for pain's arrival and preparing for devastation, Stephen gave up looking for it, and it stopped showing up. His life changed the instant he shifted the focus of his energy and attention. He not only improved his mood, but he used the raw information from his emotional signals to improve conditions for himself and the world. His emotions reconnected him with what matters and his deeper sense of purpose.

I see a lot of people who suffer from similar feelings of powerlessness when it comes to confronting issues in the world. Activists are often blinded by what is being activated inside them. When you notice what an issue calls forth in you, it is taken out of the abstract realm and into a place where you have the ultimate power to unravel its complexities. If you allow your emotions to guide you to what is important, you can begin healing this within you. Once that is in progress, you will obtain the clarity and compassion to engage others in a healing process for the external world.

INHABITING POSITIVE EMOTIONS

We become so focused on trying to avoid negative emotions that we forget to cultivate positive emotional expression in our lives. Research tells us that the pivotal difference between those with and without resilient personalities is the positivity of their emotions. Positive emotions help us thrive. They provide a buffer against depression and allow people to rebound more quickly from difficult or traumatic situations. In fact, positive emotions lead to what is known as post-crisis growth, in which one can reap benefits from life's challenges and use them to actively develop greater awareness and self-compassion.

The emotions we perceive as more positive or pleasant also have their roots in our evolutionary past. They may have accelerated our thriving by motivating us toward beneficial experiences or things that provided pleasure, but they are not necessarily primed for response at the same level of amplification as the emotions we associate with immediate survival.

Listening to thousands of personal histories over the years has taught me that exploring emotional response is a wonderful way to reconnect people with the deeper truths of their lives, and to develop positive emotions and compensatory strengths. When we embrace, feel, and integrate the proper emotional expression of all parts of ourselves, we restore inner integrity and experience the full range of our humanity.

Feminist filmmaker and author Bonnie Sherr Klein uses a wonderful turn of phrase in her book *Slow Dance*. After a second stroke, she decided to measure the quality of her life by "laughs per lived minute."

On that wonderful scale, we can definitely see that children are masters at quality of life and our best teachers on the subject of joy. Notice how love and joy are the very essence of life itself—pure spontaneous harmonizing energy released to do its job in the world.

Love and joy set your spirit free and release the ecstatic gift of yourself into the world. Cultivating joy, gratitude, and love all stimulate the production of positive neurotransmitters, like dopamine, endorphins, and oxytocin. Tapping into your positive emotions allows you to draw on nature's prescription for our ailments.

Humor reduces levels of stress hormones, such as cortisol, and is thought to enhance our immune, endocrine, and cardiovascular systems. Laughter can provide a workout for the muscles of the diaphragm, abdomen, and face. A joke can raise our spirits, shift our state, or ease our tension. If we're able to laugh during a stressful situation, we can put psychological distance between ourselves and the source of the stress. Sometimes there is nothing as healing as a good belly laugh.

DEEPER PERSONAL REFLECTION

It is useful to spend time exploring the roots of your emotions to find which have become entangled in nonproductive stories (or Post-traumatic Story Disorder).

Notice the words and the metaphors you use to describe your emotions and explore their origins.

No matter what emotion is surfacing, it can direct you to long-lost parts of yourself. Beneath every emotional pattern there is something priceless attempting to find its place in the world. When you look deeply into the content of your emotional landscape, you discover a map that can lead you to the buried treasure of your own unique expression.

DEEPER QUESTIONS FOR YOUR EMOTIONAL SELF

This is a time to notice, listen, feel, and record the responses from your Emotional Self. When you are wrestling with a perceived threat and need your Emotional Self's guidance, reflect on these questions.

- What do my emotions want me to know about this?
- What emotions arise in response to this situation, and how familiar are they? Am I opening or closing down around these emotions?
- What would happen if I allowed myself to feel the emotion (fear, sadness, shame, etc.)? What can I learn from staying present to the actual emotion as opposed to my conditioned reaction to it?
- What steps can I take to acknowledge and honor the previously unfelt content of this situation?

MEDITATION FOR YOUR EMOTIONAL SELF

Take a moment to get settled into a place where you can be free of disturbance and distraction for a few moments. Breathe into your heart as we enter this meditative journey. Let's harvest the wisdom of the deeper story beneath your emotions by reflecting on each of these in turn.

Fear. Reflect on what you learned about being safe as you were raised.

What parts of yourself did you learn to hold back in fear? What underlying desire is beneath the fear, and what deeper part of you is contained there? How would your life be different if you used your fear to direct you to what really matters to you? Is it worth cultivating courage for that? What if you were to focus on what you truly wanted instead of focusing on the fear of not having it? Think of the people you admire most. Are they focused on their fears, or are they working with their courage to fulfill their dreams?

Thank and bless your fear for reminding you of your deeper desire.

Pain and sadness. What have pain and sadness taught you about what you value and hold dear? Did they make you recognize and honor the preciousness of the moment? What have these emotions been teaching you about impermanence, accepting that there are cycles and seasons in all things? Have they taught you about what you can and cannot control? What have you discovered from those times when you were able to accept the sadness and also let go with love? Have you noticed how your empathy and compassion for others increase when you realize they share the same pain as you?

Thank and bless your pain and sadness for showing you what you value.

Anger. What parts of yourself has anger made you stand up for? What boundaries did it teach you to define? What sense of restorative justice was being called forth in you? What raw energy did anger provide to move you forward—especially in times when you were stuck and holding yourself back? Look at the big points of change in your life and notice if anger played a part in forcing you to change a direction or take that necessary next step.

Thank your anger for its clarifying determination to move forward.

Shame. Notice how shame was formed at moments of greatest vulnerability, the times when you were most in need of feeling worthy of receiving love and care. Notice if you have been denying yourself that same love and care. Look at where you feel shame and notice if you have violated your own values. What must be restored in you for you to reclaim a feeling of integrity? Honor your vulnerability by finding yourself worthy of your own loving attention.

Thank your shame for helping discover your deepest needs and define your integrity.

Doubt. Notice what part of you is being denied your own trust. How you are being called to test the soundness of your motivations? How have you learned to trust your inner knowing without becoming overly attached to it? In what way are you being called to have faith in the larger unfolding of life?

Thank your doubt for reconnecting you to the possibility of self-trust.

Forgiveness. Look at the moments in your life where forgiveness was required toward yourself and others. Consider times you needed to release yourself from the prison of statically-held negative emotions and judgments. Notice what was liberated in you when you engaged forgiveness—when you released bitterness and freed yourself to move forward in your life.

Thank your forgiveness for releasing you from the attachment to old pain and resentments.

LIVING THE DEEPER STORY OF YOUR EMOTIONS

There are many ways to feel lonely in this world, but the loneliest of all is when you become a stranger to yourself. It is only in turning toward your pain, your fears, and your longing that you truly come to know yourself, and only by courageously committing to your deepest truth can you truly become whole again.

Imagine what the world would be like if people were able to identify, express, and become accountable for their feelings, instead of unconsciously acting out. Think of how much empathy and compassion could be cultivated simply through understanding the underlying emotional needs of one another.

Imagine what it would feel like to be safe enough to really express what you feel without fear of being misunderstood or judged. We would have a genuine opportunity to come together to share our collective joys and sorrows and bear the burdens of the world together, rather than in the isolation of our inner worlds. We would cultivate self-aware children who would not continue the unhealthy patterns that have been carried across generations.

We would reinvigorate the heart of the world.

I AM

The snap, crackle, and pop of electrochemical messages zing through my nervous system and make Baryshnikov-type leaps over synapses, causing subtle changes in body temperature, nearly imperceptible shifts of surface tension on skin, momentarily suspending my breath and quickening my pulse as blood rushes and recedes, leaving pale purple splotches in its wake. I feel the catch in my throat, heat in my cheeks, and the salty sting of tears at the edges of my eyes. I convulse in wild bursts of laughter that do more for my innards than could ever be achieved with a thousand crunches at the gym. I swoon and melt, and I rage against the dying light. I would rather experience even the most devastating feelings than live in a buffered state of numbness. **I am an ecstatic emotional being. I feel; therefore, I am.**

Intuitive

CHAPTER 5

THE DEEPER STORY OF YOUR INTUITIVE SELF

"Intuition has invisible threads that connect it to the heart of all matter."

—ARTHUR KOESTLER

Every day, we are bombarded with billions of bits of sensory stimuli from which we must somehow make meaning. Just as our system is layered with instinctive responses at the survival level, our Intuitive Self is endowed with an unconscious, pattern-seeking, meaning-making capacity. It can provide us with a sudden sense of certainty in which we feel we know something without necessarily knowing how we know it.

With practice and discernment, you can learn to work effectively with the useful faculties of your intuitive self.

THE ROLE OF INTUITION IN YOUR DEEPER STORY

Function: Your intuition is a subtle sensory and energetic cuing system that bypasses conscious filtration to alert you to opportunities and dangers. It can facilitate split-second decision-making and action.

When out of alignment: You ignore intuition and cut yourself off from an important source of information and insight, or you overindulge intuitive prompts, take them too literally, jump to conclusions, assume your intuition or gut feelings are infallible forms of guidance, and react impulsively. You act without applying discernment and discrimination to the message received.

When in alignment: You are highly sensitive to your internal and external environments and responsive to subtle shifts of energy. You balance trust of your intuition with discernment. You are sensitive to congruency in yourself and others.[23] You explore intuitive nudges to discover their deeper purpose. You experience synchronicity.[24]

Key Areas of Development: Perceptive Intelligence,[25] Balanced Sensitivity and Stability, Energetic Attunement, Pattern Recognition

Dominant Questions: How can I apply subtle awareness and sensitivity in useful ways?

Arc of Development: From Insensitivity to Heightened Awareness

THE CALL OF THE INTUITIVE DIMENSION
INTUITION'S GIFTS AND LIMITATIONS

As a child, before your cognitive faculties were developed to the point where you could reason or understand cause and effect, you navigated the world on the basis of feeling and intuition. You were able to sense hidden connections between things. By the time you were old enough to go to school, you were expected to leave behind your "childish" ways of seeing and interacting with the world. You were put on notice that if you couldn't "properly" explain something you knew, it likely wasn't real; it was just a product of your imagination. In one fell swoop, both your intuition and imagination were relegated to the pile of childhood artifacts.

As we grow older, we often discover that we actually like our intuition and the sense of wonder it elicits. If you love a good mystery in whatever form—a novel, a scientific investigation, a medical diagnosis, or the laws of the universe—you will find that even in the most intellectual tasks, intuition has its place.

Think of any murder mystery. When the detective is stumped by the accumulated facts, a pivotal insight usually comes from something completely unrelated to the case—something said or seen suddenly identifies a hidden connection. The detective's intuition (and their willingness to follow it) is often what cracks the case.

> *"Intuition is a leap toward wholeness from fragmentation."*
> —ANODEA JUDITH

Intuition is experiential and visceral, a form of direct knowing. It is the uncanny ability to connect the dots and instantaneously make meaning from seemingly random input. Intuition works at the unconscious level, combining sensory and affective processes that bypass rationality to create a sense of knowing. Intuition is rapid, spontaneous, effortless, non-logical, holistic, and tacit. It cannot be voluntarily controlled.

As an evolutionary byproduct, intuition is related to, but differentiated from, our instincts. This spontaneous form of awareness does more than generate survival reactions; it helps us access hidden information, rapidly anticipate problems, and respond accordingly.

Intuition covers a lot of ineffable territory, from practical everyday nudges to being an active catalyst for scientific and artistic discovery. It awakens personal and healing insight and alerts us to dangers or opportunities. It is one of the operational mysteries of consciousness and challenges our current understanding of what it means to be sentient.

Intuition can pop in when you least expect it. Think of the times you have had a moment of certainty about something you had no business knowing—a flash of insight, gut feeling, or sense of something you had no reasonable explanation for.

There are innumerable everyday intuitive experiences, such as getting a hunch that you need to call someone only to discover they were in the process of calling you, or deciding (for no apparent reason) to vary your routine drive home, only to hear later that an accident had seriously delayed traffic on your usual route. These kinds of examples are so commonplace we rarely spend time musing on them.

Intuition can act as an early warning system. For example, Deanna watched her husband, Terry, get ready for a mountain biking trip. She was happy he was enjoying his weekly adventures with "the boys," but this time she felt concerned he might be pushing himself too hard. He was forty now, not twenty. Terry uncharacteristically brushed off her concern, calling her a worrywart. A couple of hours after he left, Deanna felt a strong alarm and "just knew" something had happened to him. A few minutes later, the phone rang, and his friends explained they were taking Terry to the hospital with what looked like a broken shoulder.

Intuition can be a lifesaver if you choose to respond to its messages. I wish I had that time I chose to dismiss an intuitive alarm in favor of being "polite" to what turned out to be a dangerous person. I got the vibe but chose to ignore it and endured a brutal assault instead. Why didn't I listen? Because I let my conditioning about being a "good person" override my intuitive warning signal.[26]

In the Western world, logic is favored over intuition. People are discouraged from expressing intuitive knowledge if they can't back up their feelings with facts. In my case, I didn't want to pre-judge a stranger. I had no logical basis for ignoring him, other than a "feeling." I had forgotten just how valuable feelings could be. In bypassing my intuitive alert and only attending to my conscious mind's many rules about how to be a good person, I had cut myself off from heeding a critical warning.

How many times have you later reflected on a signal you chose to dismiss? It's not uncommon to hear people say things like, "I *knew* there was something off with that deal," or "If only I had trusted my gut feeling about them," or "I had a feeling I should have..." Intuition is so pervasive that we often take it for granted and don't give it its due. However, if you expect it to yield precognitive abilities, or be an infallible form of guidance, you are asking too much of your intuitive self.

YOUR BRAIN ON INTUITION

We may well think we are in charge of our actions, but science has proven that our neurons make decisions at the unconscious level before we can lay claim to any sense of conscious agency. This not only challenges the notion of free will but also brings into question how we know what we know. It may turn out that intuition will someday provide a glimpse into the holistic mercurial workings of our unconscious mind.

Intuition also nudges us to reflect on the nature of time. How is it possible to have intuitive knowledge of something "before" it occurs or have access to simultaneous non-local knowledge? Perhaps intuition will provide interesting insight into the fluidity of time and consciousness...but these are subjects scientists will spend lifetimes unraveling.

Intuition is a byproduct of what is known as our brain's *bottom-up processing* system. Bottom-up processing uses your senses to take in undifferentiated stimuli, with no preconceived ideas and without reflection, and respond instantaneously to the input. By contrast, *top-down processing* takes in information and uses background knowledge or previous learning to influence your perception of the input.

As a bottom-up process, intuition is like a brief flash of light in the dark that can illuminate an otherwise hidden sense of the whole. Both intuition and synchronicity have been described as "eruptions of meaning."[27]

People who study intuition say that intuitive prompts can also be a byproduct of top-down processing, in which the mind has been predisposed through previous learning or input to suddenly grasp an intuitive understanding.

Philosophy professor Massimo Pigliucci cites scientific studies that demonstrate that people are not universally intuitive; they only tend to be intuitive in areas where they already have some established expertise.[28] He suggests that intuition is a domain-specific form of implicit knowledge that allows one to make educated guesses more likely to be correct in their field of expertise. This idea gives credence to Louis Pasteur's famous statement, "Chance favors the prepared mind."

Intuition has the power to break us free from everyday habits of thought and perception and awaken us to a sense of life's mysteries. It can bypass what we think we know and, in a moment of openness and receptivity, acquaint us with hidden connections. Daniel Seigal discusses intuition as "access to the input from the body and its non-rational ways of knowing that fuel wisdom."[29]

Great thinkers, artists, and business people alike cite intuition as a source of unexpected inspiration for their work. Steve Jobs made no bones about crediting intuition for his original design ideas.

Most people are familiar with Einstein's daydream about riding on a beam of light, which led to his theory of relativity, and the esteemed role he gave intuition in his investigative process.

> *"The intuitive mind is a sacred gift and the rational mind is a faithful servant. We have created a society that honors the servant and has forgotten the gift."*
>
> —ALBERT EINSTEIN

INTEGRATING YOUR INTUITIVE SELF

When I have a client who is stuck in logic and going around in circles, I use an exercise to strengthen their receptivity and tap into intuitive knowledge. The answer is usually there for them if they make themselves receptive to it.

Whatever their question, I encourage them to let it go, release focus, and follow their breath for a while. In the space created by following their breath, I ask them to *notice without evaluation* whatever presents itself. Things may arise as sensations, images, colors, bits of memory, specific words, sounds, fragments of songs, etc. I remind them that there is no need to do anything but notice and breathe. Nothing has to be logical or make sense as it arises.

Even in a safe situation, where nothing rests on what arises and there is nothing at stake, most clients feel awkward doing this. More often than not, on the first couple of tries they become self-conscious, worrying about getting the "wrong answer" or getting no answer at all. This is symptomatic of the kind of conditioning that insists we must have an answer for everything. I help them recall that they are not looking for answers; they are simply turning inward and noticing what surfaces. This is a process of surrendering, in which they are getting out of their own way and permitting intuitive information to flow.

Once they move past performance anxiety, learn to calm themselves, and attend to their breath, they can allow things to surface without prejudgment or interference. They often experience unexpected connections. Once intuition has presented its cues, we can play freely with the raw material, using both association and analysis.

Darren's Story

For example, Darren wanted to quit his marketing job. He said he felt "brain dead," did not enjoy his colleagues, and felt he could do much better elsewhere. This was not the career path he had anticipated. I asked him what he had envisioned for himself, and he answered that he had no idea, but this was definitely not it.

Once he was settled into his body, he asked himself what he needed to know about his situation. Then he let go of the question and just focused on his breathing. Several things presented themselves in that space. At first, he heard the maddening sound of a ticking clock and felt irritated. Next, he heard the distinctive click of a camera's shutter lens, then saw a mountain path, and had a quick flash of what looked like a Japanese symbol. These things seemed random and diverse to him initially, but as we talked about each piece and what it meant to him, it came together in a way that connected the dots beneath the surface of his conscious mind.

His irritation with the ticking clock expressed his feelings about wasting time. He had always felt he wasn't cut out for a nine-to-five existence. The shutter-click of the camera reminded him of his passion for photography. The mountain path stimulated his longing to be a modern-day nomad, documenting and photographing his journeys. The Japanese character led him to recall an article he had read about an intriguing monastery in Japan.

These intuitive promptings led Darren to decide to work a while longer to save money for a trip to Japan. Having made this decision, his attitude at work changed. He became more disciplined in his approach to projects and softened toward his coworkers.

A few months later, he traveled to Japan, where he learned to meditate. He kept a photo journal of his trip and sent me a picture of himself in monk's robes, with a shaved head and a contented look on his face that reflected the way he felt about his new path. He continued to work freelance while on the road traveling, photographing, and meditating.

There is no magic in Darren's story. All the pieces were already there for him to assemble, but he couldn't access the hidden wholeness until he stopped railing against his circumstances and opened himself to other options that were already intuitively alive within him.

Ultimately, intuition is an act of surrender. It is only when we release conscious effort and create space within ourselves that the intuitive self can emerge.

Brenda's Story

Another fun example of an intuitive nudge came from working with Brenda, an extremely delightful, albeit very serious and responsible, client. I assigned her the task of rediscovering what made her happy. To begin with, she was to go to a store that sold journals and purchase whichever one she was most attracted to. That journal is where she would record what she felt drawn to or curious about.

The next week, she related the story of her "Herculean struggle" in choosing the "right" journal. At the stationary store, she found a beautiful leather-bound journal with intriguing Celtic symbols on it. It seemed perfect: exactly the kind of thing she thought I would be proud of her for choosing. She was going to buy it, but she felt a "tug" to keep looking, and that is when her eyes caught sight of a small notebook with a sparkling image of penguins on it. It was cheap, a little garish, and didn't hold a candle to the quality of the other one, but there was something about it that just made her smile. She couldn't explain it.

After going back and forth for about half an hour, she finally relented and chose the penguin-bedazzled notebook. It turned out to be a breakthrough moment for her. She realized she had always done the "right" and "expected" thing rather than following her own preferences. Getting the penguin journal was an act of defiance—a liberation and reclamation of the silly side of her. She realized she had become too serious and stuffy and needed to loosen up. Her conditioning wanted her to choose the "tasteful" option, but her intuition told her she needed to surrender her approval-seeking and go for a sense of fun. Interestingly, it was that intuitive prompt that led her to write a beautiful children's book.

It is important to stay open to new information when it presents itself in the form of an intuitive nudge, but more importantly, you need to recognize that the intuition itself is not an ending—it is a beginning, a time to look more deeply at what has been presented and to work with it. When it comes to intuition, we cannot afford to be just daydreamers. We must also work with intuitive messages to integrate their relevance and meaning into everyday life.

BALANCING INTUITION AND LOGIC

Sometimes, intuition seems like pure magic in the way it operates, but one must be wary of thinking magically about it. When we say, "the answer lies within," we do well to recognize the double entendre in that statement.

Too often, people tell me they absolutely trust their feelings and rely solely on them for making decisions. But all feelings also involve some measure of interpretation.

Feelings are a necessary part of any decision-making process, but going on feelings alone could be problematic. We are endowed with both feelings and logic for a reason, and using these faculties to complement rather than compete with each other makes for better decisions in the long run.

If you consider yourself to be intuitive, chances are you see your intuition as being right most of the time. But do you recall the many times those sudden insights did not pan out?

Intuition is far from infallible. The raw signal of the intuitive nudge may alert you to something important, but your interpretation of that signal may or may not be correct.

As prediction-making machines, our unconscious minds quickly assess situations and often jump to conclusions. Since intuition relies on finding patterns, it can be easy to delude yourself with it. Your beliefs can prime you to see what you expect to see. Sometimes intuitions turn out to be valid, sometimes they are erroneous, and sometimes it is just downright complicated, as in this personal example.

Confusing Myself with Intuition

I was reading a book in a parked car while waiting for my friend Val to return from dropping something off to a colleague. I suddenly felt that something was wrong. I looked into the rearview to see if Val was coming, but instead, I saw a man quickly exiting the house she had gone into. He paused on the porch, looked from side to side, and then crouched down and dashed down the steps across the lawn and around the side of the building. His odd departure aroused my suspicions. Then another man came out of the house and repeated the same surreptitious behavior. My adrenaline shot up, and I leapt out of the car to investigate. I was nearly at the house when Val came out. She stopped on the porch, looked back and forth, and dashed down the steps and out to the curb. Only then did I notice the sprinkler arching back and forth over the walkway. I laughed at myself in relief.

When I approached Val, I was internally clucking my tongue at myself when she said, "Did you get my message?" Apparently, she had been sending me a mental SOS, hoping I would come rescue her. She had been cornered by her colleague and was having difficulty getting away from him until the other two men showed up and told her colleague to leave her alone. I had felt there was something wrong but had identified the wrong culprits. The men I saw as suspicious were actually the heroes in this story.

Was it my intuition that alerted me to Val's cry for help? I definitely did receive a signal that made me realize she had been gone longer than was reasonably expected. Had the mystery book I was reading primed me to see the men exiting the building as suspicious? There are no straight-forward answers, and as is often the case with intuition, all we have to go on are subjective accounts.

DEEPER PERSONAL REFLECTION

> *"There are more things in heaven and earth, Horatio, than are dreamt of in your philosophy."*
>
> —SHAKESPEARE, *HAMLET* (1.5.167-8)

Mystical experiences, visions, and sudden foresight can also fall into the zone of intuitive knowing. Stanislav Grof, one of the founders of transpersonal psychology, includes these in his broad definition of "non-ordinary states of consciousness."[30] These non-ordinary states have always played a role in healing.

Physicians have told me that patients often intuit what is wrong before they receive validation from tests. This begs the question: if they had heeded intuitive signals sooner, would they have been able to prevent or mitigate the advance of their disease?

In Penny Pierce's book *The Intuitive Way*, she spells out

what she calls the *sensitivity scale,* in which intuitive signals start out as subtle and barely perceptible vibes or vague urges, proceeding up the chain of consciousness with increasing intensity until they can't be ignored.[31] At any level, intuitive prompts can identify and direct attention to internal issues. Over time, continually unheeded signals may end up manifesting in the form of symptoms of disease, depression, or other life disruptions.

Dr. Milton E. Erickson was a hypnotherapist known for his unparalleled success using symbols and storytelling to stimulate his clients' unconscious mind to connect the relevant dots for their healing. He often used nonsense and misdirection in his stories to overwhelm the conscious mind. He trusted the wisdom of his patient's intuition to know exactly what was needed.

Indigenous medicine people use a variety of practices (drumming, chanting, ceremonies, rituals, and plant medicines) to shut off the reasoning mind so the patient can gain access to their subconscious and intuitive faculties for self-healing.

ENGAGING OUR PATTERN-FINDING BRAINS

Often, people receive intuitive signals but don't know how to interpret them. Rather than going about this literally, it is incredibly helpful to think symbolically. Stories, metaphors, and symbols are useful ways of making intuitive connections. They bring left and right brain functions together to create meaning.

One way we can strengthen our receptivity and pattern-making abilities is by working with both sides of our brain by putting vivid images together with words. Having tried this in many forms over the years, I have found the best results are achieved by having clients use image cards with interpretations to prime their intuitive system. The most readily available cards are tarot or divination cards.

You can imagine how well this exercise is received by my uber-logical clients (male and female) who are doctors, lawyers, engineers, entrepreneurs, etc. They don't want to have anything to do with this kind of "woo-woo" stuff, but I assure them this exercise has nothing to do with new age ideas or divination; it is simply an expedient way to consciously activate and engage the symbolic and pattern-recognition parts of their brain.

The clients find a deck of their own choosing—the type of cards does not matter, as long as there are vivid images and verbal interpretations. People generally choose a deck with which they have some personal resonance. Each morning they ask a question, draw a card, look at the image, and read the interpretation. As they proceed through their day, they are to notice any connections or occurrences that may relate to ideas from the card. Just as when you "discover" a new word and suddenly see it everywhere, people start to notice symbolic connections they might otherwise have missed.

This does not mean there are signs just waiting to be discovered; it means that people start intuitively using a form of selective perception to hone in on things relevant to the subject of their inquiry. This priming tool simply engages their pattern-seeking equipment.

One client who works for the Disney Company uses a similar technique in his creative brainstorming sessions with clients in which he uses image cards and has people symbolically relate those images to the subject of their inquiry.

Alan's Story

Alan, an architect, was particularly resistant to this idea. He undertook this assignment reluctantly and with skepticism. Following the instructions, he went to a large metaphysical bookstore and chose a deck of cards. He was drawn to a Viking Oracle deck because they seemed more "masculine" and he had Nordic roots. The deck combined meanings from Norse legends and runes. The first card he drew was based on the rune "Laguz," which means water. The interpretation of the card was about using emotion, intuition, and the unconscious as a source of insight. He laughed at that, but later that same day at work, his team was given a design problem in which they were asked to "work intuitively" to find a solution. These intuitive nudges or synchronicities are "meaningful coincidences." Alan admitted that he had been aware of blocking his emotional and intuitive messages, and this stimulated him to at least get curious about what he was ignoring within himself.

When people work with their intuition, they become sensitive to themselves and to the range and quality of the subjective information that is available to them as a resource. Paying attention to feedback at all levels is useful for making meaningful choices.

Sometimes, it is easier to be intuitive on somebody else's behalf because when we are listening to them, we are holding the overview position. We can see the big picture, while they are caught in the weeds of their situation. Intuition can give us a way to elevate our consciousness to illuminate the bigger picture in our own lives in that same way.

INTUITIVE MEDITATION

Take a moment to center yourself, being sure that you will remain free of disturbance and distraction for a few moments. Think of something that you would like to receive some insight about and open yourself to that possibility. Intuition cannot be coerced; it needs to be able to tell its own story in its own time. Your job is to simply seed the intuitive field with your question and stay present enough to notice what arises in response over the next several days.

To cultivate intuition you need to prepare the ground by learning how to enter states of quietude, stillness, open focus, and receptivity. When asking for an intuitive answer, you need to create space into which the message can arrive, and to be able to handle that state of emptiness. We are so used to having an answer for everything that the state of *not knowing* can make us feel awkward, humbled, and vulnerable.

Intuition requires you to suspend judgment and let go of assumptions. You need to be able to apply a level of detachment and to observe without evaluation. Even though it can arise spontaneously and provide a deep sense of certainty, intuition works best when you put a little distance between its raw signal and your immediate need to interpret it. Allow yourself to rest in a state of surrender, remaining open and truly agnostic about whatever impressions you receive. The deeper work of intuition requires incubation time to reveal itself.

It is also important not to take your intuition too literally. Your sense of wonder and curiosity are intuition's greatest allies. Allow yourself to play with intuition's presentations however they occur, whether through a brief flash of insight, distinct images, structured thoughts, diffuse sensations, strong bodily feelings, vague impressions, or as a sudden and complete knowing. Free associate, think symbolically, and explore alternative ways of interpreting whatever arises. Ask yourself what this intuitive nudge reminds you of. Are there other memories connected with it?

Reflect on decisions you have made in the past on the basis of your intuition. How accurate or relevant were your intuitive nudges? Consider the times your intuition was proven true and times it was off the mark. What accounts for the difference?

When you reflect on your intuitive experiences, are there common elements in those stories? Is there a hidden pattern being revealed through your intuition? How might you become even more sensitive and alert to useful intuitive nudges?

Intuitions sometimes arrive when you are otherwise occupied, especially when you are engaged in repetitive activities or during light trance states (like when you are driving or watching TV). They can also appear in flow states, or when you are in the timeless space of daydreaming, contemplation, or meditation.

Express gratitude to your Intuitive Self for its access to the hidden connection between all things.

DEEPER QUESTIONS FOR YOUR INTUITIVE SELF

This is a time to notice, listen, feel, and record the responses from your Intuitive Self. When you're wrestling with niggling but indistinct intuitive nudges and need your Intuitive Self's guidance, you can reflect on these questions.

- What does my intuition want me to know about this?
- What am I being called to notice or attend to?
- Am I likely to regret it if I don't directly explore this inner prompt?
- Is this situation verifying a previous insight or speaking to the future?
- What steps can I take to intuit the deeper meaning of this situation arising at this time?

LIVING THE DEEPER STORY OF YOUR INTUITIVE SELF

However we choose to define or study it at this point, intuition can be a rich source of knowledge that goes beyond our five senses, reasoning, and known storehouse of information. It connects us to practices used by ancient mystics, indigenous spiritual practitioners, and modern scientists. It provides another window of consciousness that we are free to open and explore.

When applied with a healthy dose of discernment, intuition can give you direct access to the mysterious connections made within your subconscious mind. It can prompt you in creative ways you might otherwise never consider in the everyday processing of experience.

In making us more sensitive to the subtle shifts in energy in ourselves and others, intuition helps us to monitor congruency. It is not only useful as a skill, but it facilitates a refreshing sense of wonder and curiosity about the workings of the universe beyond our conscious reach.

I AM

Lightning bolts of insight jump-start my senses, activating inner radar and alerting me to the game afoot. I swerve off the beaten track and go off half-cocked to connect the dots. Like a crazed conspiracy theorist, my intuition sees patterns in everything. Coincidence? It thinks not. Like an addict on a toot, it won't be reined in, won't listen to reason, and won't do the right thing; intuition has a mind of its own. Trading in the intangible, my intuition speaks in whispers, communicating its piece and then slipping unceremoniously out the door, leaving me to wonder. I would rather be stunned and stung by the mysteries of life than ever fall into the deadening certainty that so many people crave. **My intuition ignites my curiosity. I intuit; therefore, I am.**

Imaginative

CHAPTER 6

THE DEEPER STORY OF YOUR IMAGINATIVE SELF

"Reality leaves a lot to the imagination."

—JOHN LENNON

The infinite potential of human imagination is one of our most profound gifts. The Imaginative Self is not only a powerful ally in problem-solving, self-regulation, and coping, but it provides the internal impetus for invention, innovation, and art. It takes us beyond the limitations of our five senses, makes reality malleable, creates new perspectives, and gives us the means to explore the mysteries of life. Challenging the established boundaries of what is real and what is possible, the Imaginative Self has always felt the call to reinvent the world.

THE DEEPER ROLE OF YOUR IMAGINATIVE SELF

Function: Your imagination allows you to expand beyond the known and exercise transformative power to re-imagine and re-create your world.

When in alignment: You internally challenge the status quo by perceiving, interpreting, and expressing your unique potential. You value originality, expand your capacity for creative and divergent thinking, and turn your imagination toward finding creative solutions that serve a higher purpose. You actively and mindfully seek out imaginative perspectives through the arts and sciences to expand your world view.

When out of alignment: Imagination can disengage you from reality. It has an addictive pull that can lull you into escapism or a distracted state of passivity. As a passive consumer of the products of other's imaginations, you may end up denying or failing to engage *your own* creative power and potential. When unbounded imagination is applied without conscious awareness of its potential for unintended consequences, it can conceive inventions that could wreak havoc in the world.

Key Areas of Development: Creative Intelligence,[32] Divergent Thinking, Humor and Playfulness, Spontaneity, Aesthetics, Ethical Application of Imagination

Dominant Questions: How can I engage my imagination to create something that will expand the range of options available in the world?

Arc of Development: From Uninspired to Creatively Engaged

THE CALL OF THE IMAGINATIVE SELF

When we are young, imagining is as natural as breathing. We learn about the world through imaginative play, veering in and out of a magical landscape in which everything is alive and possesses infinite potential. Children use the same pattern-seeking processes as adults but have not yet developed the cognitive constraints that will one day narrow their vision.

For children, imagination is fully embodied, experienced as real, and imbued with meaningful sensory detail. It is not simply used for play; it also opens the door to cognitive and social awareness. Children develop empathy through pretense, play-acting various roles, and imagining themselves in the shoes of others. They are curious about everything and want to know how the world works.

By the time they are school-aged, however, being too inquisitive or imaginative starts to be actively discouraged. Busy parents and teachers experience inquiry fatigue from the constant questions and challenges that children's perspectives pose. School is designed to have you learn within strict parameters, in which there is little room for divergent thinking. Educational research indicates that by grade five or six, kids have stopped asking questions of their teachers altogether. When curiosity is no longer rewarded, it can lead to lack of engagement, boredom, and disinterest in new learning. When new ideas aren't welcomed or encouraged, imagination can atrophy.

DIVERGENT AND CONVERGENT THINKING

Schooling tends to steer kids toward *convergent thinking,* which is designed to culminate in one definitive answer. This kind of thinking draws upon amassed information that is already known to come up with the best possible solution. It's best for idea analysis and development of processes.

What tends to get suppressed along the way is *divergent thinking,* which includes imagination. This kind of thinking is spontaneous, free-flowing, complex, multi-faceted, flexible, capable of managing paradox, original, fluent, elaborative, daring, and risk-taking. Divergent thinking is great for idea generation, creative problem-solving, and opening to new possibilities.

Research has shown that we use both forms of thinking.

When we imagine and daydream, we generate ideas, but when we want to put them to use, we need to employ convergent thinking to make such ideas actionable.

To strengthen our imagination, we need free reign to think divergently. Then, we need to harness it for practical application.

Allowing Imagination to Lead

> *"Imagination is not an icing on the cake of life, but the oven in which it is baked."*
>
> —ORNA ROSS

Truly creative people are servants of their imagination, not the other way around. It is the imagination that is in charge, not the constraining Intellectual Self. This is why really creative work always has an element of something unexpected. Imaginative genius is a visitation one must yield to, but it requires discipline and a craft through which your inspiration can be channeled. Receptivity paves the way for something new to present itself, but the receiver has to show up and do the work to invite the inspiration.

At times, imagination can have a manic or tyrannical hold on a visionary. People often speak about their imagination in the same way they speak of their intuition—it is something they find themselves gripped by, an involuntary thrall rather than something they control.

There are many examples of this described by artists, musicians, writers, and dancers. My artist friend Jo says that her paintings do not come from her but through her. She says her imagination insists on having *its* vision realized, not hers, and she has no idea what will show up on the canvas until she has fully yielded to its pressure.

In his autobiography, *Music is My Mistress,* Duke Ellington talks about how at the age of fifteen, while working as a soda jerk, the rhythmic sound of a soda fountain caught his imagination and held him captive until it was translated into his first piece of music.[33]

Creative writers describe how the characters in their books take on a life of their own and determine how the story will unfold. The work of scientists and business people is just as likely to invite the unexpected visitation of imaginative genius. Discoveries of any kind are byproducts of imagination.

Imagination is the fuel for creative activity. Applying that fuel to a creative output requires some measure of convergent thinking. Truly creative people are receptive and allow their minds to open to new possibilities. Once they have been moved by their idea, they can apply the convergent thinking processes of their craft to bring it into being.

IMAGINATION IN THE ARTS AND BEYOND

Arts bridge generations and cultures, providing a window into what it means be human. Not only do the arts provide a creative outlet for the artist, but they also stimulate the imagination of those exposed to the work. The arts express original perspectives and inspire deep connections, both individually and collectively.

Intangible aspects of interiority can be made accessible to us through music, dance, literature, and the visual arts. Such offerings evoke strong feelings and deep awakenings. We can be moved, feel empathy or outrage, be swept away, overwhelmed, ecstatic, or rendered speechless. We can be stimulated, made thoughtful, or become curious about things we might never have otherwise been exposed to. Art alerts us to issues in the world, influences our perceptions, and motivates us to take action. It can break us out of our own limited perspectives and make new worlds available to us.

Imagination can be life-saving during challenging times. Inhabiting a fantasy world of one's own making (or by having access to the imagined world of others through books, movies, music etc.) can make difficult circumstances endurable. Resilience is cultivated through exposure to role models who help you imagine a better future for yourself.

But Imagination Is Not Limited to the Arts

You use your imagination all the time. Imagination is active when you dream and when you are awake. It is at work the moment you get up in the morning to envision the day ahead. The planning and goal-setting governed by the Intellectual Self would be impossible without active engagement of your imagination.

Imagination is constantly running in the background of your everyday activity, connecting the dots, making meaning out of random associations, and stoking your creative fires. It can run idly at the subconscious level only to occasionally pop through with a brilliant (if unbidden) idea, or it can be consciously invoked when you need innovative solutions.

HOW IMAGINATION CHANGES THE WORLD

Expressions of imagination are not just an internal process. Everything that exists in the world was once a figment of someone's imagination. The evidence is all around us at growing levels of complexity.

Consider how the application of imagination has already altered the world. The imaginative impulse that envisioned our first stone-scraping tools more recently conceived the super computers that our world has become dependent upon. The mud shelters of our past and the glass towers that now define our urban skylines were imagined by the same faculty. The early structures of the fur trade imaginatively morphed into a global economy. The guttural lullabies of our ancestors were transformed into symphony orchestras, and the equivalent of early cave drawings are on display in the Louvre. The stories we used to share around the fire are now consumed in the form of bestselling novels and Oscar-winning movies. No part of human culture has been left untouched by the drive to envision something *more*.

Perhaps it is the *more* idea that should give us pause when it comes to the unbounded application of imagination. Imagination has no use for the status quo; it is by nature disruptive and divergent. It can be a wild and unpredictable force in the world. Because of this, imagination is often perceived as inherently threatening. Its existence upsets tradition, routine, and so-called tried and true methods. Is the threat real or imagined? Just because we can imagine something, does that mean we should create it?

Like anything else, imagination can have a dark side.

When it is overused or applied irresponsibly, the very imagination that leads to creativity can also be destructive.

Existential Risk

It seems to me that the real risk factor lives within the undisciplined human psyche. Unrestrained human cleverness has not evolved enough to integrate other intelligences (intellectual, emotional, spiritual, and existential). Experiments and applications of unbounded imagination need an ethical framework around them that takes into consideration the potential for unintended consequences arising from those creations. This is why I believe we need a consciousness upgrade in every dimension of being.

RECONCEIVING AN ETHICAL FRAMEWORK

In 2003, I attended a symposium called *Investigating the Mind* at MIT in Boston. It was sponsored by the Mind and Life Foundation to facilitate a dialogue between the Dalai Lama, other Buddhist scholars, and luminaries from the fields of psychology and biobehavioral sciences. In the final reflections to integrate the symposium's concepts, Professor Eric Lander, who is neither a Buddhist nor a behavioral specialist but a molecular biologist, reported on an earlier discussion session that took place at the Dalai Lama's residence on the nature of life, biology, philosophy, and ethics. He admitted his trepidation when the question was asked about whether it is ethical to use animals in experiments. Knowing the Buddhist doctrine on reverence for life, he assumed there would be an outright dismissal of that possibility. He said he learned a lesson in intellectual humility that day when he heard the Dalai Lama's answer.

The Dalai Lama explained that it is not simple to say whether it is right or wrong. Although there is clearly bad karma associated with harming an animal, you also have to consider the outcome fifty years from now: will it have had a positive and beneficial effect? Dr. Lander said he understood this part of the answer, which seemed like a secular viewpoint in which things are seen through the lens of a cost-benefit analysis. But what the Dalai Lama said next really made him pause. The Dalai Lama went on to say that it would also depend on *what was in your heart* during the experiment. What was the deeper motivation of the scientist conducting the experiment?

I remember the outburst of laughter when Dr. Lander asked if we could imagine our institutional review boards using "what was in a scientist's heart" as one of the criteria for accepting or rejecting our research projects.

Then he asked, *but what if they did*? What if investigation dialogues began by asking, "Do you have a motivation to ameliorate suffering in the world?" What would change if scientists who are motivated by pure intellectual curiosity were also given a mandate to reflect upon deeper motivations behind their research as well as the consequences it might create down the road?

I believe this also speaks to the heart of accountability for all things we imagine and give birth to. It is a complex topic. We want the right to imagine freely, but we also need to create responsibly. This is where the twin engines of imagination and intellect can work together using divergent and convergent thinking. Both openness and constraint are necessary.

RESPONSIBLE USE OF PERSONAL IMAGINATION

Although we learn to drive some aspects of our Imaginative Self underground as youngsters, the imaginative impulse does not go away; there is a secret thrill in play and pretense that even adults are reluctant to relinquish. The trick is to keep our own imagining alive and work with it consciously and responsibly.

In his book on pleasure, Paul Bloom points out that the number one pastime of most Americans is participating in experiences they know are not real: in other words, acts of imagination.[34] When people are left to their own devices, they retreat to books, movies, video games, television programs, or acts of daydreaming and fantasizing. We enjoy inhabiting worlds that are not our own. Sometimes, we prefer the reduced risk involved in simulated rather than real experience. Living vicariously through our imagination gives us the chance to have a multitude of experiences with minimal personal risk.

By immersing ourselves in unfamiliar situations and problems, we learn how to work our way through them. There is also another theory about the value in the pull toward darker fiction. Children like scary tales, and adults spend hours being entertained by shows about serial killers, misuse of power, and even sexual violence. These dark subjects force us to confront and consciously integrate the shadow side of human nature.

The Movies in Our Minds

Research has shown that although we can distinguish between real and imagined worlds, once the brain systems involved in imagination are engaged, the brain produces the same kinds of responses as if we are dealing with something real. This is why we sometimes get emotionally carried away in the fictional lives of characters in books or on the screen. We have physiological responses to imagined experience. The same thing applies to our own fictions—the stories we make up in our heads.

When drama on the screen is not enough, you can activate it internally by imagining all kinds of things. Our imaginations can run wild, entertaining fears that may or may not have any basis in reality. Imagination can take us to dark places when interpretation becomes distorted due to unchecked survival and shadow responses.

Imagination fueled by immature emotional reactivity and old wounding can lead to excessive drama and acting out. If you continually fixate on painful imaginings, you solidify their impact. Imaginings based upon your wounded, self-critic, and shadow selves can activate negative self-talk, projected shame, and comparisons. Those aspects of self can run interference, block the healing potential of positive imagination, and shut down its creative potential. Ego and intellect can create challenges by refusing to let go of control so that your healthy imagination can flow freely.

Whether induced externally or created internally, our fantasies can be compelling. We have an addictive pull to the imaginal realm, where impulses, needs, and drives have unrestrained expression. This is why conscious integration of all aspects of self is necessary for the proactive application of your active imagination.

CONSCIOUSLY APPLYING IMAGINATION

Paradoxically, we both crave and resist new ideas. We

value what is original, but it also disturbs us because it forces us to reconsider fixed ideas and open ourselves to foreign and unfamiliar experiences.

Giving yourself permission to become inventive, think outside the box, engage free association, or play with random input in problem-solving situations can help you to entertain the "impossible."

Wild ideas can come out of nowhere, but they can also be ushered in times of need—hence the phrase "necessity is the mother of invention." A great example of the successful application of both divergent and convergent thinking was demonstrated when the mother of all hacks was invented to bring the Apollo 13 astronauts safely back to Earth. One of the techniques that stimulated imagination for that save was the use of reframing: creatively restating the nature of the problem.

Jim's Story

Jim called on his Imaginative Self to help resolve a problem at work. For years, there had been a good working relationship between the company's management and the union, when suddenly, for no apparent reason, communication broke down. The union initiated a series of country-wide shutdowns. Jim tried getting through to the head of the union, but years of trust had been mysteriously tossed aside. In the absence of real information to go on, Jim was curious and decided to put his Imaginative Self on the case.

He wondered how the story might look from another perspective, so he decided to write a fairy tale in which the company (the wizards) and union employees (the magicians) were engaged in an epic battle. While he was writing the story, he imagined that information was leaking across enemy lines. He wondered whom he should cast as the mole in his story, so he imagined the qualities of an actual mole. He saw it as a small, powerless creature who likes to hide.

As soon as he envisioned that, a particular employee sprang to mind. So he asked himself, what would happen if *she* held the power of the company in her hands? And then it struck him: she actually did!

This particular woman had recently been recruited from the mailroom to scan confidential company documents. On investigation, it was revealed that she had misread one of the documents and informed the union that management was planning a series of undisclosed lay-offs.

In actuality, the document was a proposed reorganization schedule in which no jobs were being cut. Ultimately, Jim shared the document with the union, and their discussions led to an entirely new level of transparency between the company and union representatives.

The answer arrived suddenly and as a surprise for Jim, but it took an imaginative restating of the problem to discover it. If you stay receptive, even in times of conflict, dissonance, or difficulty, your Imaginative Self can help save the day.

INTEGRATING YOUR IMAGINATIVE SELF

The beauty of healthy imagination is that it does not fear the unknown. It can work with confusion and take you to new places. Think of your Imaginative Self as a crucible: the alchemical melting pot in which heat transforms one substance into another. Consider what needs changing and the degree of passionate energy you are willing to expend to affect that transformation. Then, give yourself permission to play.

Here are some ways to stimulate imagination and use it for problem-solving:

- Use playful association, combining ideas, repurposing them, and looking at things from different angles and perspectives to engage your fertile imagination.
- Use your imagination as a time machine: go backward in time to supply a past version of yourself with per-

spective and knowledge that you now possess. Or go to your imagined future self to see how he or she overcomes issues you are wrestling with in the present.

- Use analogies, metaphors, and symbolic representations to restate and reframe a problem imaginatively. Change the backdrop or backstory of a problem or set it in a new context to trigger insights.
- Use wordplay to break words down into their component parts, or play with multiple meanings or interpretations of words, to provide a new way of looking at an issue.
- Stick figure drawings or nonsense poems can pop you out of your usual frame of reference and illuminate aspects of a problem or a solution that were previously elusive.
- Embodied imagination is an incredibly useful technique. Feeling and acting out various aspects of the problem, turning them into a gesture or a dance, or even taking your problem for a walk can be illuminating.

RE-IMAGINING VERSUS REPLAYING

Imagination can open you to new possibilities in challenging situations by allowing you to see the scene differently in your mind rather than replaying and reinforcing an old story. Imagine for a moment someone with whom you have had an argument. As you recall that person and the unkind things they said, experiment with seeing them in a variety of ways. You can imagine them as an object or animal, give them cartoonish features or a high, squeaky voice. This is not to induce disrespect, but to see the situation symbolically and break up your habitual pattern of perception. In reimagining the situation in your mind's eye, you can exaggerate, emphasize, or minimize details, making visual and auditory adjustments until you feel a shift in perspective. This release from the habitual negative imagining won't solve the issue, but it may just give you enough space to step back and reconsider the situation from a less defensive position. If you suspend judgment and stay open-minded, you can also imagine possible positive motivations that person may have had in behaving as they did. You can put yourself in their shoes and activate a sense of empathy for them or try out a variety of positive resolutions to the story.

USING IMAGINATION IN MENTAL REHEARSAL

Sometimes, blurring the line between the real and the imagined can have benefit. On the plus side, there is some evidence to suggest that using imagery, visuo-motor behavioral rehearsal, and symbolic mental rehearsal can prime you to achieve desired results. These techniques have been practiced and researched in the fields of medicine, psychology, biofeedback, psychoneuroimmunology, sports medicine, physical therapy, and computer training. Success largely depends on people's ability to vividly visualize and inhabit the desired kinesthetic feelings for rehearsal purposes.

Using your imagination as a simulation device can help you activate the feelings involved in achieving your desired experiences. For example, if you are striving for a goal that has been out of your reach, you might normally tell yourself a story about why you can't have that thing or focus on what is in the way of achieving your goal, instead of using your imagination to help you achieve it.

You can practice using vividly embodied imagery to visualize and imagine what it would feel like to achieve that goal. The more you practice inhabiting, feeling, and rehearsing your desired end result, the more you prime your nervous system to recognize those feelings as normal. This helps to close the gap between where you are now and where you would like to be.

No amount of visualizing without taking affirmative action will bring your goals into being but working with the power of your imagination can help to set you up for success.

THE SYNTHESIZING EFFECT OF IMAGINATION

Your imagination can creatively synthesize random bits

of input and generate new constellations of meaning. Just as "nature abhors a vacuum," so too does the imagination. Given time and space, your imagination can help you penetrate the mysteries and subconscious holdings within each dimension of yourself. If each aspect of self is allowed to take on an expressive life of its own, you can dialogue with each part to call upon its specific brand of wisdom.

Clients love working with this process because it helps to illuminate the pieces of their life's puzzle. In dialoguing with each part of yourself, you discover that, sometimes, the very things you thought were hurting you or holding you back are actually tied to a larger purpose that is trying to be fulfilled.

Using the active imagination process, you can engage each part of yourself and find clues from your deeper story.

Active Imagination

Using the Jungian technique of active imagination provides a stable environment in which you can interact with imaginal offerings. In active imagination, the goal is to discover what is alive in your subconscious mind and coax that living energy forward. To accomplish this, you need to become deeply relaxed, clear your mind, and prepare to receive whatever comes into the empty space. Suspend the need to judge anything and block out any editorial influence. Simply let whatever is going to appear to arrive, and let it do whatever it is going to do.

The objective here is to let things evolve of their own accord. Let your imaginings be *autonomous* and take on a life of their own. Follow whatever comes alive and moves within that imaginal realm. The emphasis is on what is "alive" within you: what moves. You know you are *receiving* rather than controlling or fabricating when your imagination *surprises* you and something unexpected occurs. Stay with whatever arrives for twenty to thirty minutes and then stop.

The next day, re-enter the place where you stopped, wait for it to move again, and follow it for another twenty to thirty minutes. If you do this for thirty days, you will develop a stable environment to which you can return for answers, inspiration, and guidance.

This kind of engaged imagery provides a bridge between the rational and non-rational dimensions of self.

Aisha's Story

Aisha was feeling depressed and lethargic. She felt disengaged from her life and had withdrawn from family and friends. She said she had no sense of purpose and no reason for getting up in the morning. She agreed to use her active imagination to dialogue with her soul to rediscover a sense of purpose.

She reported a lot of frustration at first just waiting for something to show up and move, but one day, she told me an unexpected story of reconnecting with her soul.

When she had relaxed and prepared herself, after a few false starts she suddenly saw an image of her grand-mother moving about her old kitchen. She followed her grandmother's movements and felt her grandmother's presence standing behind her. That strong feeling popped her out of the reverie, but she re-entered it in the same place the next day.

Feeling her grandmother behind her, she looked down and saw her own tiny hands trying to stir a mixture in a bowl. The next time she returned, they were making cookies in the shape of crescent moons. Curious about the feeling that came over her in these interactions, she decided to go to her own kitchen and do some baking, something she hadn't done for years.

As soon as she made her first crescent, she heard her grandmother's whispered prayers and remembered her explanation. She was told that each repetition was about letting go of worldly things, the hereafter, and even one-self, to prepare a pure place in which they could receive God. Aisha felt a hidden connection between her grand-mother's prayers and what she was attempting in her active imagination practice.

The next time she entered the kitchen in her imagina-tion, she saw only the mess of baking left behind and a dirty apron flung over a chair. She felt deeply discour-aged by the static image. Later that day, she decided to clean her own kitchen. Once she started, she realized how much clutter and disorganization had accumulated over the years. She started to declutter her space and let go of worldly things that no longer had purpose, giving up the notion that they might be of use "someday." As she cleaned, she began to think about all the other areas of her life that had been neglected.

She didn't want to take on her grandmother's religion but decided to create her own mantra to invoke while cleaning. Each day, she murmured her mantra while she brought a sense of order to some area of her life.

When she got to the drawer in her bedside table, she discovered a letter from her daughter-in-law and real-ized that she had something to clean up there, too. In reaching out to her, Aisha realized she had been holding on to an old story that she needed to release. In healing the rift with her son and daughter-in-law, she was able to reinstate herself as a mother and grandmother. That matriarchal role gave her a new sense of purpose in her own granddaughter's life.

The beauty of active imagination is that it is not premeditated. If you are patient, create the space, and give whatever shows up room to move, it will lead you to the answers that are already alive within you.

DEEPER PERSONAL REFLECTION

Take a moment to settle in and make sure you are free from disturbance or distraction for a few moments. We want to exercise your imagination and breathe life into it.

How you see yourself and your place in the world is an act of imagination. What are the problems you've overcome, the character-building moments, and the life-altering experiences that have contributed to how you imagine yourself? Reflect on your personal fantasies about who you are, who you want to become, or who you want to be known for by the time you leave this world.

Let's also explore inspiration for becoming the hero or heroine of your own deep story. Your inspired imagination has been active your whole life, noticing people and things that relate to the deeper story of your life. We are naturally attracted to certain qualities in others. We all have people we admire. If asked for the names of inspirational role models, you would probably list some of the usual suspects—an oft-quoted list of iconic figures.

But when you were little, your heroes were a little more home-grown. They were based on whomever awakened your curiosity and interest: a neighbor, an aunt or uncle, even a particular teacher. Maybe it was that cool guy down the street with the motorcycle, or the eccentric woman whose house was full of exotic artifacts from her travels. Specific people intrigued you and caused you to entertain thoughts about alternative ways of being.

Inspiration could have been drawn from any number of sources: cartoon characters or comic book heroes; characters from books you read, TV shows, or movies; sports figures, dancers, musical icons, or comedians. You might have been inspired by roles rather than particular people—astronauts, scientists, activists, or saviors of humanity in one form or another. Who were the stars in your personal heaven?

Who did you admire, envy, and want to be like? Who did you secretly wish were your real parents? Who had gifts, skills, wisdom, a good life, or the kind of notoriety you desired? Identify those people and what it was about them that made you dream, yearn, and aspire to something more. What part of you was being called to the surface?

As you grew older, how did your dreams evolve? Did you see yourself bringing home a gold medal, creating an amazing new invention, being a conceptual artist who changes the way we see things, a genius who eradicates world hunger, a diplomat brokering world peace, a billionaire philanthropist?

Your dreams may have been more humble. Maybe you simply wanted a happy family and a good job or to travel and learn about different cultures and parts of the world. What did fulfillment look like to you?

Explore the parts of you that identified with or were activated by these imaginary people or circumstances. Was it your wounded self, admiring someone who had overcome a tragic situation? Your ego, excited by the possibility of living up to a higher ideal? Or was it your survival self, longing for the imagined security that would come with a certain income and stature? What was your soul whispering to you about the deeper potential of your life? Who were you imagining into being?

How do those early fertile stirrings of imagination show up in your life now? What part of that imagining have you realized in some form, and what has been left behind?

Who are you becoming and how can you support that imaginal being, giving him or her room to move?

_____

DEEPER QUESTIONS FOR YOUR IMAGINATIVE SELF

This is a time to notice, listen, feel, and record the responses from your Imaginative Self. When you need your imaginative input, inspiration, and guidance, you can reflect upon these questions.

- What does my imagination want me to know about this situation?
- What image, sound, or gesture does my imagination associate with this quandary?
- What happens if I write a poem or song about this, do a stick drawing or a painting, sew, dance, or otherwise engage in imaginative play with this situation—what does this reveal?
- What steps can I take to focus my imagination toward seeing the best possible outcome of this situation?

LIVING THE DEEPER STORY OF YOUR IMAGINATION

Your Imaginative Self opens the door to new worlds from which you return with original and innovative ideas. It captivates your deep attention, inspires passion, and sparks creative problem-solving. It breaks the bonds of conditioned, conventional, and habitual thinking by challenging existing order and introducing new possibilities.

Imagination transcends the limits of time and space, taking us beyond current reality to otherwise inaccessible realms. Imagination made it possible for humanity to travel into space, so we could look back at the planet with new eyes to see the Earth as a living ecosystem.

It gives us the means to explore history or envision the future. Most importantly, imagination gets us to think beyond ourselves. As a powerful mirror of culture, it stimulates us to reconsider the way we are living and what we value. Empathic imagination lets us step into the shoes of others whom we may never have the opportunity to know directly. It helps us expand our definition of what it means to be human.

No discussion of imagination would be complete without acknowledging the many art forms it has inspired. The creative world of visual arts, music, dance, and literature are indispensable for understanding and cultivating the soul of humanity. Ultimately, imagination encourages us to call forth hidden beauty in the world.

When we are coming from a place of evolved consciousness, accountability, and wholeness, our imagination not only inspires solutions for our individual issues but stimulates ideas needed for healing the great problems of the world.

I AM

Imagination is the P. T. Barnum of the three-ring circus that is my mind: the lit fuse that shoots me from the cannon of everyday cognition. My imagination forces me to defy gravity and sanity as I loop through its rarified air, breaking bonds with the given and sending me free falling into entirely new worlds. It is the joy of the hunt, the thrill of the chase, the ecstasy of capturing and clothing the intangible with form. It is the shapeshifting trickster genius that turns life into art and art into life. It is the irrepressible urge to see, sense, and make meaning in new ways. Divine fire in the core of my being urging me to create, create, create...**I imagine; therefore, I am.**

Intellectual

CHAPTER 7

THE DEEPER STORY OF YOUR INTELLECTUAL SELF

While your Intuitive and Imaginative Selves provide the means to escape the constraints of reality, your Intellectual Self keeps you grounded in what's real. It recognizes the limitations and subjectivity of your senses. It has the inhibitory power to override emotion in favor of objective analysis. It brings focus to the issue at hand, parses fact from fiction, and uses discernment and discipline to bring your goals to fruition. Great thinkers don't run from reality; they dive right into it and are capable of finding beauty in the complexity of life as it is.

THE ROLE OF YOUR INTELLECTUAL SELF IN YOUR DEEPER STORY

Function: Intellect provides discernment, critical thinking, reality testing, and develops systems for transmitting knowledge.

When out of alignment: You are closed to new ideas and information, using limited mental models for decision-making and problem solving. You don't trust your own intellect, so in place of exercising it, you become attached to a particular bias. You pose as a skeptic without ever seriously investigating an idea before you condemn it. If intellect is over-utilized, you can get stuck in the paralysis of analysis, or too detached from feelings. If intellect is under-utilized, you may be gullible and indiscriminate.

When in alignment: You engage mental resources for discernment. You are open-minded, curious, and exploratory. You seek new learning and solutions. You use logic, reason, and evidence when assessing a situation. You check the sources and accuracy of information before arriving at conclusions.

Key Areas of Development: Objective Intelligence,[35] Critical and Systems Thinking, Logic, Reason, Problem Solving

Dominant Questions: How can I use discernment to turn knowledge into wisdom?

Arc of Development: From Ignorance to Discernment

THE CALL OF THE INTELLECTUAL SELF

Despite continuous research and debate on the topic, there is still no universally agreed-on definition of intelligence. Central to the debate is the question of whether intelligence is a single measurable ability, known as general intelligence,[36] or whether we possess multiple forms of intelligence.[37]

It is, however, generally agreed that intelligence is the ability to perceive information, learn from experience, solve problems, and use knowledge to adapt to new situations. Intelligence includes logic, abstract thought, understanding, self-awareness, communication, learning, memory, planning, creativity, and problem solving.

Your Intellectual Self creates systems to navigate, make sense of, and understand your world. This is the faculty capable of creating entire systems of knowledge and inquiry, and is responsible for developing language, social structure, cultural transmission, philosophy, morality, justice, governance, economics, technology, and science.

At the personal level, the dominant power of the Intellectual Self resides in its capacity for conscious awareness and self-regulation. Using the executive functioning areas of your brain, it helps to integrate different dimensions of cognition and behavior.[38] It governs your working memory, mental flexibility, and self-control. Your Intellectual Self becomes aware of impulses, can think about them abstractly, determines their utility, and inhibits their grip, so you can intentionally focus on achieving your goals.

To accomplish this, your intellect has the ability to override physical discomfort, interrupt responses from your survival and emotional self, limit the intrusion of intuition, refocus attention away from imagination toward concrete analysis and action, and defer gratification for the sake of moving purposefully toward established goals. It analyzes the personal costs and benefits of taking action and can marshal your will and resources to get the job done.

Intellect is not swayed by emotional reactivity, and when used appropriately, it can be your greatest ally in any emotionally charged situation. Your intellect challenges assumptions and generalizations and wants the facts of the situation before deciding how to respond.

When fully engaged, it uses painstaking analysis, investigation, and review of alternatives to do the heavy lifting involved in decision-making. It likes evidence-based answers but is open to reflecting on new possibilities.

We need the intellect's powers of discernment to keep ourselves and others reasonable, responsible, and accountable.

To satisfy the intellect's requirements, we need to look at rules and principles that underlie decisions. Understanding and clarity require effort. It takes work to get to the most objective truth possible, demanding a combination of analysis, doubt, and disinterest. After a systematic critical perspective is taken to evaluate claims and assumptions, your intellect can weigh the facts and let the evidence speak for itself.

INTEGRATING THE INTELLECTUAL SELF

Take a moment to think about how your intellect is engaged each day. You make decisions regarding your health, significant relationships, home, work, finances, leisure activities, etc. To make the most of your time and resources, your brain has to conceive your goals, to plan, prioritize, organize, and execute on each of these decisions. That means you need to be able to selectively focus on what is important.

Your Intellectual Self codifies the rules by which you live. It can prioritize your values, structure your belief system, and formalize your worldview. It can establish your intentions, set up your objectives, monitor your progress, and keep you accountable in achieving your goals. It can objectively assess your behavior to see if it is working for or against you and identify the corrections necessary to bring you into alignment with your whole self.

To achieve this, the Intellectual Self must take stock of three essential aspects:

- Where you are (the worldview and beliefs that govern your life)
- Where you want to go (your goals and highest aspirations)
- How you want to get there (the values that will motivate you and keep you in touch with what is important)

WHERE YOU ARE: RECOGNIZING YOUR WORLDVIEW

Your worldview is the way you see and interpret the world. It is the collection of thoughts, beliefs, attitudes, values, cultural and familial inputs, reinforcing assumptions, and selective perceptions that define your reality. For example, your culture can influence how you perceive the world and your place in it. In an individualist culture (such as the United States and Canada), there is greater emphasis placed on individual freedoms than in collectivist cultures (such as Japan or Korea), which focus more directly on the needs of family and community.

Your worldview is one of the filters through which you make determinations about the nature of reality. That filter (which is only partly conscious) allows you to see what you have been trained to see. In consciously examining your worldview, you may discover that it contains some inconsistencies or paradoxes.

Take a moment to reflect on the following questions:

- Are you more oriented toward a spiritual or secular view about the origin of the universe?
- What are your thoughts about the nature of reality?
- What do you think is the meaning and purpose of life?
- Do you suspect there are mysteries beyond the reach of science?
- What is the truth about human nature?
- What do you think provides the basis for human morality?
- Is some measure of faith necessary for functioning?
- How do you define justice?

The answers to these and many other significant questions help you understand components of your worldview. In general terms, few people spend much of their intellectual capital *consciously* entertaining these questions at any level of depth. Most of the answers people provide are based on inherited beliefs rather than independent thinking and investigation.

WHERE YOU WANT TO GO: BELIEFS AND VALUES

Beliefs are a shortcut that, once established, pose as reality. Many of your beliefs were encoded unconsciously during your formative years through observation and experimentation with rules. Beliefs about what is correct, appropriate, acceptable, etc. were reinforced through consequences, rewards, and punishment. Those beliefs run in the background as part of your automatic pilot (or default) system. People tend to defend, justify, and rationalize their beliefs rather than genuinely examine them.

Skeptic Michael Schermer calls the brain a "belief engine" that looks for patterns and infuses them with meaning, intention, and agency.[39] Once a belief is established, we selectively look for confirmation of that belief and delete evidence to the contrary. This is how we construct internalized models of the world and develop what is called confirmation bias.

The Pitfalls of Confirmation Bias

When evidence contrary to your belief is presented, your mind focuses on the challenge of discrediting that perspective. You look for flaws, cherry-pick the proof, and build your argument. Unfortunately, this process builds new neural pathways and memories that ultimately strengthen and entrench your original conviction. You end up reinforcing your belief rather than actually exploring it.

This process is also described as maintaining a positive illusion. Because we are able to strengthen our conviction, it gives us a sense of control and self-affirmation. We feel *right*. Feeling right may have a temporary reward associated with it, but if we actually need to change our belief (because it is undermining our ability to achieve our goals), we are better off approaching such a task with curiosity, openness to learning something new, and an objective evaluation of our conclusions.

Because the story you construct about reality is based on your beliefs, your behaviors flow from and reinforce those beliefs. As long as the world remains familiar and stable, your emotional equilibrium is intact, and it seems your beliefs are valid. However, when new or unexpected things destabilize that equilibrium, your emotions can become dysregulated, and you may be forced to re-examine your beliefs.

> *"It does take great maturity to understand that the opinion we are arguing for is merely the hypothesis we favor, necessarily imperfect, probably transitory, which only very limited minds can declare to be a certainty or a truth."*
>
> —MILAN KUNDERA

One example of non-productive interpretation and thinking about intellect itself comes from the false dichotomy perpetuated between intuitive and logical approaches to business.

Angela's Story

Angela considered herself to be a creative type. She had started a retail business based on her original clothing designs. She had a knack for predicting trends and coming up with unique but elegant products that did exceedingly well in the market. In fact, they did a little too well, and she couldn't keep up with demand. Her successful store started to falter because she didn't have the business systems in place to make it sustainable.

Angela had always resisted systematic approaches, found math boring, and didn't like the discipline involved in adhering to a structured business plan. She felt trapped when she had to consider the principles involved in running a successful business. She was certain the whole enterprise would lose its soul if she became too "bottom-line oriented." She had always believed that the intuitive and intellectual side of life were incompatible.

Fortunately, she began working with a group of spirited entrepreneurs who helped her see the light. They taught her how to put proper business practices in place, and once these were established, she could engage her intellect to design systems that were as simple and elegant as her products. She was able to manage her business sensibly and sustainably without having to sacrifice her creativity. The systematic use of her intellect not only saved her business but strengthened opportunities for the expression of her intuitive and creative aspects of self.

Through self-examination, your intellect can strip away beliefs and layers of non-productive interpretation so you can look at reality without embellishment. This is why learning not just *what* to think but *how* to think is so invaluable.

HOW YOU WANT TO GET THERE
Learning How to Think: Testing Beliefs

> *"Science is organized knowledge. Wisdom is organized life."*
>
> —IMMANUEL KANT

Your Intellectual Self can interrupt your automatic pilot to put you back in conscious control of your thought processes. It takes discipline to focus your thoughts, to suspend preconceived ideas and opinions, to reflect on things with openness, curiosity, and intellectual humility. I like this description on the art of pure thinking by Simone Weil:

"Attention consists of suspending our thought, leaving it detached, empty, and ready to be penetrated by the object; it means holding in our minds, within reach of this thought, but on a lower level and not in contact with it, the diverse knowledge we have acquired which we are forced to make use of. Our thought should be in relation to all particular and already formulated thoughts, as a man on a mountain, who, as he looks forward, sees also below him, without actually looking at them, a great many forests and plains. Above all our thought should be empty, waiting, not seeking anything, but ready to receive in its naked truth the object that is to penetrate it."[40]

Learning how to become a witness to your own thoughts, suspending your automatic responses, and employing metacognition to think about your own process of thinking allows you to move beyond assumptions and examine evidence from a place of detachment and disinterest.

The scientific method sets out principles and procedures for the systematic acquisition of knowledge. It involves recognizing and properly formulating a problem, gathering data through observation and experimentation, formulating a hypothesis, testing that hypothesis, and subjecting it to the scrutiny of others who are knowledgeable on the subject.

We build upon the learning of others, but we also add

to that knowledge base through our own learning and growth. Intellectual humility leaves the door open for a change of mind, a paradigm shift, and new discoveries. No amount of planning and predicting can take everything into account, and nothing is ever perfect. Still, employing a more mindful approach creates the possibility of greater consciousness and accountability in your responses to life's challenges.

Exercising and Strengthening Your Intellectual Self

If ever there was a time to strengthen our collective IQ, this is it. Not only are we subject to our own confirmation bias, but we are also being steered into belief bubbles through online technological algorithms. It is easy to fall prey to fake news, snake oil sales, and bad decision-making if we allow technology to do all of our thinking for us. Conveniences like GPS are great, but they can also rob us of the mental habit of orienting ourselves and developing a good sense of direction. And what if, heaven forbid, Google gets it wrong?

Our brains work on a "use it or lose it" principle, and they need to be worked to learn new things. So why not add cultivating a higher IQ to your to-do list? You can strengthen working memory and fluid intelligence by challenging yourself. Take a course on logic or systems thinking and see what problems you can solve without technology. Alternatively, physical exercise has been shown to have a beneficial effect on mental processing, so up your game by engaging in sports and physical activities. Learning a foreign language, reading books, and learning how to play a musical instrument all increase brainpower.

Rethinking Assumptions

There are many ways our habitual beliefs delude us. What may appear to be common sense is often proven to be false. Rarely do we test the validity of things that seem to be true, and in failing to test our assumptions, we miss an opportunity to think more deeply about our lives and how we want to live them. Investigation is the key.

When your beliefs and reality are at odds, each affected part of your Multi-dimensional Self yields its own brand of discomfort. Rather than running from discomfort, be willing to examine it proactively and adjust your thinking and behavior accordingly. This process of self-awareness and self-regulation helps you make healthy choices and gain greater accountability in your life. To make such choices effectively, you need to know what matters to you. So, let's explore the orienting role that values play in your life.

"Denied the comforting blanket of illusory permanence

*and absolute truth, we have the opportunity and obliga-
tion to do something extraordinary: to see the world as
it is, and to understand and appreciate that our images
will keep changing, not because they are fundamentally
flawed, but because we keep providing ourselves with
better lenses."*

—DAVID P. BARASH[41]

VALUES: KNOWING WHAT MATTERS

Values define what is important to you, provide a personal code of conduct, guide your behavior, and provide a
sense of fulfillment when you are in alignment with them.
Clarifying the priority of your values is fundamental to
making decisions that support your overall well-being.
Values help you work with the positive power of limitation.

For example, if you value optimal personal health, you
need to limit overindulgence. If you value treating others
with respect, you may have to limit reactivity and exert
more patience than you actually feel in the moment
toward another person. If you value responsible stew-
ardship of the Earth, you must consider your ecological
footprint, the energy costs of things you consume, your
method of transportation, and so on. To make holistic
decisions, it is essential to understand your values.

- Think about your past: reflect on some of the best

moments of your life. What was going on and what made these experiences so outstanding? In identifying what made these moments special, you will clarify the underlying values that were being satisfied. Make a note of those values.

· Think about your present: reflect on where you are in and out of balance in your life. What are you passionate about? What keeps you up at night? What motivates you? What is missing in your life right now? What do you feel deprived of? What would bring a greater sense of fulfillment to your life in the moment? Identify the values illuminated within your answers.

· Now think of your future. What do you want to accomplish in your life? What is on your bucket list? What will you feel sad about or seriously regret if you don't get to experience it in your lifetime? Identify the underlying values revealed in your answers.

· Think about what upsets you, irritates you, makes you angry or judgmental, and consider which of your values you believe are being challenged or transgressed in those moments.

· Think of your aspirational values—qualities you admire but may not have yet incorporated in your daily life—where you want to grow and become more proficient. Add these to your values list.

Once you have your list, group your values according to

themes and put them in order of priority. Reflect on the specific personal meaning of these values to you and make a values statement list: a set of guidelines you want to live by.

A sense of wholeness can only be achieved when you are in alignment with your values. Adhering to your values maintains your sense of integrity and helps you stay on track during times of conflict. Now let's look at your goals, some of which you may have already considered within the values exercise.

The Value of Goals

One of the things the intellect does best is to take complex subjects and break them into manageable pieces that can be weighed and balanced for their significance within the whole. The Intellectual Self's role in setting and achieving goals is to focus your mind, provide the objective overview, analyze the factors involved, set your targets, tackle the problems that will inevitably arise along the way, maintain discipline to get you there, and remind you why this is important in the first place. It can set up the goal, the process, and the means to measure your progress.

When it comes to setting meaningful goals, you need the full power of your intellect to weed through endless possibilities and analyze what will bring you optimal satisfaction.

To enlist such conscious decisions, we must come off of our automatic pilot. According to engineer and chief scientist Bob Nease, "Of the 10 million bits of information that each of our brains processes each second, only about 50 bits are devoted to deliberate thought—in other words, 0.0005%."[42] These precious fifty bits need to be marshaled toward consciously chosen goals.

Setting Goals

Well-defined goals help you draw on a vast storehouse of energy that might otherwise go untapped. Goals need to focus proactively on a specific target, rather than be used as a means to move away from undesirable circumstances or discomfort. When the vision is clear and you fully grasp the purpose of your goal, you can invest wholeheartedly in achieving it.

When you think about your goals, it is helpful to consider what the accomplishment of that goal will bring you. So, let's say you want to increase your annual income. You believe increasing your income will bring you a greater level of freedom. In that case, is the actual goal to have more money, or is it to increase your freedom? If you could have either right now, which would you choose?

There may be ways to achieve freedom that would not involve altering your income, and there may be ways of making more money that cause you to lose freedom. It is important to reflect on all of the considerations related to your goal.

Just as choosing values sets limitations, so, too, does setting a goal. Achieving a goal that might be gratifying in one area of your life might also cause an unpleasant impact on another. What satisfies your ego may prove limiting to deeper aspects of self, and so on. This is where knowing yourself, your purpose, and what you want to contribute makes all the difference.

Your goals need to be set with your Multi-dimensional Self in mind. For instance, are there any circumstances under which you would not want a particular goal? Using the Multi-dimensional Self model is useful for identifying and working effectively with potential inner conflicts that may arise in the pursuit of your goal.

Now, thinking about what matters to you, reflecting on your values and applying the above criteria, set your top three goals for the next twelve months.

One of the most critical aspects of establishing goals is to ensure that you have the resources you will need to achieve them. Do you have the information, education, skills, talent, drive, network, time, financial support, and discipline to attain your goal? If you can't answer "yes" to each of those questions, determine what you need to put in place now to make the goal achievable.

Measurement is also important. How will you know when you have achieved the goal? Over what period of time do you expect to do this? How will you track and monitor your progress along the way?

DEEPER PERSONAL REFLECTION

Choose a moment when you will be free of distraction to reflect on the quality of your thinking. Every day you are subjected to billions of bits of information out of which you somehow must decide what deserves of your attention. Your ability to think clearly and discriminately is undermined by the sheer volume of information through which you must wade each day. Advertisers compete to gain what is known as your "attention capital." Distractibility is at an all-time high, and undivided focus is becoming a thing of the past. More than ever, you need to take time to exit the "matrix," so you can think for yourself about what is truly important to you. This requires consciously applied will and discipline.

When was the last time you sat quietly and thought deeply

about the quality of your life and what would be required to either embrace it as it is, or improve it?

This is not a knee-jerk call to go for *more* out of life. In fact, part of the challenge of assessing your own satisfaction is in determining not just what you want to accomplish, but in knowing when you have reached that elusive state called satiation, or *enough*. Research shows that, typically, what people predict will bring them happiness often does not. Presence of mind and attending to what actually brings you satisfaction in the moment helps you connect with deeper truths about yourself. This requires a clear mind, presence, and quietude.

Satisfaction or fulfillment cannot be determined if you are unclear about the things that most connect you to this deeper sense of yourself. *What you want out of life* and *what you want to bring to life* can be tangibly assessed by paying attention and honoring the feedback from within you and through life's feedback.

The beauty of applied intellect is that it works like a camera lens, adjusting its aperture back and forth to focus you on both the big picture of your life and its tiniest details. You need to see both, when you are making choices. Your intellect can help you take a systems approach by looking at how everything connects in your life as a whole. Narrowing the focus can help you to look at the specific details of what is working and what isn't, so you can adapt your plans accordingly.

What does it mean to have a "good life"? Have you considered this question? What are your thoughts and beliefs about this? Do you have a guiding set of principles, values, or a philosophy that influences you in this regard?

When you apply that lens, you can consider where you are now and what you are moving toward in each aspect of your life. Consciously reflect upon the quality of life you are experiencing in each of these areas:

- Your health and overall well-being, mentally, emotionally, physically.
- Your integrity, ethics, and morality.
- Your relationships with intimate partners, family, friends, community.
- Your home, living conditions, and your environment, including your awareness and accountability for your impact on that environment.
- Your calling, career, or where you focus the majority of your productive time and attention.
- Your physical and financial safety and security.
- Your greater education: your learning, growth, and evolution, and how it might be stimulated through exposure to new models of the world.
- Your creative drive.

- Your sense of contribution.

Where are you releasing your unique strengths and skills into the world? How balanced are your life circumstances? Which areas of your life call out for greater clarity and attention? How might you create mental space to focus on your intentions in each of these areas?

DEEPER QUESTIONS FOR YOUR INTELLECTUAL SELF

This is a time to notice, listen, feel, and record the responses from your Intellectual Self. When you need your intellect's guidance, you can reflect upon these questions.

- What does my intellect want me to know about this?
- What would an objective analysis reveal in this situation?
- What have I learned from situations like this in the past that I could apply in this instance? Have others faced this situation? How have they successfully navigated this type of challenge?
- What steps can I take to be discriminate and discerning about this—focusing on facts, applying logic, and taking a systems approach to this situation?

LIVING THE DEEPER STORY OF YOUR INTELLECTUAL SELF

When you engage your Intellectual Self, you disrupt your automatic pilot and take conscious control of your life. Using discernment and discipline, you can consciously choose the rules and principles by which you live and actively work toward accomplishing meaningful goals.

What would the world be like if everyone was willing to challenge their assumptions and beliefs and work toward a more balanced perspective? With open minds and intellectual humility, we would be able to use the collective power of intellect to solve many of the world's problems. We could make a quantum leap toward a conscious evolution on the planet.

I AM

My intellect is the seeker of logical explanation, a cerebral philosopher searching for truth, an investigative reporter itching for facts beneath the story; a scientific censor demanding proofs and peer reviews; an inner skeptic keeping me from drinking my own Kool-Aid, a tireless fighter against the unknown and unknowable, a generator of endless abstraction, incessantly searching for words to concretize the ineffability of existence. I **think; therefore, *I think* I am.**

Social

CHAPTER 8

THE DEEPER STORY OF YOUR SOCIAL SELF

Humans are social animals, and connection is at the heart of our humanity. Our entire lives unfold within a relational context, and nothing has a more profound impact on well-being than our relationships. Despite the North American hubris that makes us think we can "go it on our own," as social animals, we are not only wired for connection but are dependent on it. Healthy social connectivity has a proven positive impact on physical and emotional well-being.

Through healthy reciprocal relating, we make the transition from infantile dependence through necessary individuation and on to a mature state of healthy interdependence.

To accomplish that journey successfully, we need social skills...and a little love along the way.

THE ROLE OF THE SOCIAL SELF IN YOUR DEEPER STORY

Function: Connection with others is vital for well-being; it increases the odds of survival and ensures that your individual contribution is introduced into the collective pool of humanity and the world.

When out of alignment: You feel disconnected, isolated, and alone, fail to form lasting bonds, and are unable to offer yourself to others. You develop distorted perceptions about yourself and others. At its most negative extreme, social conditioning can create separation, an "us versus them" mentality that breeds intolerance, overemphasizes conformity, and breaks human bonds, leading to dehumanization and exploitation of others.

When in alignment: You create empathetic bonds with others; engage in healthy reciprocal relationships; work and play cooperatively; share joys, sorrows, and burdens; and are able to give *and* receive support. You are motivated toward collective interest and work to make the world a better place for all.

Key Areas of Development: Social Intelligence,[43]

Interpersonal Skills, Communication, Teamwork, Appreciation of Diversity

Dominant Questions: How do I connect with others? Where do I belong? How do I fit in?

Arc of Development: From Self-Absorption to Meaningful Connection

THE CALL OF THE SOCIAL SELF

It was an act of relating that brought you into being, so from the very start, your existence depended on others.

As an infant, your survival needs may have seemed basic—food, shelter, and protection—but along with those physical needs came deeper psychosocial ones. Research has taught us about the remarkable plasticity of the brain. It is even more critical in the early years, in which every interaction plays a role in shaping your developing brain.

Early nurturing established your feelings of safety, inclusion, and belonging. Care and attention were required; you needed to be seen, heard, and responded to. Guidance was necessary for you to acquire skills and knowledge. You needed to be touched, comforted, reassured, and treated as a valued being. You needed to be loved.

How those essential needs were responded to during that vulnerable stage of dependence has a profound and enduring impact on the rest of your life. The most critical period of social nurturing occurs within the first three years of life, during the development of your nascent limbic system. That's the part of your brain that ultimately defines your personality and governs your emotional future.

> *"Investigations into the physiology of relatedness now tell us that attachment penetrates to the neural core of what it means to be a human being."*[44]

As a baby, your sensory system was designed as an open loop, requiring input from your parents. Interactions and experiences with your caregivers during this stage are not just essential for survival but are necessary ingredients for neurodevelopment and healthy regulation of your nervous system. Through this period of *physiological intermingling* with parents, your entwined systems are engaged in a process of synchronous limbic regulation. Responses such as your respiratory and heart rates can be calmed and buffered by the presence of your primary caregivers.

Through limbic entrainment, you learned to be aware of your parents' emotions and became adept at reading their moods. Your mirror neurons picked up subtle cues and you began unconsciously imitating the behavior modeled by your caregivers. As your development progressed and your frontal lobes began functioning, your interactions became increasingly conscious. Within your first few months, you learned how to elicit responses from the people around you.

This period of bonding was important, but when you reached the age of eight or nine months, an even greater need for connection with a primary caregiver began to emerge. Healthy attachment during this period is considered the most important event in a person's emotional development. It is the primary source of security, self-esteem, self-control, and social skills.[45]

Attachment theory was first expressed by John Bowlby in the 1950s. He believed that proximity to the mother was an inborn need of a child. A healthy attachment would provide both physical protection and a psychological sense of security and safety for the child. He recognized that anxiety and dysregulation occurred when an infant was separated from its mother. Crying was initially the only way a baby could keep his mother close. As he developed, he could reach out or call the mother to his side in moments of urgent need (such as in times of fear, pain, or unfamiliar circumstances). How the mother responded to these critical moments determined the degree of security and safety the child eventually developed.

The attachment period began with development of motor skills, which enabled you to move about independently. If your primary attachment figure (usually the mother) was responsive to your needs for comfort and contact, providing you a secure base to return to, then you were free to move beyond her to explore. As a result, you would develop securely and become self-reliant.

If, however, your caregiver ignored your need for closeness, you learned to detach from them, keep your distance, and distract yourself with other activities, ultimately becoming compulsively self-reliant. If the attachment figure was inconsistent in their response—at times welcoming and at other times neglectful or intrusive—you were more likely to become clingy and easily distressed. In that case, you would not develop securely, and it would be difficult for you to go forth and explore independently.

Developmental psychologist Mary Ainsworth took attachment theory to an entirely new level when she looked at how the mothering a child received during this phase would predict their emotional traits later in life. Beyond Bowlby's idea about the parent simply needing to be present as a source of security and protection, Ainsworth discovered that it was the specific degree of attunement the mother had with the child's inner state that made all the difference. A mother's ability to intuit and sense the inarticulate needs of the child (limbic resonance) and respond reliably (synchronous limbic regulation) is what influenced the child's emotional development and determined their degree of security later in life.

As it turned out, it would also prove to have an influence on health outcomes later in life as well. In the Harvard Mastery of Stress Study, conducted in the early 1950s, 126 men participated in a longitudinal study in which they were subjected to all types of stress tests. Thirty-five years later, their medical and psychological histories were obtained and analyzed. A single factor stood out as the determinant of health and well-being by mid-life, and it was called *perceptions of parental caring.* The students had been asked about the closeness and warmth they felt from their parents, and it turned out that "*All* (100%) of the participants who rated both their mothers and fathers low in warmth and closeness thirty-five years earlier had diseases diagnosed in midlife." It wasn't a measure of how loved the men *were*, but how loved *they felt they were* that had a significant impact on their lives.

The researchers concluded, "The perception of love itself... may turn out to be a core biopsychosocial-spiritual buffer, reducing the negative impact of stressors and pathogens and promoting immune function and healing."[46] The findings of this study have since been replicated.

Experiences of synchronous limbic regulation and limbic

resonance were not only responsible for initiating feelings of love and closeness with parents but also set the stage for the quality of relationships later in life. The infant's need for secure attachment later becomes the adult's need for a reciprocal loving relationship with a significant other. Because this neural template is deeply associated with survival, our attachment pattern is less flexible than other aspects of behavior.

It is important to note that not all is lost if you did not have a perfectly-formed bond with your parents; you can be significantly influenced by bonding with others later in life. You may eventually alter and rewrite your early default circuitry with new experiences, but it will require deep desire, social and emotional intelligence skills, and dedication.

Even as you mature into adulthood, your self-regulatory systems remain (at least in part) an open loop system through which your psychophysiological needs continue to intermingle with others. When you are attuned to another's regulating presence, it can affect how secure you feel in yourself and in your life.

When people say there is no pain greater than losing someone you love, they are speaking to the disruption of this mutual limbic regulation, which can be agony-inducing.

When an important relationship is cut short, not only

do you feel the pain of nerve endings uprooted and left dangling, but you go into painful withdrawal as the neurochemistry of relatedness suddenly recedes. Your system is no longer supported by the chemistry of love. Neurotransmitters such as serotonin (which has some pain-buffering qualities but is more generally recognized as a balm against depression) diminish. Opiates, which normally down-regulate pain, do not circulate at the same level, and the love hormone oxytocin (known for the role it plays in empathy, trust, and relationship-building) is suppressed.

Emotional severing is traumatizing and can have devastating effects as cortisol (the stress hormone) overwhelms your system and drives you into survival mode. Your assumptive world (the sacred beliefs you hold about the world and the way things should be) is shattered through such a loss, and for a time, your inner compass becomes directionless.

"Sometimes loneliness makes the loudest noise."

—AARON BEN-ZE'EV

Conscious loving relationships can challenge some of our most cherished ideas about ourselves, even when they are working well. It takes immense maturity, commitment, and hard work to maintain a secure and healthy relationship. We can all feel bulletproof when nothing is at stake, but ultimately, love is the one state in which we dare to risk it all.

INTEGRATING THE SOCIAL SELF: THE JOURNEY OF A LIFETIME

Even though the process of socialization begins with birth, it isn't until your cognitive skills come into play and self-awareness begins to emerge that you realize you are not actually in charge of your world. Interactions with others that were previously governed by instincts are suddenly scrutinized, and you become more strategic in your responses. You observe, experiment by pushing boundaries, and encounter consequences.

As you grow and begin to explore the world beyond home and family, you discover what is expected of you in different situations. Through engagement with friends, schoolmates, teachers, and other adults, you recognize that everyone is not the same, and you become conscious of "otherness." You begin to suspect the world might not be as friendly as previously imagined. With a certain amount of distress, you understand that those in authority not only have control over what you do, but also have a say in who you are perceived to be. Acceptance is no longer a given and becomes something you must strive for.

The things we do for love...

Waking up to your Social Self requires you to determine who you are and where you fit into the scheme of life. This means you must engage in:

- conscious consideration of your boundaries,
- exploring where you begin and end,
- discovering what you must do to invite love and acceptance,
- learning when and where it is safe to express needs and vulnerabilities,
- understanding how those needs fit into the larger realms of family and society,
- finding ways to navigate differences with others.

Social intelligence is required for negotiating this life-long learning curve.

> *"Although we are by all odds the most social of all social animals—more interdependent, more attached to each other, more inseparable in our behaviors than bees—we do not often feel our conjoined intelligence."*
>
> —THOMAS LEWIS[47]

To a certain degree, you are always exploring where you fit into society, both consciously and unconsciously discovering what aspects of yourself are acceptable under which circumstances. Within your family, peer and friendship groups, and social institutions like school or church, you learn to consider your role and status. Cultural factors such as race, ethnic origin, gender, sexual orientation, social class, and income level become important signifiers. You work hard to identify and remain conscious of potential allies and possible opponents you encounter along the way.

Social cognition improves your chances for survival. Social bonds and diverse networks enhance opportunities for learning and cooperative effort. There is safety and comfort in belonging to a team, tribe, or within groups of like-minded others (in political parties, religions, or particular orientation). We tend to cluster around commonalities.

When we form alliances, we automatically identify those who fall outside the parameters of our group. We create a class of "others" or outsiders, which can lead to comparison or even competition between "us" and "them." How you relate and respond to those who fall outside of your particular group or orienting worldview reveals the extent and maturity of your social intelligence.

Humans are not designed to be alone; fear of abandonment is hardwired into your neuro-circuitry. The threat of isolation can wreak physiological and psychological havoc. This is why banishment or being put into solitary confinement is considered the cruelest of all punishments. Being excluded from an inner circle, left out, or ostracized are particularly painful experiences to be avoided at all costs.

SOCIALIZATION THROUGH NEGATIVE JUDGMENT

When you are young, your parents attempt to protect you from creating unfavorable impressions that could lead to marginalization. This is usually accomplished by reigning in your uninhibited self-expression.

Having been socialized themselves, parents are attuned to what is deemed socially acceptable and what is not. It is extremely stressful for them to have their children run counter to what is considered publicly acceptable. Not only do they want to protect you from the opinions others might form about you, but they also want to preserve their own reputation as "good" parents. The job of keeping you in line is usually handled through expressions of disapproval.

When parents use punitive negative judgments, they leave no doubt in anyone's mind that in that specific moment, they find your behavior "distasteful."

The idea of something being "distasteful" stems from the root emotion of disgust. From an evolutionary point of view, disgust communicates a powerful aversive reaction to something foreign that has been ingested and could be potentially harmful to your system. In effect, disgust is a wrinkling and turning up of one's nose at the object in question (a move that looks a lot like snobbery and rejection). In expressing distaste, we indicate a sense of separation between ourselves and the object that has been deemed disgusting.

Socialization through the use of negative judgment defines the boundaries of acceptability. It creates distance and an artificial separation from anyone who challenges the judger's sense of what is "right" or familiar. There is a tendency to marginalize and make "wrong" what is not understood. Taken too far, this response can harden into aversion and prejudice toward any way of being that is foreign or unfamiliar.

Negative judgment is a punitive teaching device, a way of expressing distaste for something we find foreign or cannot understand. When it is directed at you, your limbic system recognizes this as a warning shot across the bow: the potential for separation or exclusion is imminent, and to remain inside the circle and regain approval, you must toe the line.

FITTING IN AND STANDING OUT

"It is well to remember that the entire population of the

universe, with one trifling exception, is composed of others."

Conformity (or at least its outward appearance) is a common strategy to avoid the risk of exclusion, marginalization, or being ostracized. Conformity can, however, drive our true nature underground (the consequences of which you will see in the next few chapters) and prevent the expression of our purpose.

While there are benefits to fitting in, it can also create a false sense of security and uniformity. If you are surrounded by people like you, you are likely living in the bubble of your own worldview, which may encourage distorted beliefs about the way things are *supposed* to be. You are missing out on the opportunity to expand your frame of reference, learn new things, and increase your repertoire of experience. It is useful to exit the bubble and invest in learning from others whose worldview differs from yours. Opening your heart and mind to others promotes the potential for communicating beyond perceived social differences.

If, on the other hand, you don't fit in or are an outlier, you have likely felt marginalized or judged by others. You may have been keeping your differences under wraps and pretending to go along with the dominant culture. Con-

THE DEEPER STORY OF YOUR SOCIAL SELF · 241

versely, you may have rebelled and fought for diversity and inclusion instead. One way or the other, I encourage you, too, to reach out and share your experience with someone who would appreciate discovering who you really are beyond the limiting definition of your *differences*.

Reaching beyond divisiveness can be hard if you are the injured party, but letting people know the real you—which involves not only communicating your hurt and anger but also who you are beyond it—is the place from which genuine connection can be fostered.

More than ever, we need to have our assumptions, prejudices, and stereotypes laid to rest. Seeing people of all kinds coming together is truly heartwarming.

One day, I was driving down Hastings Street when I saw an adorable couple sitting on a bench waiting for the bus. He was probably fourteen or fifteen years old, hair shaved on the sides with a black and pink tuft standing up on top, fully tattooed and pierced, decked out in black leather with metal studs. She was in her late seventies or early eighties, looking prim and proper, wearing her Sunday best, complete with matching hat. They were affectionately holding hands and having an animated conversation—most likely grandmother and grandson. But wouldn't it be lovely if, through all of our differences, we could all relate to each other with such acceptance and warmth?

A CASE FOR DIVERSITY

In her essay "A Fist in the Eye of God," Barbara Kingsolver makes a case for biodiversity.[49] She argues against using monocrops by pointing out that diversity allows different seeds to survive in different conditions, so that in the event of a catastrophic crop failure, there can still be "a host of surviving varietals that lie waiting in nature's fertile belly."

Evolutionary theorists posit that survival odds may also improve for the human species in populations that include diverse temperaments and types. A group that is diverse in "types" has a greater likelihood of survival during radical changes in social conditions.

Socialization often encourages conformity. Ironically, in the end, it may be our range of differences that will save us.

LEARNING TO EXPLORE DIFFERENCES

For me, the word "tolerance," when applied to differences between people, has always felt like the wrong term. Tolerance connotes putting up with something for the sake of keeping the peace rather than making a genuine effort to reach across a divide to embrace something new.

Extending love and acceptance is actually what's required, but it can be difficult to love what you don't know, so reaching out to discover others beyond your social comfort zone is important.

When you do reach out, you can't necessarily expect to be well received, especially if you are extending yourself to someone who has felt marginalized, oppressed, or made to feel "other." These people have often been gravely hurt, suffered real injustices, and felt violated. They may be extremely angry and often have good reason for feeling mistrustful toward those in the dominant culture who try to engage them. Reach out anyway. Until someone is willing to take the risk of extending themselves, nothing will change. As difficult as it may be to suspend your worldview in the face of opposition, there is nothing more worthwhile than listening and making a sincere effort to comprehend and accept a contrary one.

Working through differences to find common ground, especially in challenging circumstances, is the best way to strengthen social skills.

Often, in times of trauma or shared challenge, differences that might otherwise be emphasized become meaningless. As people work together, they discover deeper commonalities than they imagined.

LEARNING THE SKILLS OF SOCIAL INTELLIGENCE

The socialization process is necessary for some cohesion, but it is limited by the degree of consciousness applied by those people in charge of your well-being. We have to question our conditioning to look for inbuilt biases, errors of perception about ourselves and others, automatic negative judgments that prevent us from seeking others' points of view, and unnecessary barriers we place in the way of knowing others.

We need to take responsibility for our relationships with others and learn skills to create safety within ourselves and with others. When we do, we benefit from mutual self-regulation and resonance with others. We need to learn to love and appreciate others and their worldviews, and, in the process, make ourselves vulnerable in the process of exposing our deeper desire for connectedness.

MATURING SOCIAL CONSCIOUSNESS

When we are young, we must push away from our parents to define ourselves, but we also need a way to come back together into a state of healthy interdependence. It is interesting how the natural stages of life provide us with opportunities for doing that. If we have children, we get to experience some of what our parents went through, and in watching our children, we can identify with their challenges. If we care for our elderly parents, we get to experience their dependence on us.

Intimate relationships are the most challenging of all forms of social connection. It is reported that Ram Dass once said something along these lines: "If I ever catch myself falling for my own press about how enlightened I am, I only have to enter a relationship for a short time to be set straight on the subject."

In other words, relationships are difficult even for guru types. We are rendered vulnerable in our need for connection, and it feels like so much is at stake when we become intimate with another. Even if we are lucky and find a compatible partner with whom we share a loving bond, we still have to work at it and mature ourselves to keep our love alive and well. If we are on our own, our friends become the recipients of our need to give love. Giving love nurtures our own souls; it keeps us connected to what is essential and life-sustaining.

Bonds can also extend beyond the human world to include deep relationships with beloved pets and creatures of the natural world. The unconditional love of an animal can be lifesaving for the love-deprived.

Relationships of all kinds are crucial because they teach us how to move beyond preoccupation with ourselves to experience the world through another's perspective. As children, we did this naturally, but as adults, we must unlearn habits of thought and behavior to reclaim that natural state so we can consciously give and receive love.

SOCIAL CONNECTION AND WELL-BEING

We have discussed how feelings of safety and stability can be established by bonding with others through synchronous limbic regulation, and in the chapter on your Survival Self, we looked at the calming and repairing role played by your parasympathetic nervous system. Now let's look at the combined potential of these two processes in something called vagal-parasympathetic activation.

Your vagus nerve (also known as your tenth cranial nerve) allows reciprocal information to be exchanged between your brain and your body. The vagus nerve extends down from the brain stem to monitor and receive information from numerous sources in the body, including your gut (stomach and intestines), heart, liver, pancreas, gallbladder, kidney, ureters, lungs, neck (including pharynx, larynx, trachea, and esophagus), and female reproductive organs.

When we are in deep rapport with someone in moments

of wholehearted social connectedness, we are improving our "vagal tone," which means we have created an upward spiral of positive feedback from our heart, gut, and other organs to our brain, which in turn regulates our parasympathetic system. Vagal-parasympathetic activation makes our brain waves, breathing, heart rate variability, and overall system cohere in a calming response.

Heart-to-heart connection with others (tend and befriend) promotes healing by stimulating the vagal and parasympathetic response (rest and repair). Stress is reduced, your system is calmed, and empathy is engaged.

Having strong social connectivity gives you a significantly greater chance at longevity, improves your immune system, helps you recover from disease faster, reduces anxiety and depression, improves self-esteem, and makes you more open to trust and cooperation. Isolation makes you more vulnerable to anxiety, depression, and anti-social behavior.

You don't need to have a large social network; you need the internal subjective feeling of connection to others. Learning how to reach out and engage in positive social interaction not only improves your well-being but contributes to the well-being of others.

In the next several chapters, we will deal with aspects

of self that are byproducts of our socialization process. For now, you may also want to take some time to think about what you have learned about yourself through your relationships with others.

DEEPER PERSONAL REFLECTION

Take a few moments in a safe space where you will be free from disturbance or distraction. Ground and center yourself in the moment, breathing in comfort and peace and letting go of tension.

There is a growing body of scientific evidence to support the life-giving benefits of loving-kindness meditation. Proven to have positive effects on everything from reduction of stress to decreasing chronic pain and strengthening social connections and emotional intelligence, loving-kindness meditation ultimately creates compassion for yourself (which induces healing) and others (which promotes connection and harmony). The practice of sending loving-kindness to others not only relieves your own suffering but takes your heart beyond yourself and into the realm of others.

There are many ways to practice loving-kindness meditation. Doing this for even a few minutes each day can transform your relationship with yourself and others. As the Dalai Lama would say, you don't have to be

Buddhist to meditate or cultivate feelings of love and compassion.

You will be using imagery, words, and feelings. Feel free to adjust any of these things to make this a good and comfortable experience for you.

Feel gratitude for this moment of peace, for this opportunity to become present to yourself. Turn your attention toward yourself in a kind and loving way.

Soften your breath, soften your belly, and soften your heart. Feel all the love in your heart and recite these words:

- May I be filled with loving kindness.
- May I be free from harm.
- May I be healthy.
- May I be happy and have a good life.

Feel loving kindness fill and radiate through every cell in your body. Picture yourself receiving all of these good wishes.

Keep repeating the phrases until you feel yourself let go of holding back and surrender to the feelings of loving kindness. This may take several minutes.

It may feel unnatural or difficult at first but stay with being kind and forgiving toward yourself until you can hold those feelings of loving kindness. Then you can move on to another person.

Imagine someone who loves you. It may be someone close to you now or someone from your past—a child, a grandparent, even a beloved pet. Feel their love and good wishes for you. They want you to have a good and happy life. Let their loving kindness toward you deepen your gratitude toward them for the love and support they have given you.

Send your love and gratitude to that person, repeating the phrases:

- May you be filled with loving kindness.
- May you be free from harm.
- May you be healthy.
- May you be happy and have a good life.

Continue to repeat the phrases, sending your loving kindness toward them. After a few moments, you can expand to other significant people in your life: friends, relatives, and anyone who has shown love and kindness toward you. Send loving kindness to them, knowing that just as you wish to have a good life, these people do, too. Send your love and gratitude to that person, repeating the phrases:

- May you be filled with loving kindness.

- May you be free from harm.
- May you be healthy.
- May you be happy and have a good life.

Once you have practiced this for a while and you are ready to move on, you can continue to radiate loving kindness to people outside your circle: strangers, adversaries, and eventually, to all beings, knowing that each being, just like you, wants a good and happy life. Continually feeling loving kindness and extending it outward, repeat the phrases:

- May you be filled with loving kindness.
- May you be free from harm.
- May you be healthy.
- May you be happy and have a good life.

As you continue to do this on a regular basis, you will notice your attitudes softening. Eventually you will be able to hold compassion toward yourself and others. A practice of loving-kindness strengthens your social intelligence.

DEEPER QUESTIONS FOR YOUR SOCIAL SELF

This is a time to notice, listen, feel, and record the responses from your Social Self. As you explore the social realities of your life and need input and guidance from your Social Self, you can reflect upon these questions.

- What does my social self want me to know about this?
- Who is involved or affected?
- Do I feel alone, am I accepted, do I belong, do I fit in?
- Where is my support in this?
- What steps can I take to create both boundaries and healthy support for myself in this situation?

LIVING THE DEEPER STORY OF YOUR SOCIAL SELF

> *"The part of the mind that is dark to us in this culture, that is sleeping in us, that we name 'unconscious,' is the knowledge that we are all inseparable from all other beings in the universe."*
>
> —SUSAN GRIFFIN[50]

Your Social Self helps you become conscious of your inseparability from both the human and more-than-human world. By re-imagining marginality, otherness, and differences, we can weave a new story that honors the unique threads brought by each being to the great tapestry of life.

The key to harmonizing with others is in recognizing the common human needs underlying our expressed differences. We may not always fully understand or entirely agree with one another, but we can certainly extend ourselves in an effort toward acceptance. Ultimately, we heal our hearts and our lives through loving each other.

I AM

I share essential elements with billions of life forms—an ecosystem of concentric circles radiating ever outward: plant, animal, mineral, family, community, culture... Human in my desire for belonging, I am wired for connection but also made vulnerable in my desperate need for it. I reach out and retract, I fit in and stand out, I merge and move on, I am both alone and all one at the same time. **I am social; therefore, I am.**

CHAPTER 9

THE DEEPER STORY OF YOUR WOUNDED SELF

No one's life is exempt from some measure of loneliness, loss, illness, disappointment, or failure. Even though we often try to deny or outrun it, sooner or later, we have to turn and face the part of us that has been wounded. Buried within your Wounded Self is a medicine that will do more than simply resolve your pain; it will heal and integrate it to restore wholeness to your being. When we evolve our Wounded Self, we are empowered to address those same wounds that exist in the world. We begin to engage feelings of empathy, compassion, mercy, forgiveness, and ultimately, love for both ourselves and others.

"Life tears us apart, but through those wounds, if we have tended them, love may enter us."

— CHRISTIAN WIMAN

THE ROLE OF THE WOUNDED SELF IN YOUR DEEPER STORY

Function: Your wounds force you to cultivate resilience, remind you of the need for healing and reclamation, and motivate the development of empathy and compassion for self and others.

When out of alignment: Your unprocessed trauma disorganizes your nervous system and prevents healthy self-regulation. You neglect, deny, or repress pain (sometimes with the aid of substance abuse or other addictive behaviors). You may become numb, stoic, hypersensitive, self-absorbed, or lacking in perspective. You become attached to being a victim, fail to take responsibility for your own healing, blame others for your feelings or circumstances, and become disempowered. You ignore the opportunity to metabolize and transform that same wound for the world.

When in alignment: Your wounds become the whetstone against which you sharpen your skills. You work to heal your wounds and use the wisdom acquired from that healing to develop strength of character. You become attuned to the corresponding wound in the world, and desire to see this issue resolved for all.

Key Areas of Development: Healing Intelligence,[51] Self-Care, Forgiveness, Personal Accountability and Empowerment

Dominant Questions: What needs healing inside me? Where in the world does that same cry for healing exist?

Arc of Development: From Victimhood to Empowerment

THE CALL OF THE WOUNDED SELF

"There are many paths to wisdom, but each begins with a broken heart."

—LEONARD COHEN

There are times in life when pain arrives as an unwelcome visitor and stays on as an unwanted guest. Emotional wounding can feel like a blow to the solar plexus, or like having your heart ripped from your chest; it is gut-wrenching and heart-breaking at the same time. Pain has a shared pathway whether is it activated physically or emotionally. There is no emotional pain that does not have an effect on your physiology.

Wounding is caused by many things: losses, betrayals,

offenses, boundary violations, transgressions, injustices, neglect, accusations, dismissal, inequity, and abuses of power. These things shatter your expectations about life, and that shattering becomes the swan song of your innocence.

Some shattering of innocence is necessary if you are to interact with the challenges and complexities of life. It is only through the development of maturity that you begin to live with the fact that life is not always fair, and that sometimes, no matter how hard you try, it won't be enough. You need to encounter and reconcile yourself to real limitations within yourself and others. You must learn to embrace life as it is while you work toward improving it.

Early in life, you may have been wounded in ways you could not comprehend. This dysregulation of your nervous system can have severe and long-lasting effects. If the wounding is left unresolved, your life becomes organized around alternately reliving the pain and trying to avoid future recurrence of it. Feelings of fear and helplessness continue into adulthood, making you vulnerable to further trauma and reinforcement of your Post-traumatic Story.

Instinctively, your mind and body shut down around the pain, attempting to block its signal and freeze its expressive energy. To prevent its activation, you avoid vulnerability and lower your expectations of life. An identity (Egoic Self) to cover your inner turmoil must be built around the pain: a public face to show the world that you are still intact and functional.

Beneath that exterior, however, you may feel overwhelmed with sadness, angst, embitterment, or powerlessness. Other times, wounding makes you feisty, irritable, and defensive. Full of impotent rage and grief, you may externalize your pain and take it out on others. Over the long haul, inner conflict makes you battle-weary, and depending on the extremity of your struggle, you may even want to give up.

Worst of all is the terrible feeling of aloneness in your pain. When the feeling is too raw to expose, you reflexively close yourself off from the pain, but you also close yourself off from others. Even the kindest words or gestures can't come close to providing relief, so you tend to avoid them. You can feel vulnerable, exposed, hardened, and closed off all at the same time.

In your aloneness, you are left to wrestle with inevitable questions: why me, what did I do to deserve this, did I bring this on myself? You may wonder if this is your karma, if there is some price you must pay for past mistakes, or if this is simply something you must endure.

If you scrutinize your shortcomings and can't come up with a good answer for why you deserve this, you inevitably start arguing on your own behalf about why this shouldn't be happening to you. You muster arguments about how you've been a good person, how hard you've worked, and the injustice of the world. It seems patently unfair that others who are less deserving than you should be spared such pain.

No matter how hard you try to push it down or numb yourself, your wound still lingers in the background, waiting to be triggered by your next move. You may only vaguely feel it or the memory of it. Often people even wonder if their wounding was real or if they just imagined it. After pretending not to be hurt for so long, you might even convince yourself that it was not a big deal—until something happens to reawaken the pain.

Sometimes there is a sense of guilt for even having pain. After all, you might ask yourself, "Who am I to bellyache when others in this world are much worse off than me?" You may tell yourself you shouldn't be so self-indulgent, to smarten up, get over it, and just move on.

In your busy world, there is too little time for tending wounds. Sometimes you might just be so tired of working around your wound that all you can do is be annoyed with yourself when it surfaces. People often say they are bored with their painful old story.

Time does not heal all. Time creates distance, and perhaps with distance the intensity of the pain fades, but it can be easily reawakened, especially when you re-enter the vulnerable territory in which the original wound occurred. You can spend a lifetime running from pain, denying it, distracting yourself, and pretending it isn't there, but in the end, you are no further ahead, and your life is poorer because of it. There is an unlived piece of your life trapped within your wounds.

When wounds are resolved and integrated, they result in what is called post-traumatic growth. In the same way a fallen tree provides compost from which a new tree emerges, new life can emerge from the fertile ground of your wound. The healing of any wound requires letting go of the identity you built around it. When this part of your identification with the wound is released, it frees up the life force that has been restrained there. That life force contains elements of your purpose.

WAYNE'S STORY

Wayne felt wounded from as far back as he could remember. In the small blue-collar town in which he was raised, he felt isolated and different, living in fear of being discovered as gay. Neither his family nor friends had much tolerance for his sensitive nature.

At the end of high school, with the help of a school counselor, he applied for entry to a nursing program at the university in a nearby city. His father intercepted his acceptance letter in the mail and confronted him. Wayne tried to explain, but his father interrupted, accused him of being gay (in less kind words), and made it clear that this was something he believed to be repugnant. When Wayne admitted he was gay, his enraged father told him not to expect any help from him and physically threw Wayne out of the house. Traumatized and embittered, Wayne moved to the city, where he turned to alcohol and drugs to manage the pain and anger he felt toward his father.

It took him three years before he hit bottom and got into treatment. During his recovery, Wayne began to reconnect with his original calling and decided to pursue training as a nurse. Eventually, he went on to work as a palliative care nurse, a job he mostly loved. However, when he encountered patients who, like his father, were uncomfortable with the idea of a male nurse (let alone a gay one), Wayne would feel defensive and angry.

In dealing with one irascible, homophobic elderly patient, Wayne hit his limit and was seriously reconsidering his career choice. One day, when Wayne approached to give the man a bath, the patient tried to scramble out of bed to get away from him and ended up collapsing on the floor.

When Wayne lifted the man up to carry him back to bed, he noticed how frail and frightened the elderly man was, and Wayne's heart cracked open.

After that incident, he started to think about his other difficult male patients: their need to deny pain, their terror of showing weakness, and how hard they worked to be stoic for their visitors. Witnessing all that masculine vulnerability brought Wayne's father to his mind. His father had always been so tough and proud, but Wayne had never considered what it cost his father to have to show up that way. He wondered about his father's denied sensitivity and felt his heart soften toward his dad. He became determined to heal his own attitude toward his father, even if his father refused to have anything to do with him.

As in all healing, Wayne realized that he first had to do some work on loving and forgiving himself. After doing a lot of healing work, I asked him to think of the person he most loved and to connect with that feeling of love. He chose an image of his sister when she was little and focused on feeling his love for her. When the feeling of love was strong inside him, I asked him to call forth an image of his father and to direct that feeling of love toward him. Wayne did this as a daily practice, sending waves of love to his father. Over time, not only did the image of his father change, but so did Wayne's feelings. He was able to see his father as human, vulnerable, and imperfect, but even more importantly, he was able to see that his father was simply a work in progress, not the product of that one frozen moment in time so many years ago.

After some time doing this practice, Wayne decided to reach out to his father. It had been nearly thirteen years since they had spoken. Their conversation was not easy—his father was still uncomfortable with and judgmental about Wayne's sexual orientation and choice of career—but they did talk, and that was the start of a relationship that grew and improved over time. The time spent with his father had a profound impact on him. Wayne decided to become involved in men's groups who were working toward redefining masculinity, and he participated in healing dialogues about men's feelings. Wayne realized that his father—the very person he believed had denied him his true expression—ultimately led him back toward it, and he found a deep sense of purpose in sharing his story with others.

Wayne had to face, feel, and move through all the barriers he had erected around his pain, including his feelings of victimization, fear, anger, addictions, and judgments. When he did, he realized that his father, too, shared many of these same kinds of reactive feelings, even though they were expressed in a different way. Beneath their collective anguish, there was a bond between father and son that even their extreme differences couldn't extinguish, but it took a lot of love and work to find that common ground.

A WORD ON FORGIVENESS

You can't love and judge at the same time. Only in releasing the hardening of your heart that goes with judgment can you open to the love that is waiting there to be expressed.

Not all wounding stories have happy endings. People don't always come back together. Sometimes they prefer to keep their hearts closed and defend their right to their pain. Everyone has their own timing and their own process for healing; you can't force it.

You also can't protect people from their pain, rescue them, or make it better. Every individual has something specific in themselves that needs to be reclaimed in their healing. That reclamation is not a given; it is something that must be earned. In trying to rescue and solve other people's pain, you actually deny them a larger healing opportunity.

Forgiveness is about self-release. There is no forgetting a serious violation, but there is the potential for disempowering its hold on your psyche by healing it within yourself. It is not necessary to reconcile with someone who has caused you grievous harm, but through forgiveness, you can draw a powerful boundary around your experience and refuse to let it define you or rule your life.

CO-CREATING AND THE ACCEPTANCE OF RESPONSIBILITY

When a client discovered she had breast cancer, she felt confused and betrayed because she thought she had done everything "right" and should therefore be exempt from such afflictions. She had a healthy diet, had given up wheat, dairy, sugar, and so on. She exercised regularly and was in good shape. She believed that all her personal development work and her strong spiritual practice should have been enough to spare her. I empathized with her pain and confusion but knew her cancer was not about her having done something wrong. To a certain extent, all circumstances are the luck of the draw. Many factors play into the state of our health and life conditions, and nothing can provide a guarantee that you will remain safe from harm.

To think that you are responsible for everything bad that happens in your life is delusional. Nor can you take complete credit for all the good things that occur. At most, you are a co-creator, doing your best to work with the unpredictable circumstances of life. You can take responsibility for your part and become accountable for how you respond to life's difficulties, but you are not in charge of everything.

Hellen Keller was not responsible for her blindness any more than Stephen Hawking was responsible for his ALS. These people were dealt challenging hands and played them with incredible grace and fortitude. As a result, they inspired the world.

Because wounding is inherently disorienting, your usual strategies of planning, controlling, and predicting don't work. Your wounds demand a different kind of presence, which includes being able to let go of the known world, release expectations and the desire for control, and surrender to the mystery of your own heart. In doing this, you have a chance to use your wounding in a proactive way.

INTEGRATING THE WOUNDED SELF

Until recently, almost all our information about inner processes has come from studying pathology. Even now, with the technology in place to investigate healthy human responses at the neurophysiological level, we are still challenged to bridge the gap between mind, matter, and meaning. We still need metaphor to give us access to how we think, talk about, and make meaning from inner processes. This is why literature, poetry, art, music, and dance are so vital for engaging inner experience.

Using metaphor to give shape, content, and character to your pain can be revealing.

Imagine discovering a small, cringing dog living on the street, eating out of garbage cans, who runs away and hides when you try to approach it. It is dirty, covered in cuts and bruises, and has clearly been abused. Because you see its fear and vulnerability, you approach it with caution. You speak soothingly to it and try to coax it out with a bit of nourishment. You continue to do this gently and consistently to earn its trust before you expect it to come out of hiding. Your own wounds need that same type of approach.

You can't come at pain too directly. It is tender, and like that wounded puppy, it is fearful of being probed by a stranger. In cutting yourself off from your wounding, you have become a stranger to an essential part of yourself. You must learn to approach your wounds responsibly, respectfully, and tenderly.

You can use metaphor and images to make it easier to relate to your pain. You can imagine your wounds as an animal, a landscape, or even a character from a movie or a novel. What does your pain remind you of? What is it asking of you?

One client I asked this of immediately answered that the

character he most associated his pain with was Wile E. Coyote from the Road Runner cartoons. He explained that in the constant pursuit of his goals, he often inadvertently sabotaged his efforts, and they blew up in his face. This metaphor created a way for him to begin examining the deeper story of his woundedness.

In one workshop, a group of women were guided through a meditation on pain and then given some clay to work with. They were asked to make something that represented their pain. Some made things that resembled little voodoo dolls with various parts missing, some had broken hearts, and some objects were unrecognizable to anyone but its creator, but each handmade sculpture was specifically imbued with meaning for its maker. In externalizing pain in this way, these women were able to talk not just *about* it but engage with their pain *through* the meaning of the object.

Another woman spent several days making a painting as a way of coming to terms with the loss of her mother at an early age. She said that while painting, she was able to recall things about her mother she had long since forgotten, and she was surprised to discover that there were aspects of herself as a child and a youth that showed up in the painting. She came to see that she had lost parts of herself along with her mother, and she was beginning the process of recovering them. She said that for the first time she was able to re-experience the loss without being consumed by it.

Journaling, art therapy, music, or any expressive art can be a medium through which wounding can be uncovered and reintegrated.

To unearth invisible wounding, it is useful to explore the areas of life in which you struggle. Your wounds lie beneath the repetitive patterns in your life.

When your wound is trapped in your interior with no means of expression, it is compressed and restricted. To tell its stories, it needs room to move and a safe environment into which it can arrive.

SHARING YOUR PAIN

> *"There is no agony like bearing an untold story inside of you"*
>
> —MAYA ANGELOU

There is tremendous healing power in sharing your Wounded Self's stories. When sharing your story both *with* and *to* an open heart, you are not only helping yourself but are helping the listener, too. This mutual sharing builds strong bonds and releases your pain from its visceral imprisonment.

Wherever you have been wounded, seek out information about others who have experienced something similar, not on the basis of "misery loves company," but to move you from the self-centeredness that pain usually engenders. Seeing your pain as a shared part of the human condition can move you to finding solutions for the conditions that made the wounding possible. I encourage my own clients to do something meaningful to help others who have experienced the same type of wounding. Part of their own healing process comes from contributing to the healing of others.

WOUNDING IN EVERY DIMENSION OF SELF

Every part of your multi-dimensional being becomes engaged around your wounds. Wounds become embodied and can trigger a survival response. Emotions ensue as we wrestle with how and why this experience came to be. Imagination creates stories about why this happened, which through the intellect get formed into rules and beliefs. Your sense of identity is challenged, and your ego builds defenses as you navigate through the experience. Trauma impacts our ability to function at a social level, as you move into protective mode and shut down your vulnerability. Aspects of your shadow and self-critic can be called to the forefront as you turn in on yourself or project your pain outward toward others. Your dream life can become chaotic as the experience is processed at an unconscious level. Your narrative self tries to weave the meaning of this experience into the larger story of your life. Your soul is asking you to attend to the deeper story and its relationship to your purpose, so you can integrate your wound in a way that helps you to evolve.

LOVING THE WOUNDED SELF

Painful memories are like frozen moments of time. Because you tend to avoid thinking about painful things, you rarely consider revisiting these memories consciously to reclaim and integrate them into who you are today. After practicing loving-kindness meditation from the Social Self chapter, it is worth taking a few moments to choose a specific painful memory to return to and extend that same loving-kindness to the *you* being held hostage in that scenario. Simply walk back through time and find the you in the memory at the point that was most difficult, and fill that earlier you with love and compassion. Soothe and comfort that person as you allow them to release their pain, confusion, frustration, or anger. Just continue to fill them with love. Express your gratitude to them for all they have gone through so that you could grow to become who you are today. Let them know that your life has gone on, you have grown through the experience and are willing to integrate it so that they can release it now. They no longer need to hold this pain for you. Reassure them that when you reflect on the whole situation, you can see it in its larger context, and you can now see how this has contributed to your learning, growing, and evolving as a person. Stay with them until they release into your love.

In doing this on a regular basis, you can take your most painful moments and reintegrate them into your system with a powerful association of love and gratitude for what has been learned. You will discover that your life story is much more complex than you may have realized, and that only in connecting the dots can you begin to reclaim lost parts of yourself.

DEEPER PERSONAL REFLECTION

Relax into a safe place where you can be free from disturbance and distraction for a time. Feel yourself settling into your body and breathe freely and fully. Relax and let go of the need to do anything but be present.

You need to prepare the ground and invite your pain to come forward. You can welcome your pain by speaking to it gently and offering it compassion. For example, you could say:

> I am sorry for all the tension, withholding, and numbing I have done in an effort to keep from acknowledging you. I am ready now to release the hardness around my heart and create space into

which you can stretch and unfurl. I will sit, patiently breathing and showing up to receive you, creating more and more space into which you may come. I long to feel whole again and am willing to receive whatever you present to me. Please show me the part of me that is most in need of healing right now.

Take your time, breathe, and stay open to any message you may receive.

When you are physically wounded, you automatically protect the injured area. Assure this wounded part that you are offering it a safe space into which it may reveal itself. It is only in resisting pain that it becomes incapable of penetration and feels impossible to release. When you let go of resistance, soften, and open-heartedly accept your pain, you can breathe through it and receive its deeper message.

DEEPER QUESTIONS FOR YOUR WOUNDED SELF

This is a time to notice, listen, feel, and record the responses from your Wounded Self. When you need your Wounded Self's guidance to process painful experiences, reflect upon these questions:

- What does my Wounded Self want me to know about this?

- What old pain is resurfacing in this? What needs to be healed in me?
- Am I responding to this pain with awareness, empathy, and compassion?
- What steps can I take to integrate this pain in a loving way for myself?
- How can I extend that same awareness, empathy, and compassion toward others who may be experiencing this pain?

LIVING THE DEEPER STORY OF YOUR WOUNDED SELF

According to Ogalla Sioux Medicine Man Black Elk, "Everything sacred moves in a circle." Healing is a sacred circular journey in which you cycle back to your wounds time and time again to integrate their meaning into your current circumstance.

Wounds are often the wedge between a sense of entitlement and earning the right to wholeness. Only through ownership, healing, and accountability can you truly recover the fullness of your life force and its purposeful expression. When you no longer deny your wound and turn your whole being toward its embrace, you discover a treasure map leading you back to your soul.

Wounding and healing are two sides of the same coin.

Healing is not just about mending the wound; it is about reintegrating many of the aspects of self that get left behind along the way.

The process of healing is paradoxical. In freeing yourself from woundedness, you are finally autonomous and independent, which allows you to consciously recognize your essential interconnectedness and interdependence with the world.

Your empathy opens your heart to the world, and you recognize that all beings suffer, and all are worthy of mercy, love, compassion, and forgiveness.

> ### I AM
>
> There is never a way forward without reactivating some old wound. With uncanny accuracy, I unconsciously seek the perfect circumstances in my present to reawaken the pains of my past. My scars provide the treasure map showing the way to my unlived life. Delving beneath scar tissue to excavate the wound's deeper story, I uncover the corresponding wound in the world. These wounds ignite empathy and healing for me and others. **I am wounded; therefore, I am.**

CHAPTER 10

THE DEEPER STORY OF YOUR EGO

Humans are creatures of contradiction as much as we are creatures of habit. We must manage and balance many conflicting drives and urges within ourselves. The role of your Egoic Self is to provide a stable, internal idealized self-image through which the cognitive and emotional dissonance of these conflicts and contradictions can be contained.

This unassailable image acts as a center of gravity that supports our functioning in the outer world, no matter what is going on internally. It can project a united front to others even when you feel completely shattered and incongruent. It allows you to save face in such moments— and the ego's motto is, "The show must go on."

Your ego works to convince you (and others) that this

idealized image is your real self. It isn't, of course; it is simply a stand-in, a reasonable facsimile of who you *imagine* yourself to be in your best moments. There is no room for vulnerability or real-life imperfection in that image. Enticing as it is to hold this idealized version of oneself, becoming too attached to it can severely limit your opportunities for growth.

The purpose of your ego, however, is not just to simply whitewash ourselves or put a positive spin on our motives for the sake of maintaining a pleasing public persona; it also performs important self-monitoring and self-regulatory functions. Your ego recognizes when integrity and congruency are at stake. It contributes to self-reflection and moral development. With self-awareness, maturity, and integration, your ego can serve a positive role in pointing the way to integrity and authentic self-expression.

THE ROLE OF THE EGO IN YOUR DEEPER STORY

Function: Your ego's job is to maintain a stable sense of identity. It uses defensive strategies to prevent cognitive dissonance when your sense of self is being challenged.

When out of alignment: You operate from roles and a public persona rather than a deeper sense of self. You become too attached to a story or set of beliefs about yourself and use denial and defense to maintain your self-image rather than face your true nature.

When in alignment: You work to balance the congruency of your inner and outer worlds. When challenged, you seek deeper truths about yourself, consider what is in keeping with your sense of integrity, practice humility, and integrate new awareness. You work toward expressing yourself more authentically.

Key Areas of Development: Developmental Intelligence,[52] Humility, Openness, Light-heartedness, Authentic Self-Expression

Dominant Questions: What is my self-image? How attached am I to being seen a particular way? How can I best show up in each situation with humility and authenticity?

Arc of Development: From Defensiveness to Openness

THE CALL OF THE EGOIC SELF

In popular culture, the term *ego* has become synonymous with superficiality, or an over-inflated sense of oneself. While this may be true of an immature or undeveloped ego, it does not reflect the origin or purpose behind the ego's development.

An inflated sense of oneself is the most obvious manifestation of an immature ego. The inept braggart who claims, "I am the best; nobody is as good as me," is oblivious to the deep-seated unconscious insecurity that prompts such a statement. But other expressions of ego are less obvious and often fly under the radar of our scrutiny until we are challenged to account for ourselves.

When the idealized self of the ego is challenged externally or internally, our Survival, Emotional, Social, Wounded, Self-Critic, and Shadow Selves are all triggered and called to the forefront. This is when we step into the ego's roles and personas to cover our internal turmoil and show a good face to the world. At some point, everyone has felt their idealized sense of themselves shattered.

Wherever your wounds and vulnerabilities lie, your ego steps in to keep you from collapsing into cognitive dissonance and to handle the image-management requirements of the moment.

To work effectively with your ego, however, you need to understand its developmental role and how it helps you get in touch with your underlying needs.

INTEGRATING THE EGOIC SELF
THE DEVELOPMENT OF YOUR EGO

From a neurobiological point of view, the ego begins to emerge around the second year of life, as we develop the skills of reflective self-awareness: in other words, we can recognize ourselves as independent, objective entities. Up to this point, our social/emotional world has been managed in the "zone of proximal development," in which our regulatory system is entwined with and developed through interaction with others. With our newly-developed self-awareness and rudimentary cognitive skills, we learn to internalize these regulatory processes to become self-regulating.

The emergence of this self-regulation system allows for the creation of feedback channels that determine our homeostatic threshold or "set point." The set point is the optimal level of arousal required to sustain functional interactions. It allows one's system to adapt with appropriate excitatory or inhibitory responses to both internal needs and external stimuli, thus maintaining a state of equilibrium. The set point in each individual is determined not only by their innate temperament but is also directly influenced by the amount and quality of early stimulation and input they receive.

This self-regulatory system corresponds with the parasympathetically influenced maturation of the orbitofrontal cortex, which houses the executive functions of your brain.[53]

What does all of this neurobiological mumbo jumbo have to do with your ego? It is in this developmental stage that we begin to internalize the rules and expectations that lead to the creation of an idealized self-image. These rules are based on what we experience as positively or negatively reinforced around us. We are both consciously and unconsciously learning and adapting to the rules of social acceptability by observing what is rewarded or disapproved of. We are developing an internal map to enhance opportunities for reward and minimize potential disapproval. Through our ego, we identify with the good and disassociate ourselves from the bad.

SHAME AND THE EGO

We begin the process of self-monitoring in relationship to others. We internalize feedback loops that fill us with pride when we live up to our idealized self-image and activate shame when we fail to meet its expectations. The degree to which we achieve the former and avoid the latter determines our basic sense of self-esteem.

The role of the ego, however, is not just about how we experience ourselves; it is about how we imagine we are perceived in the eyes of the Other. Jean Paul Sartre pointed to this critical aspect of ego in his essay on "Being and Nothingness:"

> "I am *that Ego*; I do not reject it as a strange image, but it is present to me as a self which I am, without knowing it; for I discover it in shame and, in other instances, in pride which reveals to me the Other's look and myself at the end of that look."[54]

When our ego feels penetrated by the disapproving gaze of the Other, we feel shame and engage the self-regulatory process of "conservation-withdrawal" to maintain equilibrium. This is an inhibited state in which we passively disengage to become "unseen." This avoidance of attention is a survival strategy that allows us to heal our wounds, reinstate depleted resources, protect ourselves against the anticipated loss of self-boundaries, and reconstitute our deflated self.

Allan Shore writes, "This ubiquitous primary social emotion in which one is visible and not ready to be visible operates subtly in even the healthiest human interactions and is generated by the virtually constant monitoring of the self in relation to others."[55]

The unique potency of shame is described by psychologist and personality theorist Silvan Tompkins:

"...shame strikes deepest into the heart of man. While terror and distress hurt, they are wounds inflicted from outside which penetrate the smooth surface of the ego; but shame is felt as an inner torment, a sickness of the soul. It does not matter whether the humiliated one has been shamed by derisive laughter or whether he mocks himself. In either event he feels himself naked, defeated, alienated, lacking in dignity or worth."[56]

While shame may be the most dreaded of emotions because of its painful inward collapse, it also has a positive adaptive role to play in promoting withdrawal for the purpose of self-preservation, and for separation from potentially unhealthy or unsafe situations. It provides an opportunity for reality testing, self-correction, and adjusting one's relationship to the world.

The ego develops a range of defenses to guard against the onset of shame and the loss of pride, such as humor, distortion, displacement, repression, suppression, fantasy, isolation, dissociation, denial, reaction formation, and turning against the self. All these strategies are designed to avoid the vulnerability of being seen without the mask of persona provided by the internal idealized self.

Evan's Story

Evan was as an independent, free-spirited type raised by a family with strong conventional values. Despite occasionally running afoul of accepted protocol, he perceived himself to be like them: a good and upright character with a strong moral compass. In his forties, however, many years into what appeared to be a good marriage with a couple of kids, he fell head over heels in love with another woman. A passionate affair ensued, and he left his marriage for the woman he considered to be the love of his life.

He had not fully considered the consequences of such a move, however, and found himself on the receiving end of significant disapproval from family and friends. In desperation, he began accelerating efforts to restore both his internal and external reputation as a "good person." He overcompensated, bending over backwards to accommodate family and other members of his social network. He worked to the point of exhaustion to prove himself as the "ultimate" father, son, brother, and friend. He went out of his way to please everyone—except his new partner.

He tried to recruit her into sharing some of the guilt and shame he felt, and to participate in his reputation-restoring activities, but she refused to play along because she didn't feel the same way. She saw him as a good person and acknowledged that their affair had been an inappropriate departure for him, but she perceived others as taking advantage of his guilt for their own purposes.

When Evan inevitably became burnt out from overperforming and trying to prove he was good, he began to see his new partner as "bad and wrong," the source of all the pain and difficulty in his life. If it hadn't been for her, he would have a good life, a secure reputation, a stable family, and so on.

His ego began to convince him that he had been seduced away by her and was somehow a victim of her siren-like charms. He had completely erased the memory of his former "free-spirited" nature and the previous missteps in his life and began to see this as a single, isolated episode in which he had been unwittingly drawn into an immoral way of being.

His ego went so far as to deny ever having loved her, and he believed that the only way he could regain himself was to leave this woman and convince his family and friends that, now free of her bad influence, he had once and for all seen the error of his ways.

This is a classic case of ego defense and projection. Evan had not lived up to his internalized, idealized image of himself. In giving in to his previously denied need for feelings of passion, he had gone against his social conditioning and broken that internalized code of conduct. When that code was mirrored back to him through the disapproval of others, he desperately wanted his previous status back. Denial, displacement, and turning against himself and his lover would never restore his wholeness, but his ego was determined to see him as an innocent victim.

Evan had to turn inward to examine the truth of the needs and impulses that led him to break his marital vow. He had fallen asleep at the wheel of his marriage, had become numb, and lost touch with his need for a greater sense of aliveness and fulfillment. He needed to face that truth and acknowledge that he had been awakened by his attraction to a woman who embodied the free-spirited characteristics he had been repressing within himself.

He realized that once these feelings had been awakened, he did have choices that he had been ignoring: he could have recognized he had outgrown his marriage and taken steps to see if it could have been transformed into something new, or to end the relationship cleanly, fairly, and with respect for his wife.

He chose not to do this so that he could have the pleasure of the affair without experiencing the consequences and potential disruption to his life. It was only when his affair was discovered and he had to leave his wife that his ego became threatened. He had previously played the role of the devoted and fulfilled husband so well that he had convinced everyone it was his true nature. They didn't realize that he had been inhabiting a persona, that he was not actually happy, and they felt shocked and betrayed by that discovery. It didn't fit with the Evan they thought they knew, and therefore, they no longer knew how to trust him.

Evan had to accept the confusion he had created. He realized that no amount of displayed guilt or remorse could change or compensate for his actions. He would not be able to redeem himself or restore trust until he embraced the deeper truth of the situation. He could not alter his deep need for a more engaged life. It would only be through vulnerably admitting this need and humbly acknowledging the wrongdoing in how he went about achieving that end that he could begin to restore his integrity and reputation with himself, let alone with others. Once that was done, he began to take sincere steps to make amends with the people he had injured with his behavior. As he did this, he became more congruent, and people around him were able to regain a real sense of who he actually was.

He realized that his ego had been preventing him from experiencing any joy in the new relationship because of the shame he held about hurting others. He had to face the shame and embrace the truth of his desire for the relationship. Fortunately, his new partner was able to forgive him for his lapse of consciousness toward her, and they recommitted to a new authenticity in their partnership.

As Evan restored himself to wholeness and integrity, his happiness began to shine through, and people were finally able to see the real Evan contrasted against his former persona. This helped them put his actions into perspective. They may not have liked the way he went about it, but they could at least see some evidence of what it had done for his growth as a person.

In this case, we can see why Freud described the ego as a process through which one must navigate the demands of instinct versus the prohibitions of reality.

All along, Evan's ego was trying to cling to an idealized version of himself that prevented him from admitting his needs and taking responsibility for meeting them in a healthy way that was in keeping with his deeper sense of integrity. At the same time, the shame of going against his idealized self helped him realize where he had already been incongruent and out of integrity.

He needed to expand his self-image to include the possibility of having needs that might not be understood, accepted, or shared by others; that acknowledged his own capacity for wrongdoing and creating harm; and that, in owning his mistakes and learning from them, he could ultimately regain integrity. He needed to be real and accountable for his choices and deal more directly and honestly with the fallout of those choices. When he did all of this, he was able to re-integrate his free-spirited need for aliveness back into his self-image and express himself more authentically.

The ego can organize one's beliefs, abilities, drives, personal learning, and history into a distorted view of oneself.

Samantha's Story

Sam was a lovely yoga teacher who was trying to decide whether she should leave her "less spiritually evolved" husband. She had grown up in a family that had little tolerance for her interest in Eastern religion and spirituality. They considered her to be a "New Age flake." They were greatly relieved when she married a down-to-earth man who they assumed would keep her head out of the clouds.

Sam worked as a high school teacher and raised two children with her husband. Her family was glad she had moved beyond her "spiritual phase" and become responsible. As her kids grew and became independent, Sam started going to yoga classes. She reconnected with a sense of calling and decided to become a yoga teacher.

As she spent more time away from home in training programs, her husband complained about feeling neglected. She took this as a criticism of her interest and became defensive. She felt she had devoted her whole life to her family, and now she assumed her husband was telling her she had no right to pursue her personal calling. Of course, that wasn't what he was doing; he was simply indicating that he missed her. She felt the sting of her parents agreeing with her husband when they told her she had "gone overboard" with her new interest.

She was determined not to let anyone stand in the way of her passion. She became increasingly irritated by her husband's requests for time to do things together and perceived each request as evidence of his lack of support. Growing angrier with him, she distanced herself more with each request for closeness.

During her yoga training, Sam was learning how to become spiritually transcendent, detaching from mundane concerns and entering a rarified state of consciousness. She worked hard at tuning out her emotions and saw them as interfering with her otherwise blissful state. Over time, however, she found it harder and harder to transcend her feelings and remain detached. She concluded that her marriage was the source of her problem. A friend suggested she get some coaching before making an irreversible decision.

Through coaching, Sam identified the source of her defensiveness. She realized she actually wanted acceptance for who she was, but instead of allowing people to see what her passion meant to her, she had become reactionary and cut herself off from potential sources of support. She had also cut herself off from her own feelings and needed to begin her healing by learning to accept and express her emotions in more conscious and accountable ways.

She connected with old anger about feeling marginalized and disrespected, and found layers of unexpressed hurt simmering beneath the surface. She started working with her emotions in her yoga practice, embodying them and surrendering to their energetic flow through her system. Instead of practicing transcendence, she *descended* into the lived experience of her emotions and allowed herself to be moved by them.

As she became more comfortable accepting, inhabiting, and expressing her emotions, she felt more at home in her body and became more vibrant and animated. She reported that one of the greatest benefits of being able to feel again was that she had regained her sense of humor. As she put it, she became less ethereal and more real.

Sam continued to gain perspective and was able to see that her parents simply held a different worldview than she did. In dropping her defenses and reconnecting with herself, she was also able to reconnect with her husband, discuss her feelings, and enlist his support. Their relationship grew stronger as they worked through their feelings together.

Identity Shapeshifting

As we try on different personas and roles under different circumstances and move through various dimensions and expressions of ourselves, we are all shapeshifters. Your life story told from the perspective of your survival instincts is a different story than the one told by either your ego or your soul. Your sense of identity shifts from moment to moment, depending on which part of you is telling the story!

Egos can be useful for giving us something to live up to—if we don't become too attached to the notion. We frequently need to update our self-image to include new information about our strengths and our weaknesses. It is the job of the intellect and our self-critic to formulate our personal standards versus those we inherit from others. It is our ego's job to keep our act together and present ourselves as a coherent whole to the world.

To consider all the elements that go into developing your persona, here is a meditative exercise you can try for a week.

DEEPER PERSONAL REFLECTION

Your meditative practice is to consciously experiment with having amnesia for one week. In other words, for one week you will practice conscious presence and approach everything in your life as though you had no previous history.

When you look at your spouse, simply observe them, as if you know nothing at all about them: nothing of their habits, needs, desires, or expectations. Relate to them as though they were someone you just met. Notice how they move through their world. Notice how they relate to you, your children, your friends. If you are not in a relationship, make these observations of coworkers and friends. Approach everyone as though you were interacting with them for the first time, just the way you would with a stranger—friendly but neutral, and perhaps even curious.

Do this with yourself as well. Look in the mirror and don't see your past. See the person who gazes back at you. See yourself in a detached way.

Approach your day this way. Notice how you wake up. Observe your environment, and notice what appeals or captures your interest and what does not. Notice how you go about things: your shower, your breakfast, your interactions. Stay present with it all, simply observing and noticing what you actually do.

If your time is structured by work or the needs of others, notice how you genuinely feel about this. Are you doing these things by choice or by default? Do not judge your feelings; simply notice them. Take note of what makes you content, what stimulates you, and what bores or irritates you. Notice when your pace feels natural and when it does not. Without judging it, notice when you are being truthful and when you are not.

Observe how much of your time is governed by conscious choice. Without any sense of history governing your choices, if you had to choose all these elements of your life—your partner, your children, your coworkers, your environment, your work, your lifestyle and health, etc.— is this what you would put in place for yourself today? Write down your observations each day.

At the end of the week, take some time to reflect on your experience.

Do this without judging or justifying anything. Just allow your observations to be. Do not make a conclusion from them; remain open and curious. After reflecting, go for a walk, do some yoga, meditate, or engage in some gentle releasing activity for half an hour.

Then sit down. Close your eyes. Ask yourself, "What did this week show me about my life?" Let go, focus on your breath, and let information come to you, even if what comes doesn't appear to make any sense.

Record whatever shows up. Your messages will be symbolic. They do not have to make sense. Simply record them exactly as they show up.

Ask yourself, "What have I been pretending not to know about my life?"

Reflect on and notice what you actually did and how you actually felt, versus how you thought you would or should have felt or done, or who or what you were supposed to be or do.

What differences did you observe? When were you being fully yourself, and where did you notice yourself being incongruent, pretending to be someone you are not or playing a role? How many different personas did you inhabit over the course of the week? What reasons did you give yourself for doing these things and feeling this way? Where did your sense of your identity become challenged in this experiment?

How we want to see ourselves and how we actually show up are not necessarily the same.

DEEPER QUESTIONS FOR YOUR EGOIC SELF

This is a time to notice, listen, feel, and record the responses from your Egoic Self. When you need your ego's input and guidance in exploring who you are and who you want to become, you can reflect upon these questions.

- What does my ego want me to know about this?
- What aspect of my identity is being challenged?
- Could my reputation be affected in some way?
- How do I want others to perceive me in this situation?
- What steps could I take to become more truthful and authentic within myself and with others?

LIVING THE DEEPER STORY OF YOUR EGO

You don't have to deny or transcend your ego. You simply need to be aware of it and make conscious choices about whether this is the part you want running the show in specific circumstances. You can engage your mature ego to keep you aware of when you are incongruent or out of integrity with your authentic self. Your authentic self has nothing to do with an idealized self-image or some fabricated notion of perfection. It doesn't guard against being known; it is open to exploration by yourself and others. When you are authentic, you allow for your various quirks, kinks, vulnerabilities, and flaws. You accept the twists and turns that brought you to where you are today. You know what is important to you, and you focus on bringing a greater sense of authentic presence to everything you do.

> **I AM**
>
> The master of ceremonies that is my ego tries to maintain a united front. An over-achiever in image management, it works hard to polish and perfect my presentation to the world. Riding herd on contradictions and keeping vulnerability on a tight leash, my ego quashes the moles in my system that want to leak my imperfections to the press. Thin-skinned and defensive, my ego kicks into high gear at the slightest challenge. My ego saves face until I am ready to face my deeper self. **I am ego-bound; therefore, I am.**

Self-Critic

CHAPTER 11

THE DEEPER STORY OF YOUR SELF-CRITIC

"Sticks and stones may break my bones, but names can never hurt me."

If only that were true! Every word counts, whether it is uttered to us or from us. Words matter. They are instruments of creation; they have the power to shape lives. They can bring us together or tear us apart. They inspire, motivate, and heal, and they can also incite, negate, and destroy. Words convey information, meaning, and feeling. They help us explore and define our internal and external worlds.

Children absorb everything that is said about them, and those words become the scaffolding on which their sense of identity is built. Critical words spoken by authority figures on whom we are dependent have a powerful impact on self-perception. Even when we try to tune them out, disagree with them, or know something different, negative criticism can still cut to our core, leaving an indelible imprint that reverberates throughout our lives. The words we hold in our minds and hearts define us.

THE ROLE OF THE SELF-CRITIC IN YOUR DEEPER STORY

Function: Self-criticism prompts you to become conscious and accountable for yourself and the choices you make. Internalized critical messages can be utilized from a place of higher consciousness to assist you in developing authentic inner authority.

When out of alignment: You are unable to evaluate yourself fairly or objectively. You depend on others for self-definition, and your well-being is tied to receiving approval from others. You are hypersensitive to criticism of any kind, reactive, defensive, and inhibited. You lack accountability for your subjective sense of self.

When in alignment: You recognize the automatic nature of preconditioned thoughts. You examine the content of those thoughts to determine their value and veracity. You examine yourself and your behavior with objectivity and compassion and make a conscious choice to integrate useful feedback and release negative messages that don't apply.

Key Areas of Development: Intrapersonal Intelligence,[57] Self-Awareness, Accurate Self-Assessment, Self-Authoring

Dominant Questions: Who is in charge of my self-definition? Whose standards am I upholding?

Arc of Development: From Approval Seeking to Inner Authority

THE CALL OF THE SELF-CRITIC
THE POWER OF WORDS

Your self-critic is directly related to the power of words, so let's start our exploration of self-criticism by defining our terms. The etymological root of the word *critic* is Greek, arising from the combination of the words *kriticos* (which means "discerning judgment") and *kriterion* (which means "standards"). The job of a critic is to ensure that certain standards are upheld.

In that case, we need to understand what a *standard* is. Here's one definition:[58]

1. Something considered by an authority or by general consent as a basis of comparison; an approved model.
2. A rule of principle used as a basis for judgment.
3. An authoritative principle or rule that usually implies a model or pattern for guidance, by comparison with which the quantity, excellence, correctness, etc. of other things may be determined.

Synonyms for *standard* in its noun form include code, archetype, exemplar, par, ideal, paradigm, barometer, touchstone, benchmark, etc. In that form, a standard could be something you aspire to.

However, when you look at the synonyms for its adjective form (meaning "regular" or "approved"), a different inference emerges. Consider these synonyms: accepted, usual, staple, everyday, basic, average, stock, garden variety, boilerplate, vanilla, authoritative, popular, run of the mill, etc.

There is not much to aspire to on that list. Sure, *authoritative* and *popular* have their charm, but otherwise, that list is all about conformity, and conformity can be a double-edged sword. We need commonalities and standards that we can understand and relate to, and which create common social expectations, but we also need room for the expression of new approaches and unique ways of being.

HOW YOUR INNER CRITIC CAME TO BE

Harsh words internalized in our youth form the basis of our inner critic.[59] As a child, you heard, felt, imitated, and absorbed the words used by others that referred to you. You gradually came to understand that the quality of your life largely depended on meeting certain standards. You internalized the messages you received about yourself and your behavior. This stored information was used proactively as a guide to navigate the minefields of home and school. You learned what was considered acceptable, and what the rules, potential rewards, and potential punishments were. The more you discovered, the more time you spent in your head anticipating responses to your actions.

Your inner critic developed a self-monitoring protocol to provide a running commentary on how you were doing. With repetition and reinforcement, its internalized messages became entrenched and automatic. Your critic uses the tone of authority to get your attention when it is triggered, just as your parents did. It works in tandem with your survival circuitry, issuing internal warnings. It alerts you to potential breaches of conduct that might lead to punishment, rejection, exclusion, or ostracism.

When you learn how to use the critic's monitoring in a conscious and proactive way, it can be a useful tool for becoming accountable. But before you can do that, you have to examine the standards it is using and make sure they are *yours*, not someone else's.

Your inner critic attempts to limit your originality and keep you within the bounds of accepted standards of expression. If your essential nature is strikingly different from the family or culture in which you were raised, this undoubtedly attracted negative feedback that will have to be brought to consciousness and explored.

It is natural for parents and caregivers to attempt to bring you into alignment with the prevailing standards of the worldview they inhabit. If your way of being significantly differs from theirs, the guidance you received may have negated or dismissed aspects of self that are important to you.

Parental feedback and guidance can be protective, insightful, and honorable, but in some ways, it may also run counter to your specific needs. For example, if you are an immigrant child adapting to a culture different from that of your parents, or even a child operating at a higher level of consciousness than your parents, the feedback and corrections you were given may turn out to be more harmful than beneficial. If your beliefs about yourself are formed on the basis of that input, your view of yourself will have built-in distortions.

Your inner critic can take the positive intention behind parental messages that were intended to protect and support you, and replace them with debilitating messages that undermine confidence and self-esteem.

Jason's Story

Take Jason as an example. He was in his late thirties when he first came to see me. His father had just had a devastating stroke, and Jason's mother called to ask if he would come home to lend a hand when his father was released from the hospital. Jason hadn't been home for several years and felt anxious about being around his parents. He felt judged by them, believed he had been a big disappointment, and always felt like a failure in their presence. As much as he wanted to help out, Jason's inner critic feared that he would once again prove himself inadequate in his parents' eyes.

Jason had been a happy kid; he'd been extroverted, popular, and was a good athlete. He was good with his hands and could fix anything. As an adolescent, he loved team sports, liked to hang out at a local garage that repaired classic cars, and enjoyed helping out an older neighbor who was building a small plane. Jason was very bright, but he did not do well at school.

His parents were academically inclined and had high

expectations for him. They got Jason into the best private schools, provided him with tutors, and used their influence to ensure he got passing grades but were not happy with his performance. Suspecting he might have learning disabilities, they sent him for testing.

Jason did well enough on the tests, so his parents concluded that his attitude and extracurricular activities were the problem. To improve his academic standing, they laid down the law. He was prohibited from spending time at the garage and working on the plane. They restricted his sports activities so he could focus on schoolwork. They were certain that with strict discipline, Jason would fall into line.

Jason limped along through high school, becoming increasingly withdrawn and depressed. After graduation, he wanted to work at the garage, but his parents disapproved, not wanting him to get stuck in a "blue-collar job." They insisted he take courses at a community college to prepare for university. Jason enrolled but quickly fell behind in his work and dropped out. His parents were angered by what they perceived as his lack of motivation. Jason moved away from town, avoided his family, and took a succession of uninspiring administrative jobs.

Although he had initially been forced to give up the things that made him happy—tinkering, team sports, and working with others to solve mechanical problems—he continued to avoid those things after moving away from home. He said he "didn't waste his time on things like that anymore."

Jason's inner critic had adopted his parents' standard for success and used them to reinforce the notion that he was a failure. His actual interests, skills, and gifts had been dismissed as inferior pastimes that interfered with opportunities for "real" success, which he had been told could only be attained through academic achievement.

Jason's critic had convinced him there was something seriously wrong with his motivation. He saw himself as inherently flawed and felt ashamed. Cut off from his natural expression and plagued by self-doubt and inner criticism, he lost his enthusiasm for life.

Through our work together, Jason came to see that his inner critic had taken charge of his self-definition. He worked to restore his inner authority, adopt his own standards, and pursue the things that made him happy. He accepted his mother's request for help. He decided to focus on what he could offer rather than worrying about their approval.

Before he left for his parents' home, Jason visited a rehabilitation facility to look at equipment and learn about the mobility issues his father would face. His interest was instantly engaged. Once he got home, his family was amazed by the way he stepped up and took charge of the situation. He used his technical and mechanical abilities to build and install ramps and come up with innovative ways to deal with his father's mobility and communication challenges. He resurrected his extroversion to create a team approach to managing his father's care.

When Jason's parents expressed how proud they were of him, he smiled at the irony. The very skills that had made him seem a failure to his parents in one set of circumstances made them approve of him in another. He hadn't been seeking their approval; he had simply been expressing his true nature and felt grateful he had been given a chance to help. In valuing himself and using his gifts, he became alive again, and his parents got to see the real Jason shining through.

Jason is a classic example of how the words you dwell on become self-fulfilling prophecies. As long as he continued to focus on the idea that he was a failure, he was unable to pursue the activities in which he was naturally successful.

The stories told by your inner critic are compelling because once installed, they continue to run on autopilot until you consciously disengage them. Words can hold your spirit hostage—but they can also set it free.

INTEGRATING YOUR SELF-CRITIC
REDEEMING YOUR CRITICAL SELF

Criticism usually arises when we are being fully expressive or when we are in hot pursuit of fulfilling our desires. Expanding beyond the boundaries of the norm can attract commentary that leads to feelings of rejection, self-doubt, humiliation, guilt, shame, and unworthiness. We may be criticized for doing things that are immensely pleasing to us but irritating to others. This is one of the ways your self-critic can be very useful: it can point you to aspects of your unique expression and passions.

If your inner critic is noisy and persistent, it might be an indication of the robust way you expressed your individuality as a child. As a child, you are most likely to receive negative attention and criticism when you stand out in some way—as *when you are expressing your unique differences.*

As an infant, you were whole, intact, alive, and free, in love with yourself and your life. Three-year-old children do not feel unlovable, unworthy, or flawed. It was only through conditioning that you learned to judge and think poorly of yourself. I've never met a person who didn't love their true nature before their critic took hold and redefined it for them.

And sometimes the feedback you receive has nothing

at all to do with you; it could be the result of someone having a bad hair day, and your devastated self-esteem was simply collateral damage.

I have worked with accomplished and wealthy clients whose critics have them convinced they will never be successful enough. I have seen beautiful women and handsome men whose critics make them believe they are ugly and undesirable, and smart, capable people whose critics tell them they are imposters who will soon be discovered and exposed as frauds.

You have likely been wrestling with some aspect of your inner critic your entire life. It is easy to get caught up in it as you try to refute it. If it was saying something really true, why would you despair at its comments?

Some things are true and unchangeable. For instance, I am 5'2" tall. The standard of attractiveness in this culture indicates that women should look like models and be at least 5'7" tall. I can either accept that I am short and be okay with that—or I can add a little height with heels, but otherwise, I have no ability to change my actual height. I *do* have the ability to define my own standard of beauty.

Some people believe their critic is there to protect them, help them prepare for the worst-case scenario, keep their "ego" in check, and provide a healthy dose of humility.

It is possible to take precautions and explore potential outcomes without your critic's commentary, and a critical dose of humbling usually produces shame rather than genuine humility.

According to preliminary research at the Institute for Neuroimaging and Informatics at USC, we are estimated to have approximately 70,000 thoughts per day, so your inner critic has plenty of opportunity to say its piece. The good news is that its inescapable pervasiveness is the very thing that makes it such a powerful source for potential healing. Like a GPS system, it can be used as a navigational tool to point you toward the parts of yourself that need to be explored and reclaimed.

Your Inner GPS

The two standard approaches to dealing with the inner critic are by treating it as an enemy to be overcome or treating it as a friend to be welcomed and transformed. In my coaching, I take a third approach, which encompasses aspects of the others but is designed to use the critic as a directional tool to identify pieces of your deeper story.

When you trace each critical statement back to its origin and rewind the tape of your experience to the moment *just prior* to the criticism, you can explore what you were thinking, intending, feeling, or pursuing at that moment.

You can discover aspects of your nature that were alive and well before the critic re-defined it. This is necessary knowledge for reclaiming inner authority and setting the standards by which you choose to live.

To work effectively with the healing potential of your inner knowing, you must take back the power to define yourself in your own words, using discerning judgment (kriticos) and your own standards (kriterion).

DEEPER PERSONAL REFLECTION

Here are some ways you can mine your self-critic to reclaim your inner authority.

1. Look at the themes of your critic. Apart from the garden-variety everyday complaints, what does it most attack in you? For example, if you feel unworthy of love, write out all your thoughts about that.

2. Imagine the first time you ever encountered such an idea. Where would you have learned about people being unlovable? No child starts out thinking such a thought, so where would you have learned about it? Was it through something specific that happened to you? Did you hear someone talking about someone else and connect the dots? Feel your way back in time to find the original incident in which you concluded you were unlovable.

3. Look at yourself and the people who surrounded you during that time. What did being lovable look like? What did it mean to the people around you? Who was the model of lovability you were compared to or aspired to be like?

4. Whose standard of lovability were you supposed to uphold in that moment?

5. Is that person and their standard of lovability something you deeply believe in today?

6. Identify and write out (or create a mind map of [60]) all your inner critic's statements: all the negative thoughts you have about yourself, including ways you feel bad, wrong, deficient, ashamed, guilty, worthless, inadequate; things you negatively judge about yourself, including appearance, relationships, finances, health, parenting, etc.

7. Note the things you don't like about yourself. List all the ways you are not good enough, "too much" of something and "not enough" of another, things you feel judged for, things you were punished or reprimanded for, hurtful things others said about you, and things you were teased, bullied, or picked on about.

8. Note your fears, doubts, insecurities, and so on. If you were raised in a household in which more than one language was spoken, or in which English was not the mother tongue, make sure you also recall the negative statements communicated in that language.

9. Notice the physical sensations that accompany these

thoughts. Where do you feel them in your body? Notice what happens to your energy when these thoughts are running.

10. Notice the tone of authority with which these messages are delivered. Whose authoritative tone from childhood does your inner critic use?
11. Notice how you react to the thoughts, and any similarities to feelings you had as a child when you were being reprimanded.
12. Notice the judgmental, blaming, derogatory, and punitive nature of these statements.
13. Does the way the critic speaks to you reflect how you choose to speak to others? If not, why not?
14. If you had a friend who spoke to you in the same way your critic speaks to you, how long would you remain friends with that person?
15. Notice how your critic takes you out of the present moment by re-running negative past experiences or anticipating negative future events.
16. Notice how these thoughts affect your sense of self-esteem.

Now take a breath and ask yourself, "Is this truly who I am? Given a choice, is this who I actively choose to be?"

MEDITATION ON YOUR SELF-CRITIC

Take a moment to get settled and comfortable in a place where you will be free from disturbance or distraction, so that you can reflect on your own standards. Considering how much time and devoted energy it has taken to keep your true nature under wraps, aren't you a little curious about what was so unique and different about you that it invited such intense commentary? Breathe into your heart. You have nothing to protect or defend. Give yourself permission to feel your way through an exploration in self-definition.

Think about what made you different from your parents, siblings, friends, school system, church, community, etc. In what way did you stand out or apart from them?

Did any of your differences constitute a breach of *your own preferred standards,* or theirs?

Did you share the same worldview, perspective, or values with those who criticized you? If so, was there a difference in the level of wisdom or maturity level between you and those from whom you were differentiated?

Identify the underlying quality, intention, or need you were originally trying to express that ultimately seemed to attract criticism from others.

What positive qualities did your critic shut down in you? What else did you have to suppress in yourself to keep that part of you in check? What rewards or positive reinforcement did you receive for shutting down the expression of that part of yourself? What other skills or attributes did you develop as a result of having to keep that part of you under wraps?

How did you manage the stress caused by your inner critic, and what did you use to avoid it? Did you distract yourself from it, tune it out, numb it, or shut it down with food, alcohol, drugs, exercise, sex, TV or Netflix addiction, being a workaholic, a perfectionist—or did you utilize some other means?

Consider how much energy it has taken to suppress your natural needs, desires, and inclinations. Imagine what you could have created with an equal amount of energy and guidance devoted to teaching you how to express this part of yourself in a loving and healthy way. What would have been different in your life as a result?

What clues does your inner critic hold to your life purpose?

What do you secretly love about the part of you your critic holds in check? What would happen if you reframed each critical statement in a way that supported your true nature?

Give yourself some time to let your subconscious mind interact with the questions above and make notes that are relevant. After a day or two, return to look for patterns and strengths that are part of the self-critic's deeper story.

Reflecting on everything you have learned, rewrite YOUR definition of who you are. Keep it somewhere handy where you can frequently remind yourself of the truth about yourself and your motivations.

DEEPER QUESTIONS FOR YOUR SELF-CRITIC

This is a time to notice, listen, feel, and record the responses from your Critical Self. When assessing yourself and your performance in a specific situation, have your evolved self-critic reflect on these questions:

- What does my self-critic want me to know about this?
- What do I doubt in myself? Is there some deficit of skill or understanding that I must correct?
- Whose standard am I judging myself by?
- What steps must I take to bring myself into alignment with my own true standards and values in this situation?

LIVING THE DEEPER STORY OF YOUR SELF-CRITIC

Creating the new story of your life begins with the words you use to define yourself. You are more than the words with which others described you. Perhaps it is time for a consciousness upgrade to integrate the truth of who you are and who you are choosing to become.

Your self-critic can be an incredibly empowering faculty if consciously engaged to unearth conditioned perceptions you hold about yourself. Buried within your automatic pilot are all kinds of ideas installed by others before you had the ability to assess their validity or veracity. By consciously examining and challenging that conditioning from a place of mature consciousness, you have the opportunity to discover truths about yourself that would have otherwise gone undetected. Your self-critic not only points you to the deeper story of your true nature, it can help you to reclaim it.

Wouldn't it be great if each person had the opportunity to remember their true nature during times of stress, rather than resorting to self-criticism or criticism of others? Imagine a world in which we were each lovingly encouraged to evolve and live up to our highest standards and, in turn, were able to help each other honestly see and embrace both our gifts and our limitations.

I AM

Judge, jury, and jailor: my inner critic condemns me to life imprisonment for the crime of being myself. It holds me hostage with its constant complaints and commentary on my lack of conformity. It wants me to fit in, be like everyone else, to just be *normal*. It says its job is to protect me and keep me safe from disapproval and rejection. It has its standards and monitors my every move to keep me from ever accidentally expressing my true nature. But when I become conscious of my own standards, I take responsibility for authentically expressing who I am. **I am self-critical; therefore, I am.**

Shadow

CHAPTER 12

THE DEEPER STORY OF YOUR SHADOW SELF

In a world of duality, in which you have up and down, right and left, inner and outer, right and wrong, we also have light and shadow. In working with non-dual consciousness, you can see the complementary rather than competing role of the shadow in calling forth an individual's light. The soul's light is only made possible through its relationship with the shadow, and the soul can only be awakened through interaction with your shadow self. Your shadow is necessary for the integration of illumination.

The shadow is one of the most challenging aspects of self because it operates almost entirely beyond the reach of conscious awareness. All the negated and "unacceptable" parts of yourself manifest in unconscious self-sabotage, until you are able to bring them to consciousness and reintegrate them in healthy ways.

THE ROLE OF THE SHADOW SELF IN YOUR DEEPER STORY

Function: Your shadow is a subconscious container for negated impulses, needs, drives, and emotions. These aspects of self are hidden and suppressed until you are mature enough to consciously examine, accept, and integrate them. Embracing your shadow is critical to self-acceptance and wholeness.

When out of alignment: Unable to face the truth of your impulses, needs, or emotions, you drive them underground into your unconscious. You fear exposure and avoid vulnerability at all costs. You may believe you are unworthy of love, or, at its most extreme, may even feel unworthy to be alive and engage in unconsciously-driven self-destructive behavior. You project shadow content onto others, become self-righteous and judgmental, and try to suppress others by projecting your morality onto them. You see yourself as morally superior or more evolved than others.

When in alignment: You are in touch with self-paradox, understanding that you are not one way or another. You accept drives and desires that may be inconsistent with your ego's self-image. Shadow content is brought to consciousness to be integrated in healthy ways. Integration of your own shadow releases the need to project onto, judge, or control others. You can proactively address the underlying causes of shadow content in the world.

Key Areas of Development: Depth Intelligence,[61] Courage, Self-Trust, Vulnerability, Self-Acceptance, Release of Control

Dominant Questions: What unmet need is being protected from exposure? What vulnerability must I embrace within myself?

Arc of Development: From Self-Denying Sabotage to Active Self-Acceptance

THE CALL OF THE SHADOW

We all have secrets—things about ourselves we don't want the world to know. Things that have happened to us and within us; ill-considered or uncharitable things we have done; things we are not proud of or feel a sense of shame about; the ways in which we have failed ourselves and others: these are among the things we repress in our shadow. We unconsciously erect defenses against their unwanted intrusion.

We also have a secret self that we love. We keep this "golden shadow" under wraps, not daring to show it to the world. As children, we were smart enough to tuck away those so-called "unacceptable" parts of ourselves, and because we actually loved those parts, we buried them deep, where no one (including ourselves) would ever be able to tamper with them. We stowed them away in the last place we would ever think to look: in our golden shadow. This repressed content becomes the "unlived life" that Jung talks about. Jungian analyst Robert Johnson says: "We fight harder against the noble aspects of ourselves, the parts being called forth by our soul as part of our life purpose."[62]

We also tuck our shadow content away in pain, trauma, unhappy memories, and uncomfortable emotions. Consequently, we spend most of our lives running away from the very experiences that have the power to reconnect us with our deeper self, transform us, restore equilibrium, and put us right with the world.

The difficulty with shelving these undesirable aspects of oneself, however, is that inevitably the shelf collapses under the strain of keeping your natural impulses at bay. When the tension becomes too great, unconscious shadow content falls into our otherwise orderly lives. These disowned aspects of self reveal themselves in repetitive patterns that surface throughout your life.

Awakening to shadow content comes about in many ways. It usually erupts in feelings of discontent—times when you question your life. "Is this all there is?" "What happened to my life?" These questions signal the feeling of restriction created by the patterns you have been living with. This is when it dawns on you that some essential part of yourself has gone missing in action. Your soul wants to be free, and this is its wake-up call. For many people, that call happens when they hit mid-life (typically referred to as a mid-life crisis), but there are opportunities for bringing our shadow to consciousness at any stage of life.

In North American culture, the emphasis is on keeping everything bright, positive, and pain free. We live in denial of the shadow and are taught to drive it underground— so it manifests in our bodies as disease, discomfort, and addiction; in our minds as toxic beliefs and judgments; in our emotions as intractable and uncontrollable states of fear, revulsion, rage, and jealousy; and in our behavior as reactionary self-sabotage.

Your shadow is the master of misdirection, disowning what belongs to you and projecting it outward. Wherever a strong negative charge arises, the shadow is there—in what you judge, loathe, despise, hate, are disgusted by, or find offensive.

Your shadow also shows up in the ways you find yourself moral, upright, superior, and blame-free. When you scapegoat, engage in self-righteous battles of "good and evil," or polarize around issues of power and greed, it is there. Your shadow spawns the emotional chaos that comes with guilt, shame, separation, and deep loneliness. It becomes the dark container of all you cannot face within yourself, until you achieve the maturity to own and integrate its contents.

Whenever intense emotion is at play, your idealized self-image is likely being threatened in some way, and your shadow is being stirred beneath the surface of your ego. It takes a lot of energy to keep your shadow underground, and if you don't learn to work with its transformative power, it will eventually burst forth and wreak havoc in your life. Your shadow indicates who you choose to be and, as Thomas Moore so eloquently puts it, "The person we choose to be...automatically creates a dark double—the person we choose not to be."[63]

If you are unfamiliar with this dimension within yourself, think of examples like these:

- You witness someone doing something and/or receiving great praise for a thing you have always wanted to do but couldn't allow yourself to do, so you find yourself agitated and strongly judgmental of their performance.

- At a party, someone violates a code of conduct you hold yourself to, so you feel righteous in your condemnation of them and their behavior.
- You are highly polarized in your opinions, morally, politically, and spiritually, demonizing or condemning others who see things differently from your "correct" perspective.

Shadow aspects become dangerous when they are habitually converted into hostility. At its psychological extreme, this can cause a splintering into fragmented and dissociated parts of the self that can manifest in psychosis. At the collective, cultural, and national level, shadow selves can demonize and dehumanize others, making them the enemy of everything we stand for, and making it seem not only possible but reasonable and justifiable to go to war. We attempt to scapegoat and kill off these disowned and projected parts of ourselves. As the cartoon character Pogo would say, "We have met the enemy, and he is us."

But just as we should not demonize others, we should also refrain from demonizing the shadow. It is there to help us evolve our consciousness, and it can awaken us to possibilities and a kind of undeveloped potential that can be life-giving.

THE STORY OF LISA'S SHADOW

Lisa and Deb had been together for several years when Lisa decided she wanted to have children. Deb had never really wanted children but loved Lisa and wanted her to be happy. Deb was on a fast track in her career and made it clear that if she were to be the sole provider for their family, her job would have to be her main focus for the next few years. Lisa agreed, and they went through the donor process and had two children.

Deb worked relentlessly, as Lisa cared for the children. Lisa started to feel abandoned and neglected by Deb. Deb explained that she had to put in long hours to ensure they could maintain the lifestyle they both wanted. Lisa was grateful for the big house on the hill, their security and social stature and that Deb was so highly respected in her field. But with each new success Deb achieved, Lisa became a little angrier and withdrawn.

She became annoyed when Deb would come home and "demand" things of her and the kids. She saw Deb as being selfish, imperious, and controlling. Lisa had bonded with the kids, formed a close alliance, and developed a special secret life with them when "mean mommy" was not around.

During the day, Lisa hung out with other mothers, and at one point, she found herself quite attracted to one of them. She flirted but would never cross the line. She was too moral and upstanding, and even though she felt hurt and neglected by her partner, she saw herself as committed to sticking it out "for the sake of the kids."

When she discovered Deb was having an affair at work, she became enraged. She did everything she could to injure Deb's public and private reputation. She claimed that Deb's behavior had broken the bond of trust with their children, and Deb should feel the consequence of losing them. She spent hours talking to the children about how bad their other mom was. She told them that Deb was selfish, entitled, and uncaring. She explained that Deb didn't love really them, had never wanted them, and was deserving of nothing for what she had done to them. She forbade them from taking her calls. The children were used as unwitting pawns in the ugly divorce that followed.

Lisa's high moral stance kept her trapped in bitterness and self-righteous pain that made it impossible for her or her children to move on. She did not see that she was doing irreparable harm to her children. It was only when her daughter began to manifest disturbing symptoms that a family psychologist suggested Lisa get some help for herself.

Lisa's outrage was symptomatic of all that was repressed

within her. As a child, she had been an over-achieving superstar in school, athletics, and art, but she was never allowed to celebrate her successes. She had a brother with "challenges," and according to her parents, Lisa's successes would only make the brother feel worse about himself, so Lisa was encouraged to keep her own achievements under wraps. No matter what she did, it was never enough to get her parents' attention; all their focus went toward her younger brother. They celebrated even what Lisa saw as her brother's most meager accomplishments.

Lisa was not allowed to cultivate a sense of pride in her accomplishments, and she learned to judge anyone who did well, especially if they received a lot of recognition or were in any way "showy" about it. She had been judging Deb by that standard, and her feelings of neglect and abandonment reflected her own painful childhood.

With some support, she came to see that she, too, had withdrawn and abandoned the relationship. Deb had been working hard, and Lisa had shut down toward her rather than supporting her. Deb was responsible for breaking her commitment to Lisa in turning elsewhere for affection, but Lisa also began to see her own role in the undoing of their bond. She had complained but never shared her deeper feelings or needs with Deb.

Her morally-superior stance because she hadn't acted

on her attraction "for the sake of the children" was just another one-upmanship of Deb. She acknowledged that in her jealousy, she had recruited the kids to play out her own feelings of neglect. She had always seen herself as a good mother, never dreaming that her actions were actually harmful to her children. She gradually came to see that she was responsible for rupturing the bond of trust between the kids and Deb.

It took Lisa some time to come to terms with her shadow feelings, to grieve the loss of her sense of self, to face her personal issues instead of demonizing Deb, and to learn how to acknowledge and communicate her own needs. She worked hard to repair the damage she had done by bringing the children into her reenactment of abandonment. She became a willing partner in family therapy to help mend the bond between the kids and their other mother.

THE STORY OF SHARON'S GOLDEN SHADOW

Sharon had been a joyful kid. She was full of wild ideas and boundless energy and was always ready to get your attention. Around the age of four, her dad started suffering from clinical depression. Everything in the house became hushed. She wasn't allowed to disturb her dad, the curtains were constantly drawn, and her mother became quite severe with her if she created any noise.

When Sharon was five, her father committed suicide and her mother entered a prolonged period of grief. There was no room in the house for Sharon's childlike energy or enthusiasm, and anytime she expressed anything other than sadness, it was deemed inappropriate.

She learned how to keep her true nature under wraps and act in an "appropriate manner" around her suffering mother. She was rewarded for putting on a display of concern. Whenever she accidentally let out some happiness, she was made to feel uncaring and selfish. Sharon became so identified with her show of caring that she eventually decided to become a therapist as a career.

As the years passed, however, she began to feel depressed. She was overwhelmed and frustrated by the demands of clients. She felt like a terrible person for losing her compassion but said she no longer felt she had the ability to "fake concern" for what seemed like trivial dramas people brought to her. She began to wonder about her own mental health because she said she felt like shaking her clients and telling them to wake up.

When she did an embodied reenactment of the idea of shaking a client to get them to wake up, she came into contact with her own desire for life-enhancing joy and vitality. This was her golden shadow: the thing she had become most afraid of showing. How could she possibly feel joy when the world was full of suffering?

Sharon needed to work through many judgments about herself and others. She realized she had a deep-seated judgment about the extent to which people became attached to their suffering. She feared this meant she was uncaring and selfish, so she over-worked to "prove" to others that she was a caring person. She had suppressed her own needs for attention, believing she could only be a good person if she was selfless and fully attentive to others.

She worked hard on integrating her shadow and came up with a great strategy. To deal with how "deathly serious" she had become, she took a stand-up comedy class for psychotherapists. This gave her a healthy way to expose and express her repressed need for attention and for fun. It had never occurred to her that in bringing the joyful (as well as the empathetic) part of her to work, she could inspire healing in others. She found new fulfillment in her work when she did.

Everything we repress shows up in some other form. When we address those neglected parts of ourselves, there is a way to move forward in life. It is easy to resist the shadow, blaming, and projecting our flaws outward. Embracing the gift of our imperfections can be both humbling and liberating. Until we face and integrate the shadow side of ourselves, we remain full of fear, doubt, and judgment. Your shadow can point you toward wholeness.

INTEGRATING THE SHADOW

The job at hand is to remain aware of the shadow without becoming identified with it. Both your ego and shadow try to prevent you from admitting these aspects of self and warn against the vulnerability involved in exposing them to yourself and others. It takes a certain amount of maturity and bravery to fully face the implications of your shadow—which is why it so often becomes a feature at mid-life. This is when we are freed of the tasks of mere survival and making our way in the world and must tackle the deeper concerns that come with having a meaningful, purposeful, fulfilling life.

Because shadow content is buried within our patterns as instinctive and conditioned reflexes, we must learn to pause the Survival Self's reactions long enough to identify what part of ourselves is actually being threatened. Usually it is our persona, or ego—our conscious identification as a *certain kind* of person. This is a call to genuinely examine your values and standards to see if they are a true reflection of what matters to you. Do you consciously and authentically embody them?

PRACTICES TO EXPLORE YOUR SHADOW

To explore shadow content, you can work with both actual and symbolic information as it presents itself in your body. If there is something you find disturbing in the world, you can work with that information symbolically to explore how the disturbance is mirrored in your body. If, for example, you are upset about warfare occurring in the world, investigate and resolve the battles being waged in your own body.

If you are concerned about diminishing or overexploited resources, uncover and recover the places where your inner resources are being depleted.

If gender inequity bothers you, rebalance the way you embody the masculine and feminine energies within yourself.

You can then turn these same symbolic concerns outward to see how your worldly concerns are being enacted in your own life and relationships with others.

Another way to tackle consciousness of shadow content is to look at your unmet needs. A good reference source is Marshall Rosenberg's Non-violent Communication website, books, and courses. [64] Using his Feelings and Needs Inventory can help you identify your own unmet needs.

Shadow work is not to be taken lightly (if you'll excuse the pun). It is deep and challenging work and is best undertaken with the support of a knowledgeable therapist or guide. Over the years, I've worked with many therapists, spiritual teachers, and indigenous elders who helped me work with my shadow. We all need someone who can hold the light for us when we are in the dark—until we can hold that light for ourselves.

DEEPER PERSONAL REFLECTION

There is no other aspect of self that requires more conscious mercy and compassion than your shadow self. The work of self-forgiveness must begin here. There is a gift in our imperfection and a great equalizing humility to be had in the admission of our flaws.

Take a moment to center and ground yourself in a safe place where you can be free of disturbance and distraction for a short time. Breathe consciously and deeply into your solar plexus (the place where your survival signals are generally felt) and out through your heart, where you can connect with feelings of love and grace.

No one is perfect. Everyone has had their dark night of the soul when they needed to turn toward their shadow, including Buddha and Christ. Both were known for their acceptance of suffering and their compassion and kind response to it. Of all our suffering and shattering, shadow encounters are the most painful and also have the most potential for healing us and making us whole.

Every mentally healthy being has experienced encounters with their shadow through feelings of shame and unworthiness, times in which they wondered if they were truly lovable. We all have fears, self-judgment, negative self-talk, and ego defenses that are manifestations of shadow content. We all need to be able to accept our needs and stand in our vulnerability as strong and wholehearted beings. To do this, we must reconcile the shadow content within us.

Probably one of the most potent ways to explore that content is to make an inventory of our negative judgments and projections. What do you demonize in others? What do you demonize or reject within yourself?

What are the dreams you have abandoned along the way? Explore what needs to be brought to consciousness there. What caused you to give up? Look particularly to places where you feel a sense of shame—what deeper need is revealed beneath that wounding?

Explore recurrent patterns in your life, and mine those stories for shadow content. Consider your victim stories. See if you can identify the part of you that was disowned during the times you experienced mistreatment.

To see what is being idealized, prized, or denied in you, also look at where you feel morally superior to others.

Recognize that no one is perfect. We are all learning and growing at different rates. People operate at many different levels of consciousness. Give yourself and others the opportunity to learn, rather than condemning anyone for what is not yet known.

Breathe love into all those dark corners and see if they can be illuminated with your love.

Meditation practices that teach you to become an inner witness and hold the energy of loving-kindness help you soften defenses and promote compassion. When we can hold that energy for ourselves, we are able to offer that same mercy to the world.

DEEPER QUESTIONS FOR YOUR SHADOW SELF

This is a time to notice, listen, feel, and record the responses from your Shadow Self. When exploring the dark side of your very human nature, it is helpful to receive guidance and direction from the evolved dimension of your Shadow Self by reflecting upon these questions.

- What does my shadow want me to know about this?

- What don't I want to admit, most wish to conceal, or fear having exposed?
- What judgments do I have about myself in this?
- Am I projecting my inability to accept these parts of myself onto others?
- What steps can I take to become open and vulnerable within myself, accepting my gifts and imperfections with equal grace?

LIVING THE DEEPER STORY OF YOUR SHADOW

Imagine a world in which people were encouraged to mature their consciousness and given the support they needed to become accountable for shadow responses, both within themselves and projected toward others. Consciousness would evolve to the point where it would be impossible not to feel and take ownership for the intentional and unintended consequences created by our every action. We would feel our deep connection with others and work toward a more beautiful and just world. We would have peace, both within and without.

I AM

The shadow is the dark web of my personal filing system. It knows where the bodies are buried. Its secrets are so deeply encrypted that I can't own them, so I project their content onto those around me. Surfacing when I least expect it, it can blindside me and bring me to my knees. My shadow not only makes me face the skeletons in my closet but forces my deepest needs to consciousness, things I crave but cannot admit, even to myself. Shame is its depth sounder, warning that I am getting too close to the bone, things are about to get real, my inner being will be exposed. Alternately black and golden, my shadow illuminates me from within. **I am shadow; therefore, I am.**

CHAPTER 13

THE DEEPER STORY OF YOUR DREAMING SELF

"A dreamer is one who can only find his way by moonlight, and his punishment is that he sees the dawn before the rest of the world."

—OSCAR WILDE

Is there anything more enigmatic than the dreaming self? Part prophet, trickster, sage, and stage director, the Dreaming Self points us in directions we would otherwise not think and perhaps not even choose to look. Dreams are our intuition on steroids, with information emerging from the subterranean depths of our unconscious mind. They confront us with unpredictable events in which we are moved by forces we cannot comprehend. Dreams play a role in decision-making, problem solving, creative insight, inner guidance, healing initiation, uncovering purpose, and deepening self-awareness.

THE ROLE OF THE DREAMING SELF IN YOUR DEEPER STORY

Function: Dreams take you beyond the constraints of conscious control to access unconscious information at every level of being. Dreams illuminate issues and yield valuable insight for creative problem-solving and healing. They can prepare you to face the unknown, help you cross boundaries into other realms of experience, and give you access to archetypal or ancestral wisdom.

When out of alignment: You may not recall your dreams. If you do, you may dismiss them as irrelevant or interact with them too literally rather than gaining insight from their content. You are unable to process dream content in useful ways. You lose contact with an opportunity to experience a dimension of self that is beyond the reach of your conscious control.

When in alignment: You are able to remember your dreams. You interact with and inhabit the symbolic content of dreams, using them as a valued resource for insight, inspiration, and healing. Because dreams are unmediated by your conscious mind, they carry raw material that needs to be metabolized within your consciousness and within the world.

Key Areas of Development: Interpretive Intelligence,[65] Embodied Imagination, Working with Symbolism, Exploring Collective Unconscious, Archetypal and Ancestral Processing, Intentional Interaction with the Unconscious Realm

Dominant Questions: What part of myself am I trying to awaken through my dreams? What am I preparing for, trying to reconcile, or attempting to integrate in dreamtime?

Arc of Development: From Unconscious Processing to Subconscious Support

THE CALL OF THE DREAMING SELF

The first time I was introduced to Native American Grandmother Hazie Frasier, she looked deeply into my eyes, nodded, and with a satisfied tone said, "Ah...you're a dreamer." I couldn't help but smile at her acknowledgment. To my parents, being a "dreamer" was a sign of personal deficiency, indicating a lack of discipline and practicality. To this Elder, it meant I was endowed with a sacred gift.

Science tells us that dreams play an important role in our health and well-being, but the true purpose of dreaming is yet to be discovered. Like intuition, dreaming is involuntary and can yield a spontaneous eruption of meaning.

HOW DO WE DREAM?

Roughly one-third of your life is spent sleeping, and on average, you may spend one to two hours dreaming per night, having somewhere between four and seven dreams. Even if you don't recall your dreams, you are still having them. In fact, not dreaming may be a sign of mental illness.

We progress through a sleep cycle each night that includes four levels. During stage one, you are in a *non-REM light sleep*, which lasts from one to ten minutes.[66] During stage two, you are in another phase of *non-REM light sleep*, which lasts about twenty minutes and prepares you to enter stages three and four. In *non-REM deep sleep*, which typically starts about thirty to forty-five minutes after dropping off, your brain waves slow down, and you are difficult to arouse. Your brain waves get longer and larger. You enter stage four, the *REM* phase, within about ninety minutes of falling asleep.

During REM sleep, your eyes move rapidly, and you experience your most powerful dreams. Your heartbeat and respiration increase and may become irregular, and your brain waves speed up. When you enter REM sleep, you experience what is known as sleep paralysis, which prevents you from the dangers of acting out the scenarios in your dreams. The REM stages get longer and longer through repeated cycles throughout the night, to the point where your last REM stage can last up to an hour.

Your neural networks are extremely active during the REM stage of sleep, and your brain waves are often more active when you are dreaming than awake. Activity increases in the amygdala, cingulate, and sensory cortices. By monitoring brainwaves, researchers have been able to determine that we have dreams during non-REM sleep as well as during REM sleep.

These dream states may affect us in different ways. During REM sleep, the amygdala is highly activated, and we tend to have dreams with more intense emotional content.

Non-REM dream states tend to deal with lighter, more positive content. Research indicates that non-REM sleep is useful for learning, dream rehearsal, and memory consolidation—it's as though your brain is using past experience to try to figure out how it might relate to your future. But in REM sleep, your brain is actually trying to "live out" or gain direct experience of your future.

REM sleep has been proven to stimulate creativity. Dreams in this state are often wild and involve magical thinking. These dreams are made of loose intuitive associations strung together in a way that makes new connections and suggests novel solutions. Hence the many accounts of scientific, medical, artistic, and business ideas inspired by dreams.

The type of imagination that shows up in dreams uses a different physiology than waking imagination. The hippocampus, which is involved in recalling memories, is almost entirely shut down during REM sleep. Certain forebrain areas involved in executive functioning and logical reasoning are also offline, so our emotional processing is enhanced, and our reasoning brain is snoozing. Although our dreaming and awakened selves likely use similar associational networks to construct narratives, the everyday controls are turned off during dreams, and dreamtime imagination can take wild leaps into the unknown.

WHAT DO DREAMS DO FOR US?

In Western culture, where the focus is individualistic rather than collective, the specific content of dreams is considered to be subjective and specific. Psychoanalyst Alfred Margulies says that the perceptions of the dreamer are as unique as one's voice or fingerprints.[67] He makes the point that while the storyline of a dream may have metaphorical or mythical elements, it is the *lived experience* that provides direct access to the dreamer's inner world and coherently reflects the individual's worldview.

> *"The waking have one world in common; sleepers have each a private world of his own."*
>
> —HERACLITUS

Because so little is understood about dreams and their purpose, there is plenty of exploration and speculation by dream researchers, psychologists, anthropologists, dream workers, and dreamers alike.

Some dreamworkers believe that dreams are from our lived experience and represent a deep taproot into our soul's wisdom, and that, along with our narrative self, our dreams are engaged in the big story of our lives, designed to reveal aspects of our purpose.

Here's one example:

> *Gerald dreamed that he visited a ranch in which a wild horse was being trained in a corral. The trainer was getting rough with the horse as it bucked and reared up. Gerald (who had no previous experience with horses) felt an empathetic affinity with the horse and hopped into the corral. When the horse reared up at him in a threat-*

ening way, Gerald too stretched tall and raised his arms, trying to mirror the horse's posture. He and the horse then engaged in a slow-motion mesmerizing dance in which he felt a soul connection with the horse.

Gerald became so entranced with this dream that he ended up taking equestrian-facilitated therapy training and fell in love with working with horses. He felt his dream activated a calling he had been completely unaware of.

TYPES OF DREAMS

Various cultures believe different things about dreams, seeing them as part of a collective narrative or communication from ancestors.

For example, Cherokee Elder Grandmother Patricia says that birthing songs come to her in dreams. She sees these songs—specific songs to be given to each child at birth— as coming **from her ancestors**.

* * *

Some see dreams as a form of **empowering guidance** and a significant resource for **healing**.

Mary dreamed that she was in a CT scanner, and a

doctor told her that her cancer had metastasized, and she should make final arrangements. She walked out on a long pier, high above the ocean, climbed over the railing, and flung herself off. As she plummeted toward the water, two angels caught her. They took her back up to the pier and told her she was being given an opportunity to stay alive, but she had to really want to live, and if she undid all the unliving she had done, she would have the keys to heal the world.

This dream catalyzed a new way of being for Mary and led to significant changes in how she established boundaries and created space in her life for her own well-being.

* * *

Prodromal dreams are seen as signals alerting us to potential health issues. And nightmares can better prepare us to face threatening events in our waking life.

Linda dreamed about Elizabeth Warren being assassinated, and in the dream, she lamented, "Why do the good ones have to be taken so early?"

In her waking life, Linda needed to decide whether to have a single medically necessary mastectomy or choose a bilateral mastectomy (removing a "good" healthy breast) to prevent a future reoccurrence of breast cancer.

The question in her dream illuminated the potential for regret in having "the good one being taken so early." This question helped her to make a final decision.

* * *

Perhaps dreams are just one more thread of **interconnectivity** through which we can access unfiltered information for and from one another.

Thomas dreamed he met a painter who wanted to do his family portrait.

The dream was vivid, and when he awoke, he wrote down the name of the painter. Something in the name seemed familiar and made him curious. He realized he had probably seen it somewhere but decided to look it up. Not only did he arrange to meet the painter, but he ultimately ended up dating her sister.

* * *

Dreams can have **prophetic** elements, giving us a window into our future to prepare us for upcoming events.

Sandra had a dream about a bear that was trying to break into her house.

The next day, a large black bear wandered into her yard and broke open the door to her car to get at some food she had forgotten there.

* * *

Research has shown that dreams have a role in **memory consolidation** and **regulation of emotions**.

The night Tim discovered that his partner was cheating on him, he was so overwhelmed with anger he couldn't express himself.

> *"That night I dreamed I was a dragon flying in circles over the land but couldn't release my fire. I remember thinking that I didn't want to scorch the earth."*

This dream caused Tim to look at his repressed emotions, which ultimately led him to receive counseling. His marriage was recovered as he learned to express his deeper feelings and needs.

* * *

Dreams are **beyond the reach of our rule-bound everyday consciousness** and are not necessarily flattering or morally, aesthetically, or politically correct.

Natalie dreamed of being on a large glass throne-like toilet on an elevated stage, on which she was defecating in front of a large crowd.

Her business had failed, and she felt her dream reflected her fear of public humiliation. Interestingly, however, when she embodied the feeling of the crowd watching her, she felt their confusion rather than their judgment. She explored the possibility that people were actually confused by, rather than judging, the failure of her business. This notion gave her the courage to ask people about their response to her situation. She discovered that people still believed deeply in her abilities, and this awareness gave her the courage to try again.

* * *

Dreams present **unknown possibility** and are a rich source of information about what is hidden from our waking consciousness.

The night before she gave a presentation that she knew was incomplete, Elaine dreamed she had delivered a baby with birth defects.

Elaine recognized she had done a "half-hearted" job. Her usual high standards were abandoned, and her dream made her rethink what her energy was giving birth to. It moved her to consider whether it was time to do something different with her talents.

INTEGRATING OUR DREAMING SELF
WHAT DO WE DO WITH OUR DREAMS?

We can interpret our dreams or make up stories about them, but we are far better off letting dreams tell their own tales. They hold completely idiosyncratic and uniquely individual messages that can't be overwritten by catalogues of symbols provided by others.

While others may weigh in on the subject of your dreams, it is unlikely they will do more than scratch the surface of the dream's *feeling* significance for you. The real value to be wrested from a dream comes from being able to directly inhabit and embody its mystery, whether that dream is about you or about the world. This task is best approached with a mixture of wonder and humility as we let the dream speak for itself.

Here is an example of a dream I recorded eleven years ago while staying at a healing retreat in the mountains of Jalisco, Mexico. I offer it because it incorporates many of the dream elements suggested above.

It is daytime, and I am walking alone in the mountains. I make my way to the top of a ridge and look across the valley at a sheer cliff on the other side. Descending toward the valley floor, about three quarters of the way down, I discover a cave. I feel drawn in and enter its dark embrace. The air is cool and soft and has the lingering scent of dried herbs. The cave hums with voices, whispering in an unrecognizable language. The atmosphere is comforting and buoyant; I lean backward and feel my feet gently lift off the ground. Suspended in the air, I am floating among the voices in the dark womb of the Earth. I feel completely at home.

Moments later, I am startled by male voices approaching. The interior of the cave suddenly goes silent, and I fall to the floor. My heart thumping, I scramble out of the cavern and into the bushes. I watch as a group of men arrive, carrying a large wooden door. They affix it at the cave's entrance and seal it with a heavy metal padlock. The sound of the lock snapping shut reverberates and jars me awake.

The morning after I had this dream, I joined a group hike with our guide, Lalo. He told us we were going to a nearby abandoned orphanage. He led us to a ridge from which we could see down to the valley floor. I recognized with a start that the cliff face looked exactly like the one in my dream.

We climbed down the hillside to explore the abandoned

convent and orphanage there. The run-down facility had stacks of small rusty bed frames crammed into an otherwise empty space. Another building bore a faded portrait of the orphanage's founder, a Franciscan nun called Madre Lidia. Inside the tiny church were a few wooden pews, a small altar with a crucifix above it, and a painting of the Madonna that hung off to the side.

Lalo stepped behind the altar and gestured for us to follow. At the end of a passageway, he opened a large wooden door, and I found myself entering a cavern like the one in my dream. It was empty but for a simple wooden kneeling bench propped against a stone ledge, on which someone had left a bundle of dried herbs.

The men in our group held back, poking their heads in briefly and then withdrawing. The women of the group walked into the cave, and once we were inside, I asked Lalo to close the door behind us. We stood companionably and comfortably in total darkness. When the women spoke, their hushed tones seemed to lift and swirl around us. I suggested we explore the cave's acoustics by chanting together. Our chant continued to ring and reverberate in the cavern long after we went silent.

The women gradually left, but I stayed behind in the cave. I wanted to thoroughly feel all the elements of my dream. I surrendered to the feeling of the total darkness and drew in its deep quietude. I embodied the feeling of the cave, and I suddenly felt like a womb, expanding and stretching to accommodate someone growing inside it. I simultaneously embodied the cave, the womb, and the being who was floating and growing inside the womb. I was completely enveloped in the sensations when Lalo opened the door and said we must go. I tried to hold onto the feelings, but I had been jarred out of my reverie, and I "fell" into line with the group. Resentful of the intrusion, I hung back on the trek homeward to further explore my feelings.

I wrestled with the felt sense of the dream, the peace, the sacred feeling of being completely at home. Within the dream I felt the intrusion of others, the withdrawal of the supportive energy, and my fall. I consciously allowed myself to embody the sensation of "falling from my state of grace."

It was obvious that my response in the dream and my real-life situation were perfect reflections of one another. I knew I had tapped the dark vein of a subconscious story that was running in the background of my life.

That feeling of being disrupted from my natural state of peace was not unfamiliar. In my waking life, I often feel that the world intrudes and calls me out of my reverie, and at times, I both fear and resent that call. Reluctant to join the world of busyness and drama, I want to continue in my reverie, so I blame others for disturbing me, rather than see the world calling me forth to offer something of value—not a flattering picture of my state of consciousness.

The dream revealed aspects of my Soul, Shadow, Wounded Self, Self-critic, and Ego all struggling to find their place. My soul wanted me to take a greater level of responsibility for bringing that state of peace into the world, not hiding from the disruption of worldly affairs. I needed to balance my need for introspection with action and stop blaming others for "disturbing my peace."

Although the trip had been initiated by physical symptoms, I realized that the actual healing I needed would only occur by unlocking that cavern within me and learning how to share it with the world.

The archetypal elements in this dream could have easily been interpreted as unfinished business being communicated by either my Irish or First Nations ancestors. The themes of rebalancing masculine and feminine energies, experiencing harmony with the Earth, and the consciousness of dominant cultures confiscating and co-opting sacred space could easily fall within that category.

Interpreting a dream is not enough. Being too cerebral in

your approach, or getting too caught up in ideas about the dream's symbolic content, can distort the dream's very particular meaning and value. The real beauty in dreams is their access to a completely unconscious and unknown realm. You may never know exactly what a dream means, but you can allow that wild imaginative place to unlock mysteries within you.

There are numerous ways to cultivate your dream world so you can receive the support of your subconscious mind.

DREAM EXPLORATION PRACTICES
Dream Journals

If you keep a dream journal for a time, you will notice recurrent themes and storylines. It often helps to either write your dreams down or share them with a partner immediately on waking, because the content evaporates so quickly. Sometimes it takes years for a dream's content to truly come alive within you and having recorded it gives you the best opportunity for later reflection on what the dream was showing you.

Within the first five minutes of waking from a dream, roughly half the content is lost, and within ten minutes, up to 90 percent can vanish. This is one of the reasons why, in dream research labs, participant's stages of sleep are monitored closely, and they are awakened immediately to describe their dreams. If researchers waited until the end of the night to question the dreamers, they would undoubtedly lose most of their material. This is one reason it is beneficial to stay put when you awaken. Moving around can erase dream content, so be still and rerun the dream through before you write it down.

Stay Open

Remain open to the emotional content of your dreams. Often there is an inner message trying to break through your habitual patterns of thinking. Let your subconscious mind gather the inner material necessary to connect the dots. Don't worry about a literal deciphering but do your best to embody the feeling of each dream character and object. Becoming an object or the "other" gives an entirely different vantage point from which you can experience dream content.

Look for Themes

Reflect on the aspects of your soul purpose as revealed through common patterns and issues presented in dreams.

Title Your Dream

Dream expert Robert Moss has written numerous books

on dreams.[68] One of his useful techniques for getting to the heart of the matter is to immediately give a title to your dream, based on its feeling quality. Giving your dream a title or "bumper sticker" type phrase often gets you in touch with the felt sense of the essential message in the dream.

Ask for Guidance

Asking for dream guidance is a well-known and useful practice. Priming yourself before sleep by asking for guidance in your dreams about a particular issue is an incredibly helpful process. Prepare your space for dreaming, purify other matters from your mind, and focus on what really matters; dream guidance is not for trivial issues. Make an offering or a promise about what you will do to express gratitude if you receive your answer. Invite dream guides to interact with you. You cannot command the unknown; you can only be open to it. Be prepared to receive an answer that may seem unrelated to how you have previously perceived the issue.

Use Ritual

Creating a bedtime ritual and preparing sacred space into which dreams can arrive honors and invites your dreaming self. Prepare both sleeping and waking space. Turn off alarms to allow yourself to awaken naturally and have a pen and paper by your bedside. You can also make an auditory record of your dreams, but I don't recommend having phones by your bed. Limiting the amount of screen time before bed allows your brain to calm and prepare itself for sleep.

DEEPER QUESTIONS FOR YOUR DREAMING SELF

This is a time to notice, listen, feel, and record the responses from your Dreaming Self. Let your Dreaming Self guide you as you reflect upon these questions:

- What does my dreaming self want me to know about this?
- What is it attempting to awaken in me?
- What does this experience symbolize in my life as a whole?
- What steps can I take to engage my unconscious mind in working on this situation?
- What purpose does this dream serve in my deeper story?

MEDITATION FOR YOUR DREAMING SELF

This is a good practice when you first awaken from a dream. As you come to consciousness, keep your eyes closed and stay in the same body position so that you can reflect on your dream. Attempt to return to the dreamlike state. Become aware of your initial feelings and associations. You may wish to dialogue with the characters in the dream.

If something specific stands out about the dream—some lingering image, word, sensation, etc.—ask for guidance about the felt sense of that thing. Breathe, let go of the need to figure it out, and let yourself be awash in the feeling of it. Allow the dream to reveal itself over time.

Notice if the dream is asking something of you or if it provided any specific (or even nonsensical) advice.

Look at and reflect on the symbols in your dreams.

Realize that the images and meaning are deeply personal and look for ways they connect with your life and its deeper story.

Step out of the personal and ask what this dream might mean to the larger world. Is there some message you are receiving on behalf of the whole?

Ask your dream what part of your multi-dimensional self is trying to dialogue with you. Is there some part of yourself you have been ignoring that requires your attention?

Express gratitude toward your dreaming self and remain open to its continued recollections as they surface throughout the day.

"We are such stuff as dreams are made on, and our little life is rounded with a sleep."

—WILLIAM SHAKESPEARE, *THE TEMPEST*

LIVING THE DEEPER STORY OF YOUR DREAMING SELF

Our dreams are one of the true mysteries of consciousness and, for the most part, are beyond our conscious reach. What if we learn to honor and accept the mysteries they offer by consciously trying to interact with them in our waking lives?

If we collected our dream content over the course of a lifetime, we would undoubtedly see that they were not just the random flotsam and jetsam that washed ashore during sleep but were specifically crafted messages designed specially to come through us. Embodying dream content can be an empowering way to get in touch with the foreign content of dreams and connect with hidden aspects of our self.

Although it has been open to some dispute, Einstein is reputed to have said that the most important question we could ever ask is if the universe is a friendly place. Perhaps we should also wonder about the friendliness of the unconscious realm of our inner world and make a concerted effort to engage it more proactively.

I AM

Sleep-activated magic carpet ride, transporting me to the innermost realms where shadow and light do the dance fandango, where the infrastructure of cognizance becomes the center that cannot hold; things fall apart and coalesce in hauntingly haphazard and ludicrously liberating ways. Where a confluence of undigested images, emotions, insights, sensations, and perhaps even that bit of nibbled cheese before bed come together as cockeyed co-conspirators to awaken me to a deeper life. Where the shifting ground of being contains multitudes, harbingers of as-yet unborn parts of self. Where stories unfold without discernible setting or plot but rise and fall with such climactic vehemence that waking life becomes denouement. I awaken to myself in sleep. **I am dreaming; therefore, I am.**

Narrative

CHAPTER 14

THE DEEPER STORY OF YOUR NARRATIVE SELF

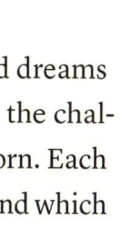

We are born into a sea of stories: the hopes and dreams of our parents, the struggles of our ancestors, the challenges of the time and place in which we are born. Each individual has a narrative center of gravity around which their sense of identity is built. Your personal stories form a distinctive narrative thread that makes you identifiably yourself.

When you ask the question, "Who am I?" all you have to draw on for understanding is the subjective experience encoded within your autobiographical memory. Those memories are curated by your Narrative Self to create a sense of meaning and purpose to your life.

You are not only a product of everything that ever happened to you but also of how you have interpreted each of these events. At first glance, your memories may seem random, confusing, and contradictory, but when you look through the eyes of your Narrative Self, you see how the dots connect to reveal purpose beneath your patterns. Once integrated, these memories illuminate the deeper story of your life.

THE ROLE OF THE NARRATIVE SELF IN YOUR DEEPER STORY

Function: Memories record your experience, and the Narrative Self interprets your world through that encoding. Your inner story and sense of self are rewritten with each new experience. This narrative lends meaning to your life and allows you to act with a conscious sense of purpose.

When out of alignment: You get caught in your personal stories, take things too personally, lose perspective, fail to recognize meaningful connections between your inner state and external circumstances, repeat patterns without understanding or learning from them, feel disempowered, and refuse to take responsibility for your own life story.

When in alignment: You can reflect on your life as

a whole. You are able to see underlying patterns and acknowledge the structuring effect of learning as your life progresses. You create meaningful connections between experiences and recognize that you are also part of a life story that is larger than your individual experience.

Key Areas of Development: Apperceptive Intelligence,[69] Intrapersonal Skills, Pattern Recognition, Memory Healing and Integration

Dominant Questions: What are the dominant stories in my life? What strengths have they cultivated in me? What do they reveal about my purpose?

Arc of Development: From Repetitive Patterns to Conscious Evolution

THE CALL OF THE NARRATIVE SELF

Our short-term and sensory memories can break down quite rapidly, but our long-term memory can store unlimited amounts of information indefinitely. To embed something within our long-term memory requires repetition, significance, a strong motivation to remember, a powerful emotional charge, or a potential threat. Our Narrative Self ensures that events of significance are not just stored in our memory but are interactively interpreted and placed in patterns of experience.

These memories are story-based. Vivid detail and emotion in a story adds context, nuance, and meaning to a factual account. Stories help us connect the dots between events and cause us to stretch beyond our own experience to gain new perspective. Through stories, the literal world and its metaphorical double can work together as powerful conveyers of meaning and influence.

It is much harder to remember a dry set of facts than to recall a compelling story. For example, if we listen to a set of facts, such as the time and date of a war, only the language-processing areas of the brain become activated. However, if we are told a story about a small group of brave people fighting for survival in the face of an advancing army, many parts of our brains become aroused as we imagine the challenges they might face. We become emotionally involved, empathizing with and possibly even rooting for them. We are engaged in not only interpreting the story but inhabiting it and anticipating its outcome. This is also true of our internalized stories. Many areas of the brain are involved as we recount the stories that form our autobiographical memory.

These encoded memories act as an interpretive filter through which all new experiences and perceptions are classified. These interpretations are organized into our self-narrative, the story we tell ourselves about ourselves. How we interpret the narrative thread of our stories determines how we feel about ourselves.

Research has taught us that neither memories nor identities are fixed objects—they are fluid and malleable, continually being altered, updated, and amended with new learning, experience, and growth. We are constantly re-creating ourselves based on new input. The memory that haunts us at one stage of life may later be perceived as funny, poignant, or even life-altering.

We have the power to reinterpret and reframe the content of our stories, as Peter did in the following example.

PETER'S STORY

Peter felt broken in every way possible. He had just gone through yet another painful relationship ending, but that wasn't his main complaint when he came to see me. He said he felt completely out of sync with the world and was trying to decide if it was worth "putting in the time just to watch everything fall apart." When I asked him to explain, he launched into a complex analysis of world politics, human dynamics, and his concern about the future of humanity. He was erudite, drawing on references from science, history, philosophy, comparative religion, psychology, and so on. I listened with rapt attention until he was complete. He had a rare interdisciplinary intelligence that was fascinating, especially since he had dropped out of high school in grade ten.

After he finished speaking, he immediately apologized for "going on and on," and insisted he should have just answered my question by saying he was "different" and didn't know how to live in the world. He said he was deeply aware that nobody really wanted to hear this stuff and that he spent way too much time thinking. He said he had pretty much given up talking because he had learned from his family, the people at work, and his various girlfriends over the years that nobody was interested.

Peter was convinced there was something wrong with him. All his memories had been marshalled into a story about how different he was and how that meant he was unworthy of people's time, attention, and love.

In working with his Narrative Self, however, a different picture emerged. Peter realized it was true that he was different from the people he had surrounded himself with. In accepting this fact rather than trying to resist it, he was able to identify that difference in a more accurate way. The truth was that Peter operated at an entirely different level of consciousness than the other people in his life. They weren't receptive or interested, because most of what Peter discussed was beyond their level of understanding.

His conclusion that "nobody" would ever be interested in him was based on feedback from a pretty limited sample of humanity. As an introvert, Peter resonated with the people in books, but in real life, he hadn't gone far enough afield to discover others who might share his interests and perspectives. Because he avoided having a computer, he was also cut off from the potential of developing an online social network of like-minded people.

Peter had done what many people do to reinforce their stories of unworthiness: he had offered his gifts to the very people who were incapable of receiving them. The measure of his worthiness was then determined by their rejection of his gifts.

He realized that to change his story, he had to change the way he did things, and that had to begin with enlarging his world. He needed to move beyond his home-based comfort zone.

He began by going to free lectures and joined a philosopher's café discussion group. He started using the computer at the library to participate in an online forum, where he regularly weighed in on a number of topics. By sharing more of himself, he became engaged in an expansive community that valued his input. He discovered that what he had previously perceived as his most painful difference had actually become his greatest asset. His desire to communicate his ideas allowed him to engage with people from around the world in a deeply fulfilling way. In offering his gifts, he discovered his value.

Painful memories often hold distortions because they focus on the responses of others rather than what matters to us. In revisiting your memories, you can empower yourself with your own interpretation and reclaim gifts that you abandoned along the way.

Keith's Story

Where Peter's intelligence had isolated him, Keith's victim story about his imagined lack of intelligence actually brought him together with others. Keith was holding back from accepting a leadership role at work because he doubted his own capability and intelligence. Keith grew up with a competitive older brother who was determined to always one up Keith. His brother frequently embarrassed Keith and belittled his intelligence.

Keith saw himself as a victim of his brother's bullying but had come to agree with his brother's assessment when it came to evaluating his own intelligence. He justified this with the fact that he had barely scraped by in school with Cs and Ds.

When he reflected on his story, Keith admitted that he had been bored to death in school. He felt chronically under-stimulated and never cracked open a book. He got his Cs and Ds with absolutely no work involved. A more likely interpretation of his marks was not that he was not smart enough but that he may have been too advanced for his assigned grade level.

Keith also admitted that he spent all of his time during and after school socializing, and this is where his other form of intelligence shone through. He had acquired prodigious social and emotional intelligence—skills that not only led to his significant success as a sales professional but opened the door to his leadership position.

In reevaluating the effect of his older brother's pushing, Keith realized that it had actually forced him to be sharp and stay on his toes. The bullying drove him to find ways to engage at a higher level of social engagement with others. Thanks, older brother! In this case, the Cs and Ds may have been facts, but the meaning Keith took from them formed a distorted story about his intelligence.

The good news was that he had the power to change his interpretation, and in doing so, was able to make a more accurate self-assessment that supported him in taking on a leadership role in which he thrived.

"The trail of memory can feel like a heavy chain, keeping us locked into the identities we have created for ourselves."

—SUZANNE CORKIN

OPERATING OUT OF OLD STORIES

Our old stories become a habitual way of thinking that, if unchallenged, continue to plague us with doubt. They can also make us so self-absorbed that we distort reality.

Lindsey had a story about how she was always abandoned in relationships. She had been in a great relationship with Claude for three years when he suddenly started having mood swings and began to change his behavior toward her. Convinced that this was a sign of his withdrawal, her Post-traumatic Story of abandonment surfaced, and she felt unloved and worthless. Lindsey's interpretation of Claude's behavior fit her story perfectly—except for the fact that the changes were induced by a rapidly growing tumor in Claude's brain and had nothing to do with her.

Virtually every romantic comedy follows the thematic line of people misinterpreting each other's intentions. An error of assumption is made by one person, who then feels injured and departs hurt and angry until, by some twist of fate (or plot), they are brought back together to discover a new understanding of events.

So how can you recognize when you are operating out of an old or inaccurate story? Check your feelings and your behavior. If you are feeling reactive or rigid, chances are you are stuck in a non-productive or post-traumatic story.

Here are some indications that you are stuck in a story rut:

- Your behavior is incongruent (words/actions do not match inner knowing).
- You feel like a victim and see others as responsible for your feelings.
- You doubt, second-guess yourself, or feel conflicted.
- You may feel guilty about or consumed with regret about your choices.
- You feel the need to justify your actions.
- You have difficulty in taking responsibility for your choices and the consequences that come with your decisions.
- Conversely, you may feel "right" and entitled to respond a certain way.
- You feel so certain about the correctness of your perspective that you block feedback or refuse to entertain other ideas.
- You have a position you are defending.
- You become reactive if questioned or challenged.
- It requires an act of will to deal with the consequences that flow from your position.

Just as you can't know another person without learning their story, you can't know yourself without considering all of the stories encoded inside you.

Every part of your multi-dimensional being has a story to tell. Your soul holds the underlying story of your purpose. Your embodied self is encoded with visceral and cellular stories, and your survival self uses fear and cautionary tales about potential risk and dangers. Your emotional self carries your stories of love, joy, and loss, and your intuitive self maintains the historical records of synchronicity and other mysterious events in your life. Your imaginative self has stories about untapped possibilities, your intellect contains stories about the workings of the universe, and your social self has stories about how you fit in and where you belong. Your wounded self holds your tales of trauma and unprocessed pain. Your ego has stories about who you want to be, and your self-critic has ones about who you are *supposed* to be. Your shadow has secret stories about what you fear and what you love about yourself. Your dreaming self uses unconscious prompts to move your story forward, and your narrative self brings all of these threads together into the evolving story of your life. Your integrated self embraces and accepts all stories as part of your evolutionary journey and transmutes them into value to offer to the world.

You have billions of bits of information encoded in the form of memories...so where do you begin?

Here are some ways to check the content of your narrative:

- Identify the memories that have most profoundly affected your sense of yourself.
- Review the list of negative comments of your self-critic. Follow the memory back to when you first acquired these kinds of thoughts and issues.
- Identify your emotional themes and note the memories you have associated with these issues. Note any memories of hurt, rejection, insecurity, loneliness, abandonment, loss, grief, sadness, depression, fear, anxiety, embarrassment, humiliation, anger, rage, destructiveness, selfishness, envy, jealousy, shame, guilt, regret, inadequacy, vulnerability, unworthiness, etc.
- Go back through the cast of characters and relationships in your life (mother, father, grandparents, siblings, teachers, neighbors, friends, significant others, bosses, coworkers, etc.). List any negative or painful memories.
- Look at the areas in your life in which you struggle, have difficulty, or wish to be different.
- Note any memories of punishment or reprimand.
- Review places you have lived, schools attended, jobs, etc.

- Reflect on any unfulfilled dreams or failures.
- Now note the memories that are closest to your heart—the memories of your most cherished moments and times when you have felt most satisfied and happy.

INTEGRATING THE NARRATIVE SELF
HEALING AND REINTEGRATING YOUR NARRATIVE

Here is a way to you can defragment the parts of yourself that have been caught up in both Post-traumatic Stories and positive experiences and integrate them into the healthy, evolving narrative of your deeper story.

Take a few moments to settle yourself in a safe place free from disturbance or distraction. Breathe and relax; adjust your body until it feels supported and comfortable.

Let's take a walk down memory lane. Begin by choosing a particularly challenging circumstance in your life in which you felt you had little control. Any kind of challenge will do—health, relationships, work, or anything else that introduced turmoil into your life. We want to review the content of that story in a way in which you can see yourself, the other people involved, and what was really going on from a new perspective.

What role does that experience play in your life now?

What impact has it had upon you? What has changed in you as a result of it? Is it a change for the better or worse?

If it is for the worse, how do you hold that memory within you? How did you greet the potential in the situation? What was the highest potential offered within that experience? Did you allow that potential to transform you or help you to evolve as a person?

What skills were being cultivated in you as a result of that experience? What qualities were being called forth in you during it? Even if the experience was difficult, painful, and irreversible, can you accept whatever it offered you? Can you think of other people who have modeled a greater level of awareness and grace in coming through such experiences? What were they doing that you would not allow yourself to do?

By giving these memories your conscious time and attention, you bring them to the foreground, where they can interact with new and current information. By bringing them up to date, you can harvest the wisdom they offer and integrate them within the context of the narrative thread that runs through your life.

Now, revisit one of your positive memories from the past. Notice what made that experience happy or satisfying. What values were being lived in that experience? What emotions were being inhabited and expressed? How did you feel about yourself at that time? Look at what was integral to your sense of purpose within that experience. How does that memory fit within the larger picture of your life?

You structure your life with stories so you can understand, transform, and integrate your experiences.

––

DEEPER QUESTIONS FOR YOUR NARRATIVE SELF

This is a time to notice, listen, feel, and record the responses from your Narrative Self. When exploring the stories that govern your life and inviting input and guidance from your Narrative Self, you can reflect upon these questions.

- What does my narrative self want me to know about this?
- What other memories or stories from my life fit with this?
- What am I trying to prove or reveal about myself in these stories?
- What steps can I take to harvest the wisdom from these stories, determine the underlying needs they reveal, and see this experience in the light of my continuous evolution?

LIVING THE DEEPER STORY OF YOUR NARRATIVE SELF

Everything within you is embedded in an intricate matrix of experience that runs from your past, through the present, and into your future. In other words, everything that happens in your life occurs within a previously established context. Your challenges are not random, nor do they exist in a vacuum—they are integral facilitative components of your unique life journey.

When you embrace your life story as an integrated whole, you discover that your soul purpose has been running beneath the visible surface of your experience like a golden thread. That thread is unbreakable and makes the illuminated manuscript of your life beautifully illustrative of your unique contribution to the world.

I AM

Inner storehouse of fact and fiction, keeper of the unspoken stories of my life, archiving bits of data and bytes of sensory stimuli, the curator of my life experience is continuously codifying, classifying, and making connections. A revisionist of memory and history, it updates, appends, arranges, and rearranges things into semi-coherent sequences. My Narrative Self fills in the blanks, taking each recognizable fragment of the mosaic that is my life and turning it into my ongoing story. **I am narrative; therefore, I am.**

Integrated
Self

CHAPTER 15

THE DEEPER STORY OF YOUR INTEGRATED SELF

Learning about, listening to, understanding, and accepting all aspects of yourself is what makes integration possible. Integration optimizes your strengths and recognizes genuine limitations. From an integrated state, you have the potential to have a profound effect on others—simply by being yourself.

Integration is experienced as a state of deep presence, having a sense of interconnectedness, living in the moment while also holding mindfulness about your impact and its ripple effect, maintaining awareness and acceptance of your limitations, operating from a mature consciousness, devoting time and energy to a calling beyond personal benefit, accepting others, and having a sense of humor and perspective.

THE ROLE OF THE INTEGRATED SELF IN YOUR DEEPER STORY

Function: Integration allows unfettered expression of one's unique potential and purpose.

When out of alignment: You are "out of integrity" within yourself, disconnected from your true essence, feel conflicted, become self-conscious and inhibited, and try to monitor and control yourself and/or others.

When in alignment: You surrender to the flow of life within you and become the living expression of your soul's purpose. You are present, accountable, and fully expressive, radiating powerful influence through example.

Key Areas of Development: Unitive Intelligence,[70] Multi-dimensional Awareness, Embodied Presence, State of Flow, and Leadership by Example

Dominant Questions: Do I fully accept and embrace all aspects of myself? What makes me feel most alive and whole? When am I most congruent and harmonious? Where do my personal gifts align with a need in the world?

Arc of Development: From Unconscious Existence to Awakened Authenticity

THE CALL OF THE INTEGRATED SELF

We know the presence of our Integrated Self in those rare moments when a higher consciousness is required to greet a particular challenge. These are the times when everything aligns within us and we are fully present to the situation at hand. We use the expression "rising to the occasion" to describe this transcendence of our habitual consciousness so we can respond from a higher truth. We spontaneously engage authentic power without effort, artifice, or control.

Many people associate an integrated state of being with spirituality but being "spiritual" does not mean you are integrated. Like everything else, spirituality can be imbalanced or distorted if it is not engaged from a place of conscious integrity.

Integrated people may be spirited, but they do not necessarily have to be spiritual. They have learned to accept and work with imperfection because they understand life is about learning and evolving. Ultimately, they are accountable.

INTEGRATED RESPONSIVENESS

That level of accountability shows up in how the Integrated Self responds. It is worth noticing the differences in response from the previous chapter where we looked at the signs of imbalanced response from the Narrative Self.

When integrated:

- You feel fully accountable for your state and your choices.
- While you accept your own truth, you are not overly attached to it and are willing to explore other perspectives.
- You are open to feedback, take it in respectfully, assess its validity, and, if appropriate, adjust accordingly.
- You realize that the choices flowing from your truth may affect others, so you communicate with those who may be affected.
- You accept that others may not approve of your choices because they have different needs and considerations.
- You listen respectfully, address concerns, and acknowledge others' rights to their perceptions and feelings.
- If, through your *best effort* in communicating, the other person cannot understand or accept your perspective, you reflect on this, take steps to gain clarity, and use your sense of integrity to make a choice before acting on your inner truth.
- You accept the consequences that come with your truth/choice.
- Your decision results in freeing up energy, making you feel more alive, more aligned, congruent, and in touch with your deeper self.

- Your choices harmonize with your sense of purpose.
- In retrospect, you see how accepting and acting on your truth led you to the next stage of your development.

MY ENCOUNTER WITH AN INTEGRATED BEING

You may recall my story at the beginning of this book, in which *The Prayer Book for the Tibetan Book of the Dead* woke me up, but I had much more healing to do beyond the galvanizing insight that text provided.

In those early post-traumatic days before returning to university, I still had moments of slipping back into depression. During those times, I wasn't sure that I could continue living with my pain. To console myself, I came up with a plan. I put what I called my *suicide card* in my back pocket. I figured if things became unbearable and I couldn't take it anymore, I could always pull that card and end the pain. Every time I sank into depression, I fiddled with that card like it was a loose tooth. It hurt like hell, but I couldn't quite leave it alone...until one day, a chance encounter woke me up to another possibility altogether.

A man got on a bus and irrevocably altered my world. He sat a few rows ahead of me, facing in my direction. There was something about him—an aura that set him apart from the other passengers. I couldn't help but stare at his astonishing face. He had chiseled features, dark olive skin, and penetrating blue eyes. A deep scar carved a path from the corner of his left eye all the way to his jawbone. It was impossible to take my eyes off him.

He got off the bus at my stop, and I followed him into a neighborhood café. Mesmerized, I watched him stride toward a group of people sitting at the back. When one of the café's regulars approached me, I asked him about the man with the amazing face. Moments later, he introduced me to Patrick.

I blurted an apology for staring at him on the bus. He looked at me in a kind way and said it was all right. Clearly, he was used to it. The next words that escaped my lips were as shocking to me as they must have been to him. I said, "It's just that I've never seen anything so beautiful. May I touch your face?"

His eyes widened in confusion, but then he smiled, and without an ounce of trepidation, I ran my fingertips from the corner of his eye down the length of his scar. We stood there looking at one another.

We spent time getting to know one another. There was an inexplicable chemistry between us that was neither romantic nor sexual. I learned a bit of his history: how he had earned his scar as a junkie inmate, and how he ultimately repaid his karmic debt by counseling drug addicts in prison.

Patrick's powerful authenticity was inspiring, and not surprisingly, I discovered he was a hero to many people. He was open, quiet, and compassionate but definitely did not take himself too seriously. He had what I can only describe as an illumined presence.

A few months after we first met, I unexpectedly ran into him downtown. It was late on a weekday morning when he came bounding across the street toward me. He seemed pale and luminous, even more oddly beautiful than usual.

Although our chance meeting surprised me, he acted as though he had been waiting for me to arrive. He said, "Thank God you're here," and swept me up in an unusually intimate embrace.

Standing back for a moment, he held me at arm's length and looked deeply into my eyes. I accepted his penetrating gaze and something in me softened. Without another word, he dashed off across the plaza.

The following day, I learned Patrick had died in his apartment shortly after our brief encounter. The official cause of death was *heart failure*, but no one who truly knew him would ever put those two words together in reference to him. Patrick's heart never failed him or anyone else.

It took me awhile to fully appreciate what he had given me, but over time, it became clear. Although I felt broken, Patrick saw me as whole. He didn't try to change or fix me, and he didn't turn away from my pain or suicidal yearnings. He taught me that scars can contain beauty and be borne with dignity. He was living proof that healing was possible.

Patrick was what I call a fully integrated being. He was totally at peace with himself and the world. He loved his life, lived it imperfectly but fully, and he left it because he was complete with it.

His departure caused me to reflect on my own unlived life and made me realize what a terrible waste it would be to leave this world without at least attempting to achieve such luminosity myself.

Sadly, I am not a luminous being, or a fully integrated person, but I no longer look for a way out of life. I continue to learn and grow as I make my way through each day. I was fortunate to encounter someone so beautifully integrated, who shared his illumination with me at the darkest time in my life. Patrick's presence called forth the life force that was withheld inside me. He inspired me to focus it on a higher vision for myself and for the world.

INTEGRATING YOURSELF

Integration begins with becoming conscious and accountable in all aspects of being. By working your way through the other chapters in this book, you should have a pretty good idea of where you are in or out of alignment in each dimension of self. Working to balance all aspects for optimal authenticity and expression of your unique gifts is what makes integration possible.

Most people find it easier to identify their weaknesses (or areas where they require additional development) than to identify things they have already mastered. When you are naturally skillful and working within your zone of optimal strength, things feel easy. Because what we are doing does not require major effort, we tend not to see what we are doing as something special or of having particular value. Think of how easy it is to brush off a compliment from someone who admires your gifts. You say something like, "It was nothing, no big deal," and so on. It isn't a big deal in the sense that it is normal for you, but it may be a very big deal to someone who has not yet achieved that level of skill.

Integrated people accept their gifts and skills without making a big deal out of them. They rarely seek credit for their impact—not because they are humble but because, in their genuine humility, they also recognize and fully accept their limitations.

It is interesting to note that of the people I consider to be fully integrated beings, not one of them would perceive themselves that way. Perhaps that is the mark of an integrated person—their total disinterest in being classified as such. They accept that there is no end to learning and growth.

YOUR ENCOUNTERS WITH INTEGRATED PEOPLE

It is not difficult to identify an integrated person. Like my friend Patrick, they stand out—not because they are seeking recognition but because they exude a rare integrity. They have a straightforward quality and speak their truth without making it the only one that counts. They don't proselytize or pretend to have all the answers. They don't interfere, try to fix, or believe they know what others need. They accept that each of us has a unique and specific path. Their words resonate because they have the full force of their soul behind them. They seek an inclusive higher ground for all and lead by example.

I am fortunate in having been mentored by a few people whom I considered to be integrated beings. Apart from Patrick, I also include my late friends Dr. Ted Merrill and Navajo Elder Leon Secatero on that list. These people fully devoted themselves to something that called forth every bit of what they had to offer, and they offered it willingly. They not only left an indelible impression on my life (and the lives of many others), but they inspired me to share more of myself with the world.

HONORING THE PEOPLE WHO ENCOURAGE YOUR WHOLENESS

You may not always be able to hold your own light, but an integrated person can, at times, loan you theirs for a while. Their presence will burn bright in you until you are ready to release your own light into the world. I believe it is important to honor those people who inspire the best in you.

- Who has been present in your life as an unconditional source of love and understanding?
- Who was able to see your *going against the grain* as an expression of your unique gift?
- Who inspired you to take a leap of faith in yourself?
- Who influenced you to stretch out of your comfort zone and be the best person you could possibly be and encouraged you to release your full life force into the world?
- Who facilitated your highest expression?

If any of these people are still alive, make sure you express your gratitude to them in some tangible way. If they have passed on, the best way to honor their memory is by continuing to build on the strengths they inspired.

DEEPER PERSONAL REFLECTION

Take a moment to settle yourself so that you can reflect peacefully without disturbance or distraction. Breathe in comfort and ease and release any tension you may be holding. This is a time to consider what it means to be fully integrated and discover the steps you can take to bring your whole being into balance.

As you have worked your way through this book, you will have come to recognize that there are no easy answers for life's difficult circumstances, but there are simple decisions you can make about how you can deal with challenge and change when it arrives.

Here is a list of some key practices you can adopt to strengthen your resilience and resolve as you move toward integration of all aspects of yourself. As you consider this list of skills, take a moment to pause, breathe, and reflect on each one, noting where in your life you are already practicing this successfully and where you might benefit from considering new approaches. Make sure that you are truly honoring yourself rather than resorting to feelings of deficiency. Give yourself permission to learn, grow, and evolve in these areas.

- Using attentiveness and deep listening both within yourself and with others.

- Staying alert to your natural inclinations and noticing what calls you.
- Embodying and embracing your feelings.
- Knowing the difference between reactivity and responsiveness.
- Grounding yourself in what is real.
- Accepting *what is* while working toward *what can be.*
- Opening yourself to opportunity and possibility.
- Using a multi-dimensional perspective, learning to see all sides of the equation.
- Applying discernment and discipline.
- Facing challenges and problems with mindful resolve.
- Embracing necessary limitations.
- Proactively working with grit and grace.
- Employing patience and persistence.
- Being imaginative, creative, playful, and resourceful.
- Letting go of the need to control outcomes and others.
- Fully accepting yourself and others.
- Maintaining healthy and reciprocal relationships.
- Giving and receiving love fully and freely.
- Communicating with care and respect.
- Seeking understanding and finding common ground.
- Being vulnerable and open to feedback.
- Offering and accepting support.
- Experiencing and expressing gratitude.
- Taking responsibility for yourself and being accountable.
- Trusting your path and letting others have their own.

- Collaborating within a co-creative community.
- Devoting yourself to a higher purpose.
- Living a life of meaning and significance.
- Making the world a better place by improving yourself first.
- Courageously standing up for what matters to you and to the world.
- Working toward healing, creating inner harmony, and peace of mind.
- Offering your gifts to the world.

And as the Dalai Lama would say, "Stop trying to be Buddhist!" Or as Lao Tzu put it, "The snow goose need not bathe to make himself white. Neither must you do anything but be yourself."

PRESCRIPTION FOR INTEGRATION

Knowing, loving, and being yourself, making room for the authentic expression of every part of your multi-dimensional being, and focusing on what matters to you is what gives your life meaning. There are no short-cuts to consciously-integrated wholeness; it can only be achieved through living fully and imperfectly, learning and evolving as you go. The best prescription I have encountered comes from yet another integrated being, the Danish multi-thinker and universalist Piet Hein:

The Road to Wisdom[71]

The road to wisdom?
—Well, it's plain
and simple to express:
Err
and err
and err again
but less
and less
and less.

DEEPER QUESTIONS FOR YOUR INTEGRATED SELF

This is a time to notice, listen, feel, and record the responses from your Integrated Self. When exploring the deeper story of your life, you can reflect upon these questions.

- What does my integrated self want me to know about this?
- What underlying theme or pattern am I trying to integrate?
- What would it be like to completely love and accept myself, even with this issue?
- What can I offer to the world as a result of integrating

my self-awareness, forgiveness, acceptance, and love around this issue?
- What role does this issue serve in my life, and how is it tied to my higher purpose?

LIVING THE DEEPER STORY OF YOUR INTEGRATED SELF

Coming full circle now, you can reflect upon how your life can be altered by working with the gifts of each dimension of yourself within each experience you have. Having integrated and evolved your evolving consciousness, you would now be:

- Living your soul's purpose.
- Inhabiting your body's wisdom.
- Rewiring your survival mechanisms.
- Wholeheartedly embracing your emotional nature.
- Applying the subtle workings of your intuition.
- Employing the creative genius of your imagination.
- Utilizing the discerning power of your intellect.
- Grounding yourself in social interdependence.
- Working with the catalytic energies behind your wounding, ego, inner critic, and shadow to inspire higher consciousness.
- Activating the subconscious value in your dreams.
- Rewriting the narratives with which you make sense of yourself and the world around you.

In accepting and working with every part of your multi-dimensional self, you would be integrated and committed to living a fully conscious and accountable life.

And that, my friend, is a rare and beautiful thing.

I AM

Comfortable and content in body, mind, and spirit, wholeheartedly here for myself and for the world, open to life, nothing to deny or resist, all systems and senses in supportive synchrony; cooperating, consensual, conscious, and connected. Taking my purpose seriously but my sense of self lightly, with grace, humor, and humility, I accept responsibility for the indelible imprint of my presence on the face of eternity. All in, I gratefully embrace the gift of life. **I am integrated; therefore, I am.**

CONCLUSION

As Nietzsche so eloquently put it, "Language is not the adequate expression of all realities." I am certain the words I've shared in this book do not begin to approximate the immensity and complexity of your journey toward wholeness. At life's most ecstatic and excruciating turning points, words always fall short—but however inadequately, we still need to transmit our experience.

Sharing our stories encourages empathy, and we need a lot more of that in the world. We can't embrace what we don't understand, and no matter how prescient we may think we are, we can never truly know what motivates another person until we have heard their story.

Despite the many forms of insurance people purchase every year as a hedge against life's potential disasters, I believe that the best insurance anyone can possess is elevated consciousness. Everyone feels vulnerable when they are stuck and unable to move forward. These are the most pivotal moments of our lives, because they hold the potential for something new to emerge. They are also the times when we most need encouragement, empathy, and compassion from others and ourselves. So rather than running from your challenging moments, I hope you will more willingly turn toward them with grace and gratitude for the awakening they offer and find the hidden wisdom within them.

As a fellow traveler on the road toward integrated consciousness, I thank you for sharing this part of your journey with me.

APPENDICES

APPENDIX 1

THE DEEPER STORY QUESTIONS FOR EACH ASPECT OF SELF

Identify and write down an issue you would like to gain insight about. Take a moment to get settled and quiet and breathe into your heart. With the issue in mind, ask yourself these questions. Take time to pause, breathe, notice, listen, feel, and record the responses from each part of you.

ENSOULED SELF

- What does my soul want me to know about this?
- Is the way I am handling this issue a consistent expression of my true nature?
- How might this issue be related to my highest aspirations or sense of purpose?
- What steps can I take to align myself with my soul's guidance?

- What deeper story is my soul trying to awaken in me?

EMBODIED SELF

- What does my body want me to know about this?
- What physical sensations are present?
- What are my senses telling me?
- What steps can I take to become grounded and embodied—to become present to the authentic strength within me?

SURVIVAL SELF

- What does my survival self want me to know about this?
- Is there a part of me that feels threatened?
- What is at stake?
- Am I accurately assessing this situation, or am I caught in a Post-traumatic Story response?
- What steps can I take to calm my nervous system so I can gain better perspective in this situation?

EMOTIONAL SELF

- What do my emotions want me to know about this?
- What emotions arise in response to this situation, and how familiar are they?
- Am I opening or closing down around these emotions?

- What would happen if I allowed myself to feel the emotion (fear, sadness, shame, etc.)? What can I learn from staying present to the actual emotion as opposed to my conditioned reaction to it?
- What steps can I take to acknowledge and honor the previously unfelt content of this situation?

INTUITIVE SELF

- What does my intuition want me to know about this?
- What am I being called to notice or attend to?
- Am I likely to regret it if I don't directly explore this inner prompt?
- Is this situation verifying a previous insight, or speaking to the future?
- What steps can I take to intuit the deeper meaning of this situation arising at this time?

IMAGINATIVE SELF

- What does my imagination want me to know about this?
- What image, sound, or gesture does my imagination associate with this quandary?
- What happens if I write a poem or song about this, do a stick drawing or a painting, sew, dance, or otherwise engage in creative play with this situation—what does this creative work reveal?

- What steps can I take to focus my imagination toward the best possible outcome of this situation?

INTELLECTUAL SELF

- What does my intellect want me to know about this?
- What would an objective analysis reveal in this situation?
- What have I learned from situations like this in the past that I could apply in this instance?
- Have others faced this situation? How have they successfully navigated this?
- What steps can I take to be discriminate and discerning about this, focusing on facts, using logic, and applying a systems approach to this situation?

SOCIAL SELF

- What does my social self want me to know about this?
- Who is involved or affected?
- Do I feel alone, do I belong, am I accepted, do I fit in? Where is my support in this?
- What steps can I take to create both boundaries and healthy support for myself in this situation?

WOUNDED SELF

- What does my wounded self want me to know about this?
- What old pain is resurfacing in this? What needs to be healed in me?
- Am I responding to this pain with awareness, empathy, and compassion?
- What steps can I take to integrate this pain in a loving way for myself, extending that same awareness, empathy, and compassion toward others who experience this pain?

EGO SELF

- What does my ego want me to know about this?
- What aspect of my identity is being challenged?
- Could my reputation be affected in any way?
- How do I want others to perceive me in this situation?
- What steps can I take to become more truthful and authentic within myself and with others?

SELF-CRITIC

- What does my self-critic want me to know about this?
- What do I doubt in myself? Is there some deficit of skill or understanding that I must correct?
- Whose standard am I judging myself by?
- What steps must I undertake to bring myself into

alignment with my own true standards and values in this situation?

SHADOW SELF

- What does my shadow want me to know about this?
- What don't I want to admit, or do I most wish to conceal, or fear having exposed?
- What judgments do I have about myself in this?
- Am I projecting my inability to accept these parts of myself onto others?
- What steps can I take to become open and vulnerable within myself, accepting my gifts and imperfections with equal grace?

DREAMING SELF

- What does my dreaming self want me to know about this?
- What is it attempting to awaken in me?
- What does this experience symbolize in my life as a whole?
- What steps can I take to engage my unconscious mind in working on this situation?
- What purpose does this dream serve in my deeper story?

NARRATIVE SELF

- What does my narrative self want me to know about this?
- What other memories or stories from my life fit with this?
- What am I trying to prove or reveal about myself in these stories?
- What steps can I take to harvest the wisdom from these stories, determine the underlying needs they reveal, and see this experience in the light of my continuous evolution?

INTEGRATED SELF

- What does my integrated self want me to know about this?
- What underlying theme or pattern am I trying to integrate?
- What would it be like to completely love and accept myself, even with this issue?
- What can I offer to the world as a result of integrating my self-awareness, forgiveness, acceptance, and love around this issue?
- What role does this issue serve in my life, and how is it tied to my higher purpose?

APPENDIX 2

Multiple Intelligences

APPENDIX 3

ARCS OF DEVELOPMENT

Ensouled: From Unconscious Individuality to Interconnected Consciousness

Embodied: From Head-Driven to Fully Embodied

Survival: From Mindless Reactivity to Mindful Responsiveness

Emotional: From Numb to Fully Expressive

Intuitive: From Insensitivity to Heightened Awareness

Imaginative: From Uninspired to Creatively Engaged

Intellectual: From Ignorance to Discernment

Social: From Self-Absorption to Meaningful Connection

Wounded: From Victimhood to Empowerment

Ego: From Defensiveness to Openness

Self-Critic: From Approval Seeking to Inner Authority

Shadow: From Self-Sabotage to Awakened Authenticity

Dreaming: From Unconscious Processing to Subconscious Support

Narrative: From Repetitive Patterns to Conscious Evolution

Integrated: From Fragmentation to Integrated Wholeness

APPENDIX 4

SYMPTOM, PROCESS, INTEGRATED RESULT

SYMPTOM / ASPECT OF SELF TO BE EXPLORED	TRANSFORMATIVE PROCESS	INTEGRATED RESULT
Tuned out/On automatic (Embodied/Intuitive/Intellectual)	Becoming Conscious	Being Present and in the Moment
Feeling Stuck/Confused (Critic/Soul/ Imaginative)	Perspective Taking	Clarity
Anxious/Afraid/Doubting (Survival/Emotional/Critic)	Assessing and Taking Risks	Self-Trust
Hypersensitive/Reactive (Survival, Embodied)	Self-Regulation	Grounded and Centered
Rejected/Self-Judging (Wounded/ Ego/Critic)	Self-Reflection	Self-Awareness
Lonely/ Isolated (Social/Wounded)	Empathy and Compassion	Accepting of Self and Others
Ashamed/Unworthy/Unloved (Shadow/Survival/Ego/Integrated)	Embracing Imperfection	Self-Love

SYMPTOM / ASPECT OF SELF TO BE EXPLORED	TRANSFORMATIVE PROCESS	INTEGRATED RESULT
Disconnected/Outlier (Social/Ego)	Reaching Out	Connected within a Community
Listless/Procrastinating (Survival/Soul/Embodied)	Facing Challenges	Openness to Possibility
Negative/Pessimistic/Frustrated (Critic/Shadow/Intellectual/ Imaginative)	Focusing on Goals	Creatively Engaged
Victimized/Blaming/Projecting (Shadow/Integrated)	Being Accountable	Empowered
Burdened/ Obligated/Resentful (Embodied/Intellectual/Social)	Honest Communication	Clear Boundaries
Lacking/Craving/Wanting More (Soul/Imaginative)	Experiencing Gratitude	Generously Offer Your Gifts
Confused/Struggling/Failing (Soul/Intellect)	Aligning with Purpose	Succeeding on Your Own Terms

APPENDIX 5

THEREFORE, I AM

There are few statements that have resonated over the centuries, such as Descartes' famous declaration, "I think; therefore, I am." It was an acknowledgement of human sentience, and the important role consciousness plays in all aspects of our lives. For me, however, that statement always felt incomplete. Human beings are so much more than their thought processes, and despite its magnificent powers, the human mind has often been given too exalted a role within the range of human gifts. If we truly want to be integrated and whole, we need a new model. This is my response to Mr. Descartes...

Therefore, I Am

...with respect for Rene Descartes

ENSOULED SELF

A spark of consciousness carried me into this world and clothed itself in my being, its immaterial essence and animating presence binding me to the web of life. Interwoven within the fabric and fate of all that is, my soul's imminent guiding force insists that I live up to the sacred potential of life. **I am ensouled; therefore, I am.**

EMBODIED SELF

My body is a sentient miracle composed of earthly elements and stardust—the bridge between spirit and matter. I bump up against the world in my skin suit, but boundaries blur in this sensory symphony called life. I exchange a continuous flow of energy and information with forests and streams; riding waves of light and sound, my heartbeat harmonizing with the rhythms of the earth. Gravity anchors me, but my backbone defies the pull, and muscles engage to carry me upright through the landscapes of my life. Rooted in physicality and part of the living ecology of the Earth, **I am embodied; therefore, I am.**

SURVIVAL SELF

Every day, beyond my conscious awareness, my survival is negotiated at a purely organic level. Swirling strands of recombinant DNA bark out their orders—cells are born, proliferate and die, while electrochemical sparks ignite my brain, heart, and gut. Elements combine, cooperate, and conspire to sustain my vital energy. Muscles and reflexes at the ready, sensitive and alert to environmental cues. I evolve in safety, bursting forth in animated glory like a butterfly shedding its chrysalis, but with the remotest of perceived threats, I instinctively recoil and regress cocoon-ward. I am an organism with a biological imperative to survive. **I survive; therefore, I am.**

EMOTIONAL SELF

The snap, crackle, and pop of electrochemical messages zing through my nervous system and make Baryshnikov-type leaps over synapses, causing subtle changes in body temperature and nearly imperceptible shifts of surface tension on skin, momentarily suspending my breath, and quickening my pulse as blood rushes and recedes, leaving pale purple splotches in its wake. I feel the catch in my throat, the heat in my cheeks, and the salty sting of tears at the edges of my eyes. I convulse in wild bursts of laughter that do more for my innards than could ever be achieved with a thousand crunches at the gym. I swoon and melt, and I rage against the dying light. I would rather experience even the most devastating feelings than live in a buffered state of numbness. **I am an ecstatic emotional being. I feel; therefore, I am.**

INTUITIVE SELF

Lightning bolts of insight jumpstart my senses, activating inner radar and alerting me to a game afoot. I swerve off the beaten track and go off half-cocked to connect the dots. Like a crazed conspiracy theorist, my intuition sees patterns in everything. Coincidence? It thinks not. Like an addict on a toot, it won't be reined in, won't listen to reason, and won't do the right thing; intuition has a mind of its own. Trading in the intangible, my intuition speaks in whispers, communicating its piece and then slipping unceremoniously out the door, leaving me to wonder. I would rather be stunned and stung by the mysteries of life than ever fall into the deadening certainty that so many people crave. **Intuition ignites my curiosity. I intuit; therefore, I am.**

IMAGINATIVE SELF

Imagination is the P. T. Barnum of the three-ring circus that is my mind: the lit fuse that shoots me from the cannon of everyday cognition. My imagination forces me to defy gravity and sanity as I loop through its rarified air, breaking bonds with the given and sending me free falling into entirely new worlds. It is the joy of the hunt, the thrill of the chase, the ecstasy of capturing and clothing the intangible with form. It is the shape-shifting trickster genius that turns life into art and art into life. It is the irrepressible urge to see, sense, and make meaning in new ways. Divine fire in the core of my being, urging me to create, create, create...**I imagine; therefore, I am.**

INTELLECTUAL SELF

My intellect is the seeker of logical explanation, a cerebral philosopher searching for truth, an investigative reporter itching for facts beneath the story, a scientific censor demanding proofs and peer reviews, an inner skeptic keeping me from drinking my own Kool-Aid, a tireless fighter against the unknown and unknowable, a generator of endless abstraction, incessantly searching for words to concretize the ineffability of existence. **I think; therefore, *I think* I am.**

SOCIAL SELF

I share essential elements with billions of life forms—an ecosystem of concentric circles radiating ever outward: plant, animal, mineral, family, community, culture. Human in my desire for belonging, I am wired for connection but also made vulnerable in my desperate need for it. I reach out and retract, I fit in and stand out, I merge and move on, I am alone and *all one* at the same time. **I am social; therefore, I am.**

WOUNDED SELF

There is never a way forward without reactivating some old wound. With uncanny accuracy, I unconsciously seek the perfect circumstances in my present to reawaken the pains of my past. My scars provide the treasure map showing the way to my unlived life. Delving beneath scar tissue to excavate the wound's deeper story, I uncover the corresponding wound in the world. These wounds ignite empathy and healing for myself and others. **I am wounded; therefore, I am.**

EGOIC SELF

The master of ceremonies that is my ego tries to maintain a united front. An over-achiever in image management, it works hard to polish and perfect my presentation to the world. Riding herd on contradictions and keeping vulnerability on a tight leash, my ego quashes the moles in my system that want to leak my imperfections to the press. Thin-skinned and defensive, my ego kicks into high gear at the slightest challenge. My ego saves face until I am ready to face my deeper self. **I am ego-bound; therefore, I am.**

SELF-CRITIC

Judge, jury, and jailor: my inner critic condemns me to life imprisonment for the crime of being myself. It holds me hostage with its constant complaints and commentary on my lack of conformity. It wants me to fit in, be like everyone else, to just be *normal*. It says its job is to protect me, keep me safe from disapproval and rejection. It has its standards and monitors my every move to keep me from ever accidentally expressing my true nature. But when I become conscious of my own standards, I take responsibility for authentically expressing who I am. **I am self-critical; therefore, I am.**

SHADOW SELF

The shadow is the dark web of my personal filing system. It knows where the bodies are buried. Its secrets are so deeply encrypted that I can't own them, so I project their content onto those around me. Surfacing when I least expect it, it can blindside me and bring me to my knees. My shadow not only makes me face the skeletons in my closet but forces my deepest needs to consciousness, things I crave but cannot admit, even to myself. Shame is its depth sounder, warning that I am getting too close to the bone, things are about to get real, my inner being will be exposed. Alternately black and golden, my shadow illuminates me from within. **I am shadow; therefore, I am.**

DREAMING SELF

Sleep-activated magic carpet ride, transporting me to

the innermost realms where shadow and light do the dance fandango, where the infrastructure of cognizance becomes the center that cannot hold; things fall apart and coalesce in hauntingly haphazard and ludicrously liberating ways. Where a confluence of undigested images, emotions, insights, sensations, and perhaps even that bit of nibbled cheese before bed come together as cockeyed co-conspirators to awaken me to a deeper life. Where the shifting ground of being contains multitudes, harbingers of as-yet unborn parts of self. Where stories unfold without discernible setting or plot but rise and fall with such climactic vehemence that waking life becomes denouement. I awaken to myself in sleep. **I am dreaming; therefore, I am.**

NARRATIVE SELF

Inner storehouse of fact and fiction, keeper of the untold stories of my life, archiving bits of data and bytes of sensory stimuli, the curator of my life experience is continuously codifying, classifying, and making connections. A revisionist of memory and history, it updates, appends, arranges, and rearranges things into semi-coherent sequences. My narrative self fills in the blanks, taking each recognizable fragment of the mosaic that is my life and turning it into my ongoing story. **I am narrative; therefore, I am.**

INTEGRATED SELF

Comfortable and content in body, mind, and spirit, whole-heartedly here for myself and for the world, open to life, nothing to deny or resist, all systems and senses in supportive synchrony; cooperating, consensual, conscious, and connected. Taking my purpose seriously but my sense of self lightly, with grace, humor, and humility, I accept responsibility for the indelible imprint of my presence upon the face of eternity. All in, I gratefully embrace the gift of life. **I am integrated; therefore, I am.**

ADDITIONAL RESOURCES FOR EACH ASPECT OF SELF

RESOURCES FOR THE ENSOULED SELF

Adrienne, Carol. *The Purpose of Your Life: Finding your Place in the World Using Synchronicity, Intuition and Uncommon Sense*. New York: Eagle Brook, 1998.

Frankl, Viktor. *Man's Search for Meaning*. Beacon Press: United States, 1959.

Hillman, James. *The Soul's Code: In Search of Character and Calling*. New York: Random House, 1996.

Kornfield, Jack. *Meditation for Beginners*. Boulder CO: Sounds True, 2008.

Langer, Ellen. *Mindfulness*. Boston: DeCapo Lifelong Books, 1989.

Macy, Joanna. *World as Lover, World as Self.* Berkeley, CA: Parallax Press, 1991.

thecontemplativemind.org http://www.contemplativemind.org/

Seigel, Daniel. *The Mindful Brain.* New York: W.W. Norton, 2007.

Taylor, Jill Bolte. *My Stroke of Insight: A Brain Scientist's Personal Journey.* New York: Penguin Group, 2006.

RESOURCES FOR THE EMBODIED SELF

Abrams, David. *The Spell of the Sensuous: Perception, Language in a More-Than-Human World.* New York: Pantheon Books, 1996.

Blakeslee, Sandra, and Blakeslee, Matthew. *The Body Has a Mind of Its Own: How Body Maps in Your Brain Help You Do (Almost) Everything Better.* New York: Random House, 2007.

Heer, Dain. *Embodiment: The Manual You Should Have Been Given When You Were Born.* Le Vergne, TN: Lightning Source Inc., 2013.

Mate, Gabor. *When the Body Says No: The Cost of Hidden Stress.* Toronto: A.A. Knopf Canada, 2003.

Nuland, Sherwin B. *The Wisdom of the Body.* New York: Alfred A. Knoff, 1977.

Shepherd, Philip. *New Self, New World: Recovering Our Senses in the Twenty-First Century.* Berkeley, CA: North Atlantic Books, 2010.

Shepherd, Philip. *Radical Wholeness: The Embodied Present and the Ordinary Grace of Being* Berkeley, CA: North Atlantic Books, 2017.

RESOURCES FOR THE SURVIVAL SELF

Chodron, Pema. *When Things Fall Apart: Heart Advice for Difficult Times*. Boston: Shambhala, 1997.

De Becker, Gavin. *The Gift of Fear: Survival Signals that Protect Us from Violence*. Boston: Little, Brown & Co., 1997.

Kabat-Zinn, Jon. *Full Catastrophe Living: Using the Wisdom of your Body and Mind to Face Stress, Pain, and Illness*. New York: Delacorte Press, 1990.

Manley, Wani Iris. *Get Out of Survival Mode and Live the Life You Really Want*. CreateSpace Independent Publishing Platform, 2016.

Peyton, Sarah. *The Resonant Self: Guided Meditations and Exercises to Engage your Brain's Capacity for Healing*. New York: W.W. Norton & Co., 2017.

RESOURCES FOR THE EMOTIONAL SELF

Barrett, Lisa Feldman. *How Emotions Are Made: The Secret Life of the Brain*. Boston: Houghton Mifflin Harcourt, 2017.

DeSteno, David. *Emotional Success: The Power of Gratitude, Compassion, and Pride*. Boston: Houghton, Mifflin, Harcourt, 2017.

Ekman, Paul. *Emotions Revealed: Recognizing Faces and Feelings to Improve Communication and Emotional Life*. New York: Henry Holt, 2007.

Goleman, Daniel. *Emotional Intelligence*. New York: Bantam Books, 1995.

McLaren, Karla. *The Language of Emotions*. Boulder, CO: Sounds True, 2010.

Pert, Candace. *Molecules of Emotion: Why You Feel the Way You Feel.* New York: Scribner, 1997.

Watt-Smith, Tiffany. *The Book of Human Emotions: From Ambiquphobia to Umpty—154 Words from Around the World for How We Feel.* London: Profile Books, 2015.

RESOURCES FOR THE INTUITIVE SELF

Chabris, Christopher and Daniel Simon. *The Invisible Gorilla and Other Ways Our Intuitions Deceive Us.* New York: Random House, 2009.

Gigerenzer, Gerd. *Gut Feelings: The Intelligence of the Unconscious.* New York: Viking, 2007.

Gladwell, Malcolm. *Blink: The Power of Thinking Without Thinking.* New York: Little, Brown and Co., 2005.

Love, Martha Char and Robert Sterling. *Increasing Intuitional Intelligence: How the Awareness of Instinctual Gut Feelings Fosters Human Learning, Intuition, and Longevity.* CreateSpace Independent Publishing Platform, 2015.

Pierce, Penny. *The Intuitive Way: The Definitive Guide to Increasing Your Awareness.* New York: Simon & Schuster, 2009.

RESOURCES FOR THE IMAGINATIVE SELF

Adams, Kathleen. *Journal to the Self: 22 Paths to Personal Growth.* New York: Warner Books, 1990.

Cameron, Julia. *The Artist's Way: A Spiritual Path to Higher Creativity.* New York: Jeremy P. Tarcher, 2002.

DeBono, Edward. *Lateral Thinking: Creativity Step by Step.* London: Penguin UK, 1970.

DeBono, Edward. *The Six Thinking Hats*. London: Penguin UK, 1985.

Gilbert, Elizabeth. *Big Magic: Creative Living Beyond Fear*. New York: Riverhead Books, 2015.

Henry, Todd. *The Accidental Creative: How to Be Brilliant at A Moment's Notice*. New York: Portfolio/Penguin, 2011.

Kleon, Austin. *Steal Like an Artist: 10 Things Nobody Told You About Being Creative*. New York: Workman Publishing Company, 2012.

Pressfield, Stephen. *The War of Art: Break through the Blocks and Win Your Inner Creative Battles*. New York: Warner Books, 2002.

Tharp, Twyla. *The Creative Habit: Learn it and Use it for Life*. New York: Simon & Schuster, 2003.

RESOURCES FOR THE INTELLECTUAL SELF

Ariely, Dan. *Predictably Irrational: The Hidden Forces that Shape our Decisions*. New York: Harper, 2008.

Duhigg, Charles. *The Power of Habit: Why We Do What We Do in Life and Business*. Toronto: Doubleday Canada, 2012.

Goleman, Daniel. *Focus: The Hidden Driver of Excellence*. New York: Harper, 2013.

Gardner, Howard. *Frames of Mind: The Theory of Multiple Intelligences*. New York: Basic Books, 1983.

Kahneman, Daniel. *Thinking Fast and Slow*. Toronto: Doubleday Canada, 2011.

Nash, Laura, and Stevenson, Howard. *Just Enough: Tools for Creating Success in Your Work and Your Life*. New Jersey: John Wiley & Sons Inc., 2004.

Newport, Cal. *Deep Work: Rules for Focused Success in a Distracted World*. New York: Grand Central Publishing, 2016.

Pentland, Alex. *Social Physics: How Good Ideas Spread—The Lessons from a New Science*. New York: Penguin Press, 2014.

Thaler, Richard H. and Sustein, Cass R. *Nudge: Improving Decisions about Health, Wealth, and Happiness:* New Haven: Yale University Press, 2008.

RESOURCES FOR THE SOCIAL SELF

Goleman, Daniel. *Social Intelligence: The New Science of Human Relationships*. New York: Bantam, 2007.

Kauth, Bill and Alowan, Zoe. *We Need Each Other: Building Gift Community*. Ashland, OR: Silver Light Publications, 2011.

Le Botton, Alain. *The Course of Love: A Novel*. New York: Simon & Schuster, 2016.

Lewis, Thomas B., Amini, Fari, and Lannon, Richard. *A General Theory of Love*. New York: Random House, 2000.

Licata Matt. *The Path is Everywhere*. Boulder, CO: Wandering Yogi Press, 2017.

Pennebaker, James W. *The Secret Life of Pronouns: What Our Words Say About Us*. New York: Bloomsbury Press, 2011.

Rosenberg, Marshall. *Non-Violent Communication: A Language of Life*. Encinitas, CA: PuddleDancer Press, 2003.

RESOURCES FOR THE WOUNDED SELF

Badenoch, Bonnie. *The Heart of Trauma: Healing the Embodied Brain in the Context of Relationships*. New York, W.W. Norton, 2017.

Levine, Peter. *Walking the Tiger: Healing Trauma*. Berkeley, CA: North Atlantic Books, 1997.

Levine, Stephen. *Healing into Life and Death*. New York: Doubleday, 1987.

Mate, Gabor. *The Return to Ourselves: Trauma, Healing, and the Myth of Normal*. Audio. Boulder, CO: Sounds True, 2018.

Richo, David. *When the Past is Present: Healing the Emotional Wounds That Sabotage Our Relationships*. Boston: Shambhala, 2008.

Sieff, Daniela F. *Understanding and Healing Emotional Trauma: Conversations with Pioneering Clinicians and Researchers*. London/ New York: Routledge, 2015.

Tipping, Colin. *Radical Forgiveness: A Revolutionary Five-stage Process to Heal Relationships, Let Go of Anger and Blame, Find Peace in Any Situation*. Boulder, CO: Sounds True, 2009.

Van der Kolk, Bessel. *The Body Keeps the Score: Brain, Mind and Body in the Healing of Trauma*. New York: Viking, 2014.

RESOURCES FOR THE EGO SELF

Baggini, Julian. *The Ego Trick*. London: Granta, 2012.

Holiday, Ryan. *Ego is the Enemy*. New York: Penguin, 2016.

King, Alexander. *Freedom from Yourself: Rumi's Selected Poems from Divan Shams Tabrizi*. Australia: Balboa Press, 2014.

Metzinger, Thomas. *The Ego Tunnel: The Science of the Mind and the Myth of the Self*. New York: Basic Books, 2009.

RESOURCES FOR THE SELF-CRITIC

Andreas, Steve. *Transforming Negative Self-Talk: Practical, Effective Exercises*. New York: W.W. Norton, 2014.

Earley, Jay, and Weiss, Bonnie. *Freedom from Your Inner Critic: A Self-Therapy Approach*. Boulder, CO: Sounds True, 2013.

Forrest, Emma. *Your Voice in My Head: A Memoir*. Toronto: Random House, 2011.

Stone, Hal and Stone, Sidra. *Embracing Your Inner Critic: Turning Self-Criticism into a Creative Asset*. San Francisco: HarperSanFranciso, 1993.

Young, Jeffrey, and Klosko, Janet. *Reinventing Your Life*. New York: Dutton, 1993.

RESOURCES FOR THE SHADOW SELF

Brown, Brene. *The Gifts of Imperfection: Let Go of Who You Think You're Supposed to Be and Embrace Who You Are*. Center City, Minn.: Hazelden, 2010.

Edwards, Aleta. *Fear of the Abyss: Healing the Wounds of Shame & Perfectionism*. Otto, NC: Red Pill Press, 2016.

Ensler, Eve. *In the Body of the World*. Toronto: Random House Canada, 2013.

Johnson, Robert A. *Owning Your Own Shadow: Understanding the Dark Side of the Psyche*. San Francisco: HarperOne, 2009.

Solomon, Andrew. *Noonday Demon: An Atlas of Depression*. New York: Scribner Classics, 2015.

Stossel, Scott. *Age of Anxiety: Fear, Hope, Dread and the Search for Peace of Mind*. New York: Alfred A. Knopf, 2013.

Zweig, Connie. *Meeting the Shadow: The Hidden Power of the Dark Side of Human Nature*. New York: Tarcher Perigee, 1991.

RESOURCES FOR THE DREAMING SELF

Aizenstat, Stephen. *Dream Tending: Awakening to the Healing Power of Dreams*. New Orleans: Spring Journal, Inc., 2011.

Johnson, Robert A. *Inner Work: Using Dreams and Active Imagination for Personal Growth*. New York: Harper Collins, 1986.

Jung, C.G., Hull, R.F.C., Trans. William McGuire. *The Undiscovered Self/Symbols and the Interpretation of Dreams*. New Jersey: Princeton University Press, 2010.

Mindell, Arnold and Mindell, Amy. *Dreambody*. Portland, Oregon: Lao Tse Press, 1982.

Moss, Robert. *Dreaming the Soul Back Home: Shamanic Dreaming for Healing and Becoming Whole*. Novato, CA: New World Library, 2012.

Taylor, Jeremy. *The Wisdom of Your Dreams: Using Dreams to Tap into your Unconscious and Transform Your Life*. New York: Jeremy P. Tarcher/Penguin, 2009.

RESOURCES FOR THE NARRATIVE SELF

"Biology of Story." Buchbinder, Amnon. http://biologyofstory.com/#/, accessed June 20, 2018.

Brockmeir, Jens and Carbaugh, Donal (ed). *Narrative and Identity, Studies in Autobiography, Self and Culture*. Amsterdam, NL: John Benjamins Publishing Company, 2001.

Gottschall, Jonathan. *The Storytelling Animal: How Stories Make Us Human*. Boston: Houghton Mifflin Harcourt, 2012.

McAdams, Dan P. *The Stories We Live By: Personal Myths and the Making of the Self.* New York: Morrow, 1993.

Qi Wang. *The Autobiographical Self in Time and Culture.* Oxford: Oxford University Press, 2013.

Simms, Andrew (ed). *Knock Twice: 25 Modern Folk Tales for Troubling Times.* CreateSpace Independent Publishing Platform, 2017.

RESOURCES FOR THE INTEGRATED SELF

Csikszentmihaly, Mihaly. *Flow: The Psychology of Optimal Experience.* New York: Harper Perennial, 1990.

Jenkinson, Stephen. *Die Wise: A Manifesto for Sanity and Soul.* Berkeley, CA: North Atlantic Books, 2015.

Turner, Toko-pa. *Belonging: Remembering Ourselves Home.* Salt Spring Island, BC: Her Own Room Press, 2017.

White, John (ed). *The Highest State of Consciousness.* Guildford, UK: White Crow Books, 2012.

Wilber, Ken. *Integral Psychology: Consciousness, Spirit, Psychology.* Boston: Shambhala, 2000.

ABOUT THE AUTHOR

GAEL MCCOOL is an author, inspirational teacher, and transformational life coach who helps her clients become conscious, accountable, and whole. She is a Registered Clinical Counselling Hypnotherapist and a certified life coach specializing in social, emotional, and spiritual intelligence. She has been in practice in Vancouver, BC for over thirty-five years.

NOTES

1   Spiritual Intelligence: "The ability to behave with wisdom and compassion, while maintaining inner and outer peace, regardless of the situation." Wigglesworth, Cindy. *SQ21: The 21 Skills of Spiritual Intelligence*. New York: Select Books, 2012.

2   Nondualism refers to an evolved state of consciousness, which transcends dichotomies of "I-thou" or either/or thinking.

3   Watts, Alan. *The Book on the Taboo Against Knowing Who You Are*. New York: Random House, 1989.

4   Hillman, James. *The Soul's Code: In Search of Character and Calling*. New York: Ballantine Books, 1996.

5   McNeley, James K. *Holy Wind in Navajo Philosophy*. Tucson: The University of Arizona Press, 1988.

6   Houston, Jean. *The Possible Human*. New York: Jeremy P. Tarcher/Putnam Penguin Group, 1982.

7   Rael Joseph, and Marlow, Mary Elizabeth. *Being and Vibration*. North Carolina: Millichap Books, 2012.

8   Jaynes, Julian. *The Origins of Consciousness and the Breakdown of the Bicameral Mind*. New York: Houghton Mifflin Harcourt Publishing Company, 1976.

9   Ralph Waldo Emerson. *Self-Reliance and Other Essays*. New York: Dover Publications, 1993.

10   Oliver, Mary, "Wild Geese" in *Dream Work,* 1986.

11   Jong, Erica. *Fear of Fifty*. New York: Jeremy P. Tarcher/Penguin Group, 1994.

12 Sensate Intelligence: the ability to feel or apprehend physically, by means of the senses.

13 Oliver, Mary. *Dream Work*. New York: Atlantic Monthly Press, 1986.

14 Adaptive Intelligence: The ability to adapt toward positive modes of survival.

15 Mindfulness: Focusing awareness on the present moment, while calmly acknowledging and accepting your feelings, thoughts, and bodily sensations.

16 Ackerman Diane, *A Natural History of Love*. New York: First Vintage Books, 1995. pg. 141

17 Affective Intelligence: The ability to know and express emotions in healthy ways.

18 Damasio, Antonio R. *Descartes' Error, Emotion Reason and the Human Brain*. New York: Avon books, 1994.

19 Ekman, Paul. An Argument for Basic Emotions. "Cognition and Emotion," 6 (3/4), University of California, 1992, San Francisco (169-200).

20 Goleman Daniel, *Emotional Intelligence: Why It Can Matter More Than IQ*. New York : Bantam Books, 1995.

21 Schachter, S. "The interaction of cognitive and physiological determinants of emotional state," in *Advances in Experimental Social Psychology*, ed. L. Berkowitz. New York: Academic Press, 1964, 49-79.

22 Burns, David. *Feeling good: The New Mood Therapy*. New York: Penguin Books, 1981.

23 Congruency: One's internal response and external behavior are in agreement and expressed harmoniously (congruently).

24 Synchronicity, a term coined by psychologist Carl Jung, describes "meaningful coincidences:" events that occur without apparent causal relationship but that seem to be related in a meaningful way.

25 Perceptual Intelligence: The ability to have or show sensitive insight.

26 If you ever receive an intuitive nudge that involves your safety in any way, act on it immediately. You can decipher the value of the signal after the fact.

27 Sheldrake, Rupert. Lecture at the "Synchronicity, Psyche and Matter Symposium." Joshua Tree, California, 2014.

28 Pigliucci, Massimo. *Answers for Aristotle: How Science and Philosophy Can Lead Us to a More Meaningful Life*. Philadelphia: Basic Books, 2012.

29 Seigel, Daniel J. *Pocket Guide to Interpersonal Neurobiology: An Integrative Handbook of the Mind*. New York: W.W. Norton & Company, 2012.

30 Grof, Stanislav. *Psychology of the Future: Lessons from Modern Consciousness Research*. Albany: State University of New York Press, 2000.

31 Peirce, Penny. *The Intuitive Way: The Definitive Guide to Increasing Your Awareness*. New York: Atria, a division of Simon & Schuster, Inc., 2009 (109).

32 Creative Intelligence: The ability to engage imagination and produce original ideas.

33 Ellington, Duke. *Music is My Mistress*. Garden City, N.Y: Doubleday, 1973.

34 Bloom, Paul. *How Pleasure Works: The New Science of Why We Like What We Like*. New York: W.W. Norton and Company Inc., 2010.

35 Objective Intelligence: The ability to remain objective (free from the influence of personal feelings or opinions) in considering and representing facts.

36 Charles Spearman identified g: a single underlying intelligence factor he believed accounted for the variety of observable abilities, which was later used as the basis for IQ testing.

37 In Frames of Mind: The Theory of Multiple Intelligences, Howard Gardner divides intelligences into specific modalities rather than a single factor.

38 Executive functioning involves complex cognitive processes as part of a meta cognitive system. Located primarily in the forebrain, it includes the dorsolateral prefrontal cortex, the anterior cingulate cortex, and the orbitofrontal cortex.

39 Schermer, Michael. *The Believing Brain*. New York: St. Martin's Press, 2011.

40 Weil, Simone. *Waiting for God*. New York: Harper Perennial, 2009.

41 Barash, David P. "Paradigms Lost." https://aeon.co/essays/science-needs-the-freedom-to-constantly-change-its-mind. 27 October, 2015. Accessed 24 March 2018.

42 Nease, Bob. *The Power of Fifty Bits: The New Science of Turning Good Intentions into Positive Results*. New York: Harper Collins, 2016.

43 Social Intelligence: The ability to get along with and to engage cooperatively with others.

44 Lewis, Thomas; Amini, Fari; and Lannon, Richard. *A General Theory of Love*. New York: Vintage Books, 2000 (76).

45 Elliot, Lise. *What's Going On In There? How the Brain and Mind Develop in the First Five Years of Life*. New York: Bantam Books, 1999.

46 Ornish, Dean. *Love and Survival*. New York: HarperCollins, 1998 (33-34).

47 Lewis, Thomas, Amini, Fari, and Lannon, Richard. *A General Theory of Love*. New York: Vintage Books, 2000 (98).

48 Holmes, John Alexander. *Wisdom in Small Doses*. Chicago: The University Publishing Company, 1927.

49 Kingsolver, Barbara. *Small Wonders*. New York: HarperCollins Publishers, 2002.

50 Griffin, Susan. *Pornography and Silence: Culture's Revenge Against Nature*. New York: Open Road Integrated Media, 2007.

51 Healing Intelligence: The ability to restore to health and wholeness.

52 Self-Developing Intelligence: The ability to rebalance your sense of self and maintain a healthy sense of identity as you develop and mature.

53 Schore, Allan N. *Affect Regulation and the Origin of the Self: The Neurobiology of Emotional Development*. Hove, UK: Lawrence Erlbaum Associates, 1994 (360).

54 Satre, Jean Paul. *Being and Nothingness*. New York: Washington Square Press, 1992 (261).

55 Schore, Allan N. *Affect Regulation and the Origin of the Self: The Neurobiology of Emotional Development*. Hove, UK: Lawrence Erlbaum Associates, 1994 (360).

56 Tomkins, Silvan. "Shame." In *The Many Faces of Shame*, DL Nathanson (Ed.). New York: Guilford Press, 1987 (161).

57 Intrapersonal Intelligence: The ability to be introspective; to understand one's inner world, internal awareness of thoughts, feelings, and responses.

58 WordReference.com: Random House Learner's Dictionary of American English, 2018.

59 Internalized negative thoughts about one's self, also known as negative self-talk.

60 A mind map is a visual diagram to organize information so that you can see how each part relates within the whole.

61 Depth Intelligence: The ability to explore and work effectively with the unconscious content of the psyche.

62 Johnson, Robert, and Ruhl, Jerry Michael. *Balancing Heaven and Earth: A Memoir of Visions, Dreams and Realizations*. New York: Harper Collins Publishers, 1998.

63 Moore, Thomas. *The Care of the Soul*. New York: Harper Collins, 1992.

64 https://www.cnvc.org/

65 Interpretive Intelligence: The ability to translate and embody dream content and symbolism into relevant insight.

66 REM: Rapid Eye Movement, which indicates a deeper dream state.

67 Margulies, Alfred. *The Empathetic Imagination*. New York: W.W. Norton and Company, 1989.

68 Moss, Robert. *Active Dreaming: Journeying Beyond Self-Limitation to a Life of Wild Freedom*. Novato, California: New World Library, 2011.

69 Apperceptive Intelligence: The ability to understand something perceived in terms of previous experience.

70 Unitive Intelligence: The ability to inhabit a spacious mode of non-dual perception and expression.

71 Hein, Piet. *Grooks*. Denmark: Hodder & Stoughton Ltd., 1966.

Made in the USA
Middletown, DE
17 November 2020